HAMLET

WILLIAM SHAKESPEARE

HAMLET

With Contemporary Essays

Edited by JOSEPH PEARCE

IGNATIUS PRESS   SAN FRANCISCO

This edition of *Hamlet* follows the Alexander Text
of the Complete Works of William Shakespeare, first published in 1951.
This edition was first published in 2008.

Cover art:
Michail Vrubel, *Hamlet and Ophelia*
Russian State Museum, St. Petersburg, Russia

Photo credit: Scala / Art Resource, N.Y.

Cover design by John Herreid

ISBN 978-1-58617-261-9
Library of Congress Control Number 2008926772
Printed in India ∞

Tradition is the extension of Democracy through time; it is the proxy of the dead and the enfranchisement of the unborn.

Tradition may be defined as the extension of the franchise. Tradition means giving votes to the most obscure of all classes, our ancestors. It is the democracy of the dead. Tradition refuses to submit to the small and arrogant oligarchy of those who merely happen to be walking about. All democrats object to men being disqualified by the accident of birth; tradition objects to their being disqualified by the accident of death. Democracy tells us not to neglect a good man's opinion, even if he is our groom; tradition asks us not to neglect a good man's opinion, even if he is our father. I, at any rate, cannot separate the two ideas of democracy and tradition.

—G. K. Chesterton

Ignatius Critical Editions—Tradition-Oriented Criticism for a new generation

CONTENTS

Contents

INTRODUCTION

Joseph Pearce
Ave Maria University

And let me speak to th' yet unknowing world
How these things came about. So shall you hear
Of carnal, bloody, and unnatural acts;
Of accidental judgments, casual slaughters;
Of deaths put on by cunning and forc'd cause;
And, in this upshot, purposes mistook
Fall'n on th' inventors' heads—all this can I
Truly deliver.

(5.2.371–78)

The first documentary record of Shakespeare's *Hamlet* is its entry in the Stationers' Register on July 26, 1602, but the play itself seems to have been written and performed as early as 1598.[1] Shakespeare's principal source for the play was an earlier play of the same name, based on an old Norse folktale, that scholars now call the *Ur-Hamlet*, meaning "original *Hamlet*", which was probably written by Thomas Kyd, best known for his *Spanish Tragedy* (c. 1589). Although Kyd's play has been lost to posterity, it seems certain that it was performed regularly by the Chamberlain's Men (Shakespeare's acting troupe) during the early 1590s, and, as such, it is very likely that Shakespeare acted in it during that period. He would therefore have known the earlier play very well and was evidently prompted to write his own version of it. It is reasonable to conjecture that he chose to do so as a reaction against the tone or content of the original. Shakespeare had already been provoked into writing his

[1] The play is mentioned in a marginal note of an edition of Chaucer published in 1598, but allusions in the play itself to events that happened after this date suggest that the final version of the play was not completed until as late as 1602.

play *King John* as a reaction against an earlier play entitled *The Troublesome Reign of King John*, and, a few years later, he would write *King Lear* to counter a similar bias in a play entitled *The True Chronicle History of King Leir and His Three Daughters*. It seems probable, therefore, that Shakespeare wrote *Hamlet* to counter aspects of the earlier play with which he disapproved and to which he wished to make a literary riposte. Since the *Ur-Hamlet* is no longer extant, it is impossible to know what exactly Shakespeare found objectionable in the earlier version, but the fact that Kyd was tried and imprisoned for atheism in 1593 suggests that Shakespeare sought to "baptize" the drama with his own profoundly Christian imagination.

As for the play itself, it is perhaps the most popular and well-known of all Shakespeare's works and is also the longest and arguably the most difficult to understand. It has certainly puzzled generations of critics and continues to confuse and confound its readers with infuriating conundrums. Who exactly is Hamlet? Is he a noble and conscientious young man struggling heroically against "the slings and arrows of outrageous fortune", or is he a hopelessly melancholic procrastinator? And what of the Ghost of Hamlet's father? Is he who he says he is, or is he (or it) a demon hell-bent on bringing murder and anarchy to the kingdom of Denmark? And then there is Ophelia. Does Hamlet love her, or is his love, like his madness, merely feigned? And is Ophelia an innocent lamb who is slaughtered by the sins of others, or is she in some way culpable for her own madness and death? On a panoramic level, does the play present a moral vision of reality signaling the triumph of Christian hope, or does it point to the chasm of nihilistic despair?

These puzzles, according to Peter Milward, "are more than enough to turn *Hamlet* from a revenge tragedy to a problem play. No wonder we are left at the end with a feeling rather of bewilderment than of catharsis! No room is left for tears, as at the end of *King Lear*, but only for scratching of the head."[2]

---

[2] Peter Milward, *Shakespeare's Meta-drama: Hamlet and Macbeth* (Tokyo: Renaissance Institute, 2003), p. 18.

There is no denying that *Hamlet* presents us with a difficult puzzle that *seems* insoluble. Yet things are not always what they seem, as Hamlet reminds his mother:

Seems, madam! Nay, it is; I know not seems.
'Tis not alone my inky cloak, good mother,
Nor customary suits of solemn black,
Nor windy suspiration of forc'd breath,
No, nor the fruitful river in the eye,
Nor the dejected havior of the visage,
Together with all forms, moods, shapes of grief,
That can denote me truly. These, indeed, seem;
For they are actions that a man might play;
But I have that within which passes show—
These but the trappings and the suits of woe.

(1.2.76–86)

In these few words, Hamlet is exhibiting a deep understanding of metaphysics. He is echoing Aristotle and Saint Thomas Aquinas in his distinction between the *essence* of things and their *accidental* qualities. At its deepest level of meaning, *Hamlet* works on this metaphysical and ontological level. The play deals with *definitions*, with the meanings of things, and with the difference between those things that essentially *are* and those that only *seem* to be. It is about what things *mean*, not about what things *seem*. And it is about learning to discover the difference between the two. It is the quest for the definite amid the clouds of unknowing.

In order to understand *Hamlet* as Shakespeare understood it, we need to see the play through the playwright's profoundly Christian eyes. This inescapable truth was understood by the Shakespearean critic E. M. W. Tillyard, who emphasized Shakespeare's breadth of spiritual vision in *Hamlet*:

I doubt if in any other play of Shakespeare there is so strong an impression of the total range of creation from the angels to the beasts.... This way of looking at creation is powerfully traditional and Christian; and in *Hamlet* if anywhere in Shakespeare we notice the genealogy from the Miracle Plays with their setting of Heaven, Purgatory, and Hell, as for instance in the hero's description of himself as a fellow "crawling between heaven and earth".... *Hamlet* is one of the most medieval as well as one of the most acutely modern of Shakespeare's plays. And though the theme of spiritual regeneration may be absent from the plot, the setting includes the religious consciousness most eminently.[3]

The only questionable aspect of Tillyard's otherwise excellent appraisal of the "religious consciousness" of the play is his assertion that "spiritual regeneration may be absent from the plot". This is not the case. Hamlet begins, tempted to suicide, in the Slough of Despond, bogged down by the sins of others more than by his own transgressions, and ends with firm resolution and a serene resignation to the will of God:

> Not a whit, we defy augury: there is special providence in the fall of a sparrow. If it be now, 'tis not to come; if it be not to come, it will be now; if it be not now, yet it will come—the readiness is all. Since no man owes of aught he leaves, what is't to leave betimes? Let be.
>
> (5.2.211–16)

Hamlet has come a long way from the suicidal despondency of his first soliloquy in Act 1 to this willing acceptance in Act 5 of the benignity of God's providence and his knowledge that "the readiness is all". In between, he has descended Dantelike into the infernal depths and, like Dante, emerges through purgatorial fire into the gracious acceptance of the love of God. This is "spiritual regeneration" at its most sublime, albeit Shakespeare, unlike Dante, leaves his vision of paradise offstage, apart from the scantiest of glimpses offered in passing as the plot unfolds.

It is perhaps the "readiness" of Hamlet in the play's final scene that provides the other key to solving the puzzle at the play's beguiling heart. If the quest for true meaning, inherent

[3] E. M. W. Tillyard, *Shakespeare's Problem Plays* (London: University of Toronto Press, 1950), pp. 29–30.

in the discernment of that which is from that which seems, is the means by which Hamlet finds himself, then the "readiness is all" is the ultimate end, the very purpose of the play itself. The play reaches its own readiness, its own ripeness, in the readiness of Hamlet to put his trust in God. Hamlet's conversion of heart makes him ready to meet whatever Providence may bring. His "readiness" has made him ripe for the picking—and ripe for the pricking by Laertes' envenomed foil. He is ready to meet his Maker and is therefore ready to die. "If it be now", so be it—or "let be", to employ Hamlet's precise words. Since "let be" is most commonly rendered in English usage as "Amen", it elevates these words from the level of mere dialogue with Horatio to the level of prayer, i.e., dialogue with God. Hamlet's words represent a doxology, offering formal praise to God for his revealing to Hamlet of the ultimate truth that makes sense of all the apparent contradictions that have bedeviled the play's unraveling. If, as Hamlet now believes, "there is a special providence in the fall of a sparrow", he knows also, from the following words from Matthew's Gospel, from which these lines are plucked, that he has nothing to fear from death: "Fear not, therefore; you are of more value than many sparrows."[4] Hamlet's resolve, his resolution, is the resolution of the problem that the play poses. The resolution of the seemingly insoluble problems of life is to be found in Christ alone.

At this point, one is sure to meet the objection of many that such a solution is not only too simple but too simplistic. What of the questions posed at the outset? What of the apparent bloodlust of Hamlet? What are we to make of the Ghost's own apparent bloodlust? And what of poor Ophelia, canonized so eloquently by Samuel Johnson as "the young, the beautiful, the harmless, and the pious"?[5] And what of Hamlet's relationship with Ophelia, in which Hamlet treats her, in

[4] Matthew 10:31.
[5] Samuel Johnson, *Johnson on Shakespeare: Essays and Notes Selected and Set Forth with an Introduction by Walter Raleigh* (London: Oxford University Press, 1908), p. 196.

Johnson's judgment, "with so much rudeness, which seems to be useless and wanton cruelty"?[6] If Hamlet is a hero, how are we to account for his apparent murderous hatred and his "wanton cruelty"?

These are good questions that will have to be answered if we are to make sense of the play.

Let us begin with Hamlet himself. We are informed on several occasions that he had studied at Wittenberg, the university at which Martin Luther taught, which is generally considered to be the birthplace of the Protestant Reformation. Clearly, since Wittenberg is gratuitous to the development of the plot and is not present in the folk tradition that serves as the play's source, Shakespeare has deliberately infused an element of contemporary religious controversy into the play. And yet he does so in a way that suggests that his sympathies are not with the Reformers or, at least, that he regards them with a marked ambivalence. Hamlet's pun on the Diet of Worms[7] in his description of Polonius' corpse is decidedly distasteful (4.3.19–23), and while it is true that the good and noble Horatio studied at Wittenberg, it is equally true that the corrupt and ignoble spies Rosencrantz and Guildenstern were also alumni of the same university.

If Hamlet appears to be a Protestant of sorts, it is curious that the Ghost of his father is indubitably Catholic. We know as much from the Ghost's description of his own death:

> Cut off even in the blossoms of my sin,
> Unhous'led, disappointed, unanel'd,
> No reck'ning made, but sent to my account
> With all my imperfections on my head.
> O, horrible! O, horrible! most horrible!
>   (1.5.76–80)

---

[6] Ibid.

[7] *Diet of Worms*: a general assembly of the estates of the Holy Roman Empire, held in Worms, a small German town, in 1521, at which Martin Luther famously defended his *Ninety-Five Theses*.

The archaisms *unhous'led*, *disappointed*, and *unanel'd* refer to the Catholic sacraments of Communion, penance (confession), and extreme unction (last rites, or anointing of the sick), all of which were snatched away from him by his sudden death, leaving him cut off in the blossoms of his sin, with all his imperfections on his head. It is for these unabsolved sins that he is being punished, not for the fact that King Claudius has not been punished for murdering him. It is imperative that this crucial fact is noted and remembered because it saves us from the error of believing that Hamlet has to avenge his father so that his ghost can rest in peace. This is emphatically not the case. Hamlet's "vengeance" is demanded by Justice, by the moral law, and has nothing to do with his father's punishment for his own sins. The Ghost's sins will be "purg'd away" through suffering regardless of whether Hamlet brings King Claudius to justice.

It should also be remembered that the Ghost sees things differently from every other character in the play. He has the eyes of eternity. He sees things as they *are* and not merely as they *seem* from the perspective of those trapped in the tunneled vision of time. The living *believe* that something is true or false; the dead *know* the true from the false. The Ghost is, therefore, our most reliable witness to that which *is*, as opposed to that which merely *seems*. This is made clear from his bloodcurdling intimations of what awaits the sinner after death:

> But that I am forbid
> To tell the secrets of my prison-house,
> I could a tale unfold whose lightest word
> Would harrow up thy soul, freeze thy young blood,
> Make thy two eyes, like stars, start from their spheres,
> Thy knotted and combined locks to part,
> And each particular hair to stand an end,
> Like quills upon the fretful porpentine.
> But this eternal blazon must not be
> To ears of flesh and blood.
>
> (1.5.13–22)

Clearly the Ghost sees and knows things far beyond the ken
of those who have not yet shuffled off this mortal coil. Unless,
of course, the Ghost is not what he seems but is a demon from
Hell. This, then, is another crucial question. Is the play's most
reliable witness to the really real really reliable?

Horatio gives us the first clue that the Ghost is genuinely
the purgatorial spirit of Hamlet's father when he tells Hamlet
that the Ghost had a "countenance more in sorrow than in
anger" (1.2.231), suggesting a penitential spirit from Purgatory, not a demon loosed from Hell—and suggesting also that
his desire is for justice, not vengeance. Yet the Ghost could be
a liar, a fake father posing as a penitent, and Hamlet himself
is unsure whether the Ghost is friend or foe. Mindful of his
earlier words to his mother that he knows not "seems"—those
"actions that a man might play", i.e., feign—but that he
demands to know what something *is*, "that within which passes
show", he demands to know of the Ghost whether he is really
his father's spirit or whether he is a deceiving demon wearing
"but the trappings and the suits of woe":

> Angels and ministers of grace defend us!
> Be thou a spirit of health or goblin damn'd,
> Bring with thee airs from heaven or blasts from hell,
> Be thy intents wicked or charitable,
> Thou com'st in such a questionable shape
> That I will speak to thee.
>
> (1.4.39–44)

The Ghost answers that he is "thy father's spirit",

> Doom'd for a certain term to walk the night,
> And for the day confin'd to fast in fires,
> Till the foul crimes done in my days of nature
> Are burnt and purg'd away.
>
> (1.5.9–13)

The Ghost is, therefore, a soul in Purgatory, "a spirit of health"
destined for Heaven once his sins are purged, and not a "goblin
damn'd". But do we believe him? Is he what he seems? What,

for instance, are we to make of his demand that Hamlet is to avenge his death? Is it plausible that "a spirit of health" would demand an eye for an eye instead of follow Christ's commandment that we love our enemies and turn the other cheek? Is the Ghost guilty of a bloodlustful desire for revenge that exposes him as an infernal impostor posing as Hamlet's father? Or is he merely seeking justice? This is another crucial question.

Although the Ghost uses the word "revenge", he is referring to the fact that there is a cold-blooded murderer on the loose who has escaped the justice of the law. Is the ministration of justice and the desire that the criminal should pay for his crime reprehensible or unchristian? Should King Claudius go unpunished? Is it not Hamlet's duty to unmask the criminal and the crime? Surely there can be no question that he has a duty to expose King Claudius' heinous actions once the Ghost has told him of the crime.

This follows if, of course, the Ghost is telling the truth. Hamlet is at first convinced that he is, declaring after their first meeting that it is "an honest ghost" (1.5.138). And yet Hamlet is healthily skeptical and devises the staging of a play not only to "catch the conscience of the King" but to test the veracity of the Ghost.

> The spirit that I have seen
> May be a devil; and the devil hath power
> T' assume a pleasing shape; yea, and perhaps
> Out of my weakness and my melancholy,
> As he is very potent with such spirits,
> Abuses me to damn me. I'll have grounds
> More relative than this. The play's the thing
> Wherein I'll catch the conscience of the King.
> (2.2.594–601)

It is evident from such lines that Hamlet's procrastination and apparent inability to act are not a damnable weakness on his part but that, on the contrary, they are born of virtuous circumspection and a determination that he is the minister of justice, not the perpetrator of injustice. His delay is the triumph of prudence over prejudice, of that which *is* over that which *seems*. And lest we forget Shakespeare's purpose in highlighting the reason for Hamlet's tardiness, we are reminded once again that Hamlet must know that the guilty party is indeed King Claudius and not the Ghost before he can act with a clear conscience:

> If his occulted guilt
> Do not itself unkennel in one speech,
> It is a damned ghost that we have seen,
> And my imaginations are as foul
> As Vulcan's stithy.
>
> (3.2.78–82)

In the event, of course, the King's guilt is exposed and the Ghost is indeed shown to be "honest".

It is almost time to turn our attention to the unfortunate Ophelia, but before we do so, it is necessary to know more about her father, Polonius, and her brother, Laertes.

Like the Fool in *King Lear*, Polonius is a pragmatist par excellence. His worldly philosophy, as expounded in his advice to his son, is devoid of all supernatural insight and divorced from any Christian concept of virtue. The "few precepts" that he gives to Laertes are all designed to further his son's worldly advancement and are summarized in the phrase "This above all—to thine own self be true" (1.3.78). Such a phrase, imbued with the fashionable humanism of the late Renaissance, has little to do with the Christian humanism of Shakespeare or Saint Thomas More and more to do with the secular humanism of Niccolò Machiavelli. There is no discernible Christianity in Polonius' "precepts", merely self-centeredness enshrined, and his philosophy of pragmatic relativism has no room for any truth beyond the self. It is, therefore, interesting that Shakespeare exhibits his own contempt for such a philosophy through his incarnation of it in such a disreputable character.

If Polonius is clearly depicted as one of the play's villains, his son, Laertes, is an altogether more complex character. In contrast to the banality of Polonius' precepts, Laertes' advice

to his sister with regard to her relationship with Hamlet is full
of astute political philosophy.

> Perhaps he loves you now,
> And now no soil nor cautel doth besmirch
> The virtue of his will; but you must fear,
> His greatness weigh'd, his will is not his own;
> For he himself is subject to his birth:
> He may not, as unvalued persons do,
> Carve for himself; for on his choice depends
> The sanity and health of this whole state;
> And therefore must his choice be circumscrib'd
> Unto the voice and yielding of that body
> Whereof he is the head. Then if he says he loves you,
> It fits your wisdom so far to believe it
> As he in his particular act and place
> May give his saying deed; which is no further
> Than the main voice of Denmark goes withal.
>
> (1.3.14–28)

Laertes is fearful of his sister's relationship with Hamlet and
urges her to share his fear: "Fear it, Ophelia, fear it, my dear
sister" (1.3.33). He knows that as prince and heir to the realm,
Hamlet must always put his duty before his desire. Answer-
able, ultimately, to his duties to the state of Denmark, Hamlet
is not in a position to allow his heart to rule his head. Since
Ophelia is not of royal lineage, she should not expect that
Hamlet will marry her, and, as such, she should preserve her
honor by distancing herself from the relationship. These words
are painful for Ophelia, but she sees the wisdom that they convey and reluctantly agrees to heed her brother's advice:

> I shall the effect of this good lesson keep
> As watchman to my heart.
>
> (1.3.45–46)

Clearly we should have a great deal of sympathy for poor
Ophelia, but is she really "the young, the beautiful, the harmless, and the pious" icon that Samuel Johnson makes of her?

And what of Hamlet's treatment of her "with so much rudeness ... and wanton cruelty"? Is Ophelia an innocent lamb
slaughtered on the altar of other men's sins? Or does she share
some measure of blame for her own fate?

Taking her father's and her brother's advice, Ophelia dis-
tances herself from Hamlet's advances, thereby adding to
Hamlet's sense of desolation. She is, however, hardly to blame
for heeding the advice and warnings of her own family, or for
being obedient to her father's wishes, especially if her brother
is correct in his assessment that Hamlet can never marry her.
But let us see things from Hamlet's perspective. His troubled
state of mind as he enters what has become known as the nunnery scene is made apparent by the near-suicidal depths to
which he plunges in his famous soliloquy:

> To be, or not to be—that is the question;
> Whether 'tis nobler in the mind to suffer
> The slings and arrows of outrageous fortune,
> Or to take arms against a sea of troubles,
> And by opposing end them?
>
> (3.1.56–60)

This is Hamlet at his most angst-driven, weighing up the
options of suffering the injustices heaped upon him or of rising in rebellion against them. To suffer in stoic silence, or to
rise up in anger against the tyrants? That is the question.

> For who would bear the whips and scorns of time,
> Th' oppressor's wrong, the proud man's contumely,
> The pangs of despis'd love, the law's delay,
> The insolence of office, and the spurns
> That patient merit of th' unworthy takes,
> When he himself might his quietus make
> With a bare bodkin?
>
> (3.1.70–76)

Hamlet's predicament has brought him to the brink of suicide, and we should note that the "pangs of despis'd love" are

included among the list of those burdens weighing heavily on his mind. It seems, therefore, that Ophelia's spurning of him has added to his other cares. It is only Hamlet's Christian conscience, or at any rate his fear of Hell, that keeps him from acting upon his desire to end his own life.

> Who would these fardels bear,
> To grunt and sweat under a weary life,
> But that the dread of something after death—
> The undiscover'd country, from whose bourn
> No traveller returns—puzzles the will,
> And makes us rather bear those ills we have
> Than fly to others that we know not of?
>
> (3.1.76–82)

It is from these depths of despondency that Hamlet first sees Ophelia, reading a book of prayers, and his initial reaction is anything but cruel.

> The fair Ophelia.—Nymph, in thy orisons [prayers]
> Be all my sins rememb'red.
>
> (3.1.88–89)

And yet almost immediately, his mood changes. The (feigned) madness comes upon him, and he speaks in most unkind riddles to his former love. Surely this is nothing but "wanton cruelty". Yet his crime of cruelty, though real, is a *crime passionel*, a crime of passion, especially if he suspects or knows that Ophelia is now working against him as a spy, gathering information on her father's and King Claudius' behalf. Does Hamlet know that Polonius and King Claudius are listening to their conversation? In the absence of stage directions, it is difficult to know for certain, but the text itself offers tantalizing clues that Hamlet does indeed know that Ophelia has betrayed him to his enemies. "Ha, ha! Are you honest?" he asks suddenly, prompting a nervous response from Ophelia, who has perhaps given herself away as a very unconvincing spy. Later he asks, suddenly and for no apparent reason, "Where's your father?" prompting another nervous and lying response from Ophelia. In this context, Hamlet's cruel words to Ophelia take on new life, and his repeated insistence that Ophelia enter a nunnery takes on new significance. It is not simply that he will not marry her and that therefore she might as well resign herself to celibacy; it is that she would be better off in a convent than in the damnable intrigues and treacheries of the King's court. Better to live the religious life than to stand con-demned as a spy in the service of a murderer.

Perhaps Ophelia's character is defined by her weakness. It was her weakness that led her to respond to Hamlet's wooing of her, forgetful of the fact that it was very unlikely that he would ever marry her; it was weakness that led her to betray Hamlet through her role as the bait that enabled King Claudius and Polonius to eavesdrop on their conversation; and perhaps it was this very same weakness that led to her final loss of reason. She is certainly a great tragic figure, but we should not allow her tragic beauty to distract us from the deeper elements of the play. Hamlet does not allow himself to be distracted by her beauty, and nor should we. He is intent on answering the deeper ques-tions at the dark heart of the drama, and so should we be.

The deepest elements of the play are to be found, as we have seen, in the difference between that which *is* and that which only *seems* to be. It is the difference between those who choose to be and those who choose not to be. This is the ques-tion to which we must now return.

Immediately after Hamlet exits from the nunnery scene, Ophelia refers to him as "[t]h' observ'd of all observers" (3.1.154), a reference to his popularity and to his being the model of courtliness and scholarship that others observed in order to emulate. He is the "glass of fashion" (3.1.153). The reader, however, sees the irony in her words because, of course, Hamlet's every word and movement in the preceding conversation has been observed from behind the arras by King Claudius and Polonius. The fact is, and as Hamlet knows, the whole of King Claudius' court is a network of spies, making it difficult to discern those who *are* who they say they are—the honest, genuine, or real—from those who *are not* who they say they are—those who only *seem* to be honest, genuine, or real. It is Hamlet's suspicion that Ophelia belongs in the latter group that fuels his anger against her.

In his almost obsessive pursuit of truth and justice, i.e., the things that truly *are* because they are rooted in an immutable moral law, Hamlet is confronted by those who are living a lie and dealing in deceit. This conflict between the moral object and the morally objectionable is particularly evident in Act 2, which is dominated by spies and espionage.

The second act begins with Polonius sending the aptly named Reynaldo[8] to spy on Laertes. He offers Reynaldo elaborate advice on the art of espionage, telling him how to deceive with deftness and dexterity and how to subvert with subtlety and suggestiveness. By the time that Reynaldo leaves on his mission to spy on Polonius' own son, we have lost any vestiges of sympathy for Polonius. We see him for what he is, a master of intrigue who will even betray his own children in order to achieve his goals. Indeed, no sooner has Reynaldo left to spy on Laertes than Polonius begins to hatch the scheme to use his own daughter as bait, enabling him and the King to spy on Hamlet. We see Hamlet's contempt for Polonius in his words of scathingly cryptic condemnation of him as a "fishmonger", a slang expression for one who procures prostitutes for another's use. Polonius is a fishmonger: one who procures spies (prostitutes in the sense that they sell themselves into sin) for King Claudius.

In the same enigmatic "fishmonger" passage (2.2.173–93), we see Hamlet complain that only one man in ten thousand is "honest", i.e., that only a very small number of men *are* what they *seem*, whereas the rest, living a lie, *are not* what they *seem*. To be or not to be. That is the question. But what of the conundrum in the same passage, about breeding maggots in a dead dog? And why is Ophelia dragged into the conversation? Hamlet is obviously referring to the corruption and decadence of

---

[8] Although Reynaldo is derived from "king" and is etymologically unrelated to *renard* (fox), the pun is surely intentional.

King Claudius' court and of the "fishmongers" who prosper therein. The "dead dog" is Denmark, the "something rotten" to which Marcellus refers in the opening act (1.4.90), and the maggots are presumably the sort of people who thrive amid such corruption, particularly perhaps the omnipresent spies. But what of Ophelia? His introduction of her into the conversation immediately following the graphic description, pregnant with allegorical applicability, of maggots and "good kissing carrion" suggests that Hamlet already suspects that the fishmonger, Polonius, had procured his daughter's services for the King as a spy. If this reading is correct, it makes sense of the punning on "conception" as meaning both "understanding" and "becoming pregnant". If Polonius lets his daughter "walk i' th' sun", i.e., serve that power that breeds maggots in a dead dog, Polonius may conceive, i.e., gain the knowledge that he wants, but in doing so, his daughter might also conceive, i.e., be defiled by her involvement in "kissing carrion".

It seems that spies are everywhere, and Hamlet's discovery that Rosencrantz and Guildenstern, his two trusted friends from Wittenberg, have sold their souls to his murdering uncle adds to his angst-ridden sense of foreboding. If his own friends prove false, whom can he trust? Later in the play, speaking of Rosencrantz and Guildenstern, Hamlet decries the whole business of espionage and denounces those who prostitute themselves to it.

> Why, man, they did make love to this employment;
> They are not near my conscience; their defeat
> Does by their own insinuation grow:
> 'Tis dangerous when the baser nature comes
> Between the pass and fell incensed points
> Of mighty opposites.
>
> (5.2.57–62)

If the "honesty" of spies is not what it seems, nor is the "madness" of Hamlet. Many of his most incisive observations are made under cover of such madness, and seeing the sagacity amid the folly is part of the secret to understanding the play. Not only is Hamlet perfectly sane, even when he is at his most distraught, but it almost seems on occasion that he is the only sane character among a menagerie of moral misfits. Take, for instance, his response to Polonius' supercilious comment that he will use the newly arrived players "according to their desert".

> God's bodykins, man, much better. Use every man after his desert, and who shall scape whipping? Use them after your own honour and dignity: the less they deserve, the more merit is in your bounty. Take them in.

(2.2.523–27)

Here we see that Hamlet's sanity is rooted in a profoundly Christian understanding of the dignity of the human person and in the love and mercy of God. These are not the words of a madman but of a man maddened by the moral madness that surrounds him. "The time is out of joint", he laments at the end of Act 1, adding with resentful anger that he "was born to set it right" (1.5.189–90). His sanity is the antidote to the poison that courses through the sin-cankered plot of the play. Without his heroic struggle to make sense of the madness surrounding him, nothing would make sense at all. Everything would be madness.

Even if we accept that Hamlet is more "sane" and virtuous than many of the characters that surround him, we are still uncomfortable at the sheer passion of his invective against the vice that is prevalent in the rottenness of Denmark. His angry words shock us with their unbridled candour and apparent bloodlustful desire for vengeance. Nonetheless, and in spite of any temptation to be judgmental, we should employ a degree of circumspection, worthy of Hamlet himself, before we condemn the speaker too harshly. We need to remind ourselves that the man on whom he seeks vengeance has murdered his father and has subsequently wedded his mother. This is enough to awaken hellish thoughts in the best of men, even if it is not enough to justify them. And we should remember that Hamlet is not a static character throughout the unfolding of the play. He begins in a state of near-suicidal melancholy but experiences the "slings and arrows of outrageous fortune" with passionate circumspection until he arrives at the settled serenity and sagacious resignation of the final act. He is on a journey, a pilgrim en route from a close encounter with Hell, via Purgatory, to a glimpse of the Heaven that beckons offstage. In the midst of this journey, we should not expect our hero to behave impeccably, without a blemish on his character. He is, as he says of himself, "very proud, revengeful, ambitious, with more offences at my beck than I have thoughts to put them in, imagination to give them shape, or time to act them in" (3.1.124–28). He is a miserable sinner, though more sinned against than sinning, who finds himself "crawling between earth and heaven" (3.1.128). He is, in fact, very much like the rest of us, except perhaps that he has more reason than most of us for being angry with the situation in which he finds himself. The key point, however, is that even at his most earthy, he never loses sight of Heaven. He knows right from wrong, and virtue from vice, and tries to do what a good and virtuous man is called to do. He does not always succeed, and occasionally he allows imprudent passion to overpower his usual prudent circumspection. Such moments are, however, the exception and not the rule.

Hamlet knows that unbridled passion is wrong, whether it be in the service of lust, as in the case of the "incestuous" relationship between his mother and King Claudius, or whether it be in the service of hatred, as in the case of some of his own thoughts and words. This is made abundantly plain in his complaint to his mother that "reason panders will" (3.4.88), i.e., that reason panders to our desires instead of our desires being governed by reason. Once again, we see the recurring conflict between that which is and that which only seems to be. If our desires are governed by reason, we are subjecting the subjective to the objective, and, in so doing, we ensure that that which *seems* to be is mastered by that which *is*. If, on the other hand, "reason panders will", we are subjecting the objective to the subjective, and, in so doing, that which *is* is sacrificed to that which *seems* to be. Put plainly, there is a natural moral law, existing in reality, i.e., not invented by man, which transcends and trumps our desires. Something is right or wrong, whether we like it or not. We can be fooled by our desires into believing that what we want is good for us, whereas in fact it is harmful. It *seems* to be good, but it *is* in fact harmful. The whole of *Hamlet* turns on this inescapable distinction between reason and will, between that which is and that which seems to be, and the test of success is the extent to which the protagonists conform their will to reason. This is Hamlet's struggle throughout the play, and we see at the end that he succeeds.

It is intriguing that Hamlet makes this distinction between reason and will, with all that it implies, during his impassioned meeting with his mother, and even more so in the context of the reappearance of the Ghost. Why is it that Hamlet can see the Ghost but his mother cannot? It is not because the Ghost is only a figment of Hamlet's imagination, as his mother believes, because we know that Horatio, Bernardo, and Marcellus have also seen it. Is it because Hamlet's mother is blind to the spiritual truth that the Ghost represents? Has her disordered will usurped her reason to the extent that she no longer perceives the spiritual basis of reality? In losing her reason, has she lost her faith?

Hamlet's response to her blindness and misperception is unequivocal:

> It is not madness
> That I have utt'red. . . .
> .   .   .   .
> Mother, for love of grace,
> Lay not that flattering unction to your soul,
> That not your trespass but my madness speaks:
> .   .   .   .
> Confess yourself to heaven;
> Repent what's past; avoid what is to come;
> And do not spread the compost on the weeds,
> To make them ranker. Forgive me this my virtue;
> For in the fatness of these pursy times
> Virtue itself of vice must pardon beg,
> Yea, curb and woo for leave to do him good.
> (3.4.141–42; 144–46; 149–55)

The conclusion that must be drawn from this exchange between mother and son is apparent enough. The Ghost exists, whether we like it or not and in spite of any belief to the contrary by those who have made themselves morally blind through a pandering of the will. Not only is the Ghost real, but his involvement is crucial to the unfolding of the whole plot. If it had not been for the intervention of the "honest Ghost", Hamlet would never have known of the King's treachery and murder; he would never have known that any justice was necessary. The Ghost, who can be nothing but "honest" because he comes from the eternal realm, where everything *is* and nothing merely *seems* to be, is absolutely necessary to inject a healthy dose of supernatural objectivity into the picture. As a soul in eternity, and therefore closer to the presence of God, he is the most *real* character in the whole play. He sees more than anyone else because he sees what *is* and not what *seems* to be. His very presence tears apart the petty Machiavellian schemes of relativists, such as King Claudius and Polonius, ripping their "seems" to the seams. He shines forth the heavenly light of Purgatory into the twilight zone of lies, half-truths, and deception into which Denmark had fallen.

But what of Hamlet's death? And what of Ophelia's? Can we really be satisfied by their destruction? Perhaps not. In an ideal world, the innocent would not fall victim to the sins of others. But we do not live in an ideal world but in a fallen one, and this is the world in which Shakespeare and all his characters reside. Shakespeare is not writing Christian fantasy but Christian realism, and this entails martyrdom and suffering on the part of the innocent. This is the real world in which Shakespeare found himself. Why would the playwright whitewash such grim realities from his plays? And why would we want him to? *Hamlet* is not a fairy story. There is no guaranteed "happy ending" in this life, and if we are indeed to live "happily ever after", it is in the next life, not in this one. "Happily ever after" happens offstage, after the final curtain has fallen, and Shakespeare's great gift is the way in which he is always pointing offstage to the deeper reality that is beyond it.

So, at last, we come to Hamlet's death and the promise of his resurrection.

The honorable Horatio is, appropriately, the first person to speak following the death of the prince whom he had served so loyally:

> Now cracks a noble heart. Good night, sweet Prince,
> And flights of angels sing thee to thy rest!
>
> (5.2.351–52)

Horatio's words, ending in *requiem*, are a translation, with only a minor alteration, from the Latin of the *In paradisum*, the antiphon of the burial service following the Requiem Mass: *In paradisum deducant te angeli. . . . Chorus angelorum te suscipiat, et cum Lazaro quondam paupere aeternam habeas requiem.* It is surely no coincidence that Hamlet's own last words, uttered immediately before these, are "[T]he rest is silence", in which "rest" quite clearly signifies both *cetera* and *requies*.[9] Thus Shakespeare ends his play by offering a Requiem Mass for the "noble heart" of his hero. This *is* a truly happy ending, even if it *seems* to be a tragedy.

---

[9] Gerard Kilroy, "Requiem for a Prince: Rites of Memory in *Hamlet*" (unpublished manuscript). *Cetera* as in *et cetera* (and the rest); *requies* as in *requiescant in pace* (rest in peace).

So, at last, we come to Hamlet's death and the promise of his resurrection.

The honorable Horatio is, appropriately, the first person to speak following the death of the prince whom he had served so loyally:

> Now cracks a noble heart. Good night, sweet Prince,
> And flights of angels sing thee to thy rest!
>
> (5.2.351–52)

Horatio's words, ending in *requiem*, are a translation, with only a minor alteration, from the Latin of the *In paradisum*, the antiphon of the burial service following the Requiem Mass: *In paradisum deducant te angeli. . . . Chorus angelorum te suscipiat, et cum Lazaro quondam paupere aeternam habeas requiem*. It is surely no coincidence that Hamlet's own last words, uttered immediately before these, are "[T]he rest is silence", in which "rest" quite clearly signifies both *cetera* and *requies*.[9] Thus Shakespeare ends his play by offering a Requiem Mass for the "noble heart" of his hero. This *is* a truly happy ending, even if it *seems* to be a tragedy.

---

[9] Gerard Kilroy, "Requiem for a Prince: Rites of Memory in *Hamlet*" (unpublished manuscript). *Cetera* as in *et cetera* (and the rest); *requies* as in *requiescant in pace* (rest in peace).

TEXTUAL NOTE

There are three different "original" texts of *Hamlet*: the First Quarto, dating from 1603; the Second Quarto, dating from the following year; and the First Folio of 1623. The First Quarto is sometimes called the Bad Quarto because it is clearly a pirated version that differs from the two later authoritative editions. This edition follows the Alexander Text (named after the Shakespearian scholar Peter Alexander), which is internationally accepted as authoritative and is based on the First Folio.

Hamlet, Prince of Denmark

DRAMATIS PERSONAE

Claudius, king of Denmark
Hamlet, son to the former and nephew to the present king
Polonius, lord chamberlain
Horatio, friend to Hamlet
Laertes, son to Polonius
Voltemand ⎤
Cornelius ⎥
Rosencrantz ⎥ courtiers
Guildenstern ⎥
Osric ⎥
A Gentleman ⎦
A Gentleman
A Priest
Marcellus ⎤ officers
Bernardo ⎦
Francisco, a soldier
Reynaldo, servant to Polonius
Players
Two Clowns, gravediggers
Fortinbras, prince of Norway
A Norwegian Captain
English Ambassadors
Gertrude, queen of Denmark and mother of Hamlet
Ophelia, daughter to Polonius
Ghost of Hamlet's father
Lords, Ladies, Officers, Soldiers, Sailors, Messengers,
    and Attendants

ACT 1

Scene 1.   *Elsinore. The guard-platform of the Castle.*

Francisco at his post. Enter to him Bernardo.

Bernardo. Who's there?

Francisco. Nay, answer me. Stand and unfold[1] yourself.

Bernardo. Long live the King![2]

Francisco. Bernardo?

Bernardo. He.   5

Francisco. You come most carefully upon your hour.[3]

Bernardo. 'Tis now struck twelve; get thee to bed,
          Francisco.

Francisco. For this relief much thanks. 'Tis bitter cold,
          And I am sick at heart.

Bernardo. Have you had quiet guard?

Francisco.   Not a mouse stirring.   10

Bernardo. Well, good night.
          If you do meet Horatio and Marcellus,
          The rivals[4] of my watch, bid them make haste.

Enter Horatio and Marcellus.

Francisco. I think I hear them. Stand, ho! Who is there?

---

[1] *unfold*: show or identify.
[2] *Long live the King!* perhaps a password.
[3] *most carefully upon your hour*: i.e., at the exact time you are supposed to.
[4] *rivals*: companions or partners.

Horatio. Friends to this ground,[5]

Marcellus. And liegemen[6] to the Dane.[7]   15

Francisco. Give you good night.

Marcellus. O, farewell, honest soldier!
  Who hath reliev'd you?

Francisco. Bernardo hath my place.
  Give you[8] good night.   *Exit.*

Marcellus. Holla, Bernado!

Bernardo. Say—   20
  What, is Horatio there?

Horatio. A piece of him.

Bernardo. Welcome, Horatio; welcome, good Marcellus.

Horatio. What, has this thing appear'd again to-night?

Bernardo. I have seen nothing.

Marcellus. Horatio says 'tis but our fantasy,
  And will not let belief take hold of him   25
  Touching this dreaded sight, twice seen of us;
  Therefore I have entreated him along
  With us to watch the minutes of this night,[9]
  That, if again this apparition come,
  He may approve our eyes[10] and speak to it.

Horatio. Tush, tush, 'twill not appear.   30

---

[5] *this ground:* i.e., Denmark.
[6] *liegemen:* loyal subjects.
[7] *Dane:* i.e., the king of Denmark.
[8] *Give you:* a colloquial form of the salutation "God give you".
[9] *to watch . . . this night:* to stand watch through the night.
[10] *approve our eyes:* corroborate what we claim to have seen.

Bernardo.   Sit down awhile,
  And let us once again assail your ears,[11]
  That are so fortified against our story,
  What we have two nights seen.

Horatio.   Well, sit we down,
  And let us hear Bernardo speak of this.   35

Bernardo. Last night of all,
  When yond same star that's westward from the pole
  Had made his course[12] t' illume that part of heaven
  Where now it burns, Marcellus and myself,
  The bell then beating one—

Enter Ghost.

Marcellus. Peace, break thee off; look where it comes
        again.   40

Bernardo. In the same figure,[13] like the King that's dead.

Marcellus. Thou art a scholar;[14] speak to it, Horatio.

Bernardo. Looks 'a[15] not like the King? Mark[16] it,
        Horatio.

Horatio. Most like. It harrows[17] me with fear and wonder.

Bernardo. It would be spoke to.[18]

Marcellus.   Question it, Horatio.   45

Horatio. What art thou that usurp'st[19] this time of night
        Together with that fair and warlike form

---

[11] *assail your ears:* try to persuade or convince away your incredulity.

[12] *his course:* perhaps inferring that the "star" is in fact a planet.

[13] *same figure:* exact likeness.

[14] *Thou art a scholar:* Horatio is identified as an educated man who speaks Latin, the proper language for speaking to ghosts and for conducting exorcisms.

[15] *'a:* he.

[16] *Mark:* attend or note its location, position, and appearance.

[17] *harrows:* distresses, torments, or (more literally) rakes my soul with terror.

[18] *speak to it . . . It would be spoke to:* Ghosts could not begin conversations.

[19] *usurp'st:* A supernatural creature has come into nature.

In which the majesty of buried Denmark[20]
Did sometimes[21] march? By heaven I charge thee,
    speak!

Marcellus. It is offended.

Bernardo.   See, it stalks away.   50

Horatio. Stay! speak, speak! I charge thee, speak!

                                            [*Exit Ghost.*]

Marcellus. 'Tis gone, and will not answer.

Bernardo. How now, Horatio! You tremble and look pale.
    Is not this something more than fantasy?
    What think you on't?   55

Horatio. Before my God, I might not this believe
    Without the sensible and true avouch[22]
    Of mine own eyes.

Marcellus.   Is it not like the King?

Horatio. As thou art to thyself:
    Such was the very armour he had on   60
    When he the ambitious Norway[23] combated;
    So frown'd he once when, in an angry parle,[24]
    He smote the sledded Polacks[25] on the ice.
    'Tis strange.

Marcellus. Thus twice before, and jump[26] at this dead
    hour,   65
    With martial stalk[27] hath he gone by our watch.

---

[20] *majesty of buried Denmark*: i.e., the dead king.
[21] *sometimes*: formerly.
[22] *avouch*: avowal, assurance.
[23] *Norway*: i.e., the king of Norway.
[24] *parle*: parley; interaction, conversation.
[25] *sledded Polacks*: a poleax weighted with lead like a sledgehammer. This has
been mistaken as a reference to Polish troops on sleds.
[26] *jump*: precisely.
[27] *stalk*: march, attitude of walking.

Horatio. In what particular thought to work[28] I know not;
But, in the gross and scope of mine opinion,[29]
This bodes some strange eruption[30] to our state.

Marcellus. Good now,[31] sit down, and tell me, he that
    knows,   70
Why this same strict and most observant watch[32]
So nightly toils[33] the subject[34] of the land;
And why such daily cast[35] of brazen cannon,
And foreign mart[36] for implements of war;
Why such impress[37] of shipwrights,[38] whose sore task   75
Does not divide the Sunday from the week;[39]
What might be toward,[40] that this sweaty haste
Doth make the night joint-labourer with the day:[41]
Who is't that can inform me?

Horatio.   That can I;
At least, the whisper[42] goes so. Our last king,   80
Whose image even but now appear'd to us,
Was, as you know, by Fortinbras of Norway,
Thereto prick'd on by a most emulate[43] pride,

[28] *In what particular thought to work*: for what reason.
[29] *in the gross and scope of mine opinion*: as far as my current understanding allows me.
[30] *eruption*: disruption, upheaval.
[31] *Good now*: if you please.
[32] *watch*: wakefulness, alertness (both military- and labor-related).
[33] *toils*: causes to toil.
[34] *subject*: subjects.
[35] *cast*: casting in a foundry (into the mold of a cannon).
[36] *foreign mart*: foreign markets.
[37] *impress*: forced service, conscription.
[38] *shipwrights*: shipbuilders.
[39] *Does not divide the Sunday from the week*: The work continues even on Sundays.
[40] *toward*: impending, looming.
[41] *Doth make the night joint-labourer with the day*: The work continues through the night.
[42] *whisper*: rumor.
[43] *emulate*: emulous; a jealous rivalry, the attempt to match or surpass by imitation.

Dar'd to the combat; in which our valiant Hamlet—
For so this side of our known world[44] esteem'd
    him—   85
Did slay this Fortinbras; who, by a seal'd compact,[45]
Well ratified by law and heraldry,[46]
Did forfeit, with his life, all those his lands
Which he stood seiz'd of,[47] to the conqueror;
Against the which a moiety[48] competent[49]   90
Was gaged[50] by our king; which had[51] return'd
To the inheritance of Fortinbras,
Had he been vanquisher; as, by the same comart[52]
And carriage[53] of the article design'd,[54]
His fell to Hamlet. Now, sir, young Fortinbras,   95
Of unimproved[55] mettle[56] hot and full,
Hath in the skirts[57] of Norway, here and there,
Shark'd up[58] a list of lawless resolutes,[59]
For food and diet,[60] to some enterprise
That hath a stomach in't;[61] which is no other,   100
As it doth well appear unto our state,[62]
But to recover of us, by strong hand

[44] *this side of our known world*: i.e., western Europe.
[45] *seal'd compact*: formal agreement.
[46] *law and heraldry*: the established rules of combat.
[47] *stood seiz'd of*: was possessed of.
[48] *moiety*: equivalent portion of land.
[49] *competent*: adequate, satisfactory.
[50] *gaged*: wagered.
[51] *had*: would have.
[52] *comart*: bargain, covenant.
[53] *carriage*: tenor, sense.
[54] *article design'd*: terms of the agreement.
[55] *unimproved*: unproven, untried.
[56] *mettle*: spirit, resilience.
[57] *skirts*: outskirts or outlying territories.
[58] *Shark'd up*: put together rashly or thrown together indiscriminately.
[59] *lawless resolutes*: villainous or desperate characters.
[60] *diet*: daily pay.
[61] *That hath a stomach in't*: testament to the boldness and danger of the undertaking.
[62] *our state*: i.e., Denmark.

And terms compulsatory,[63] those foresaid lands
So by his father lost; and this, I take it,
Is the main motive of our preparations,   *105*
The source of this our watch, and the chief head[64]
Of this post-haste[65] and romage[66] in the land.

Bernardo. I think it be no other but e'en so.
    Well may it sort,[67] that this portentous[68] figure
    Comes armed through our watch; so like the King   *110*
    That was and is the question of these wars.

Horatio. A mote[69] it is to trouble the mind's eye.
    In the most high and palmy[70] state of Rome,
    A little ere[71] the mightiest Julius[72] fell,
    The graves stood tenantless, and the sheeted dead[73]   *115*
    Did squeak and gibber[74] in the Roman streets;
    As, stars with trains of fire,[75] and dews of blood,[76]
    Disasters in the sun;[77] and the moist star[78]
    Upon whose influence[79] Neptune's empire[80] stands
    Was sick almost to doomsday[81] with eclipse;[82]   *120*

---

[63] *compulsatory:* compulsory; enforced by law or force.

[64] *head:* reason, source.

[65] *post-haste:* great speed.

[66] *romage:* bustling activity, commotion.

[67] *sort:* be fitting, appropriate.

[68] *portentous:* ominous, as a portent of things to come.

[69] *mote:* speck; here, a speck of thought.

[70] *palmy:* prosperous.

[71] *ere:* before.

[72] *Julius:* Gaius Julius Caesar (100–44 B.C.), Roman emperor; assassinated.

[73] *sheeted dead:* corpses wrapped in burial cloths.

[74] *squeak and gibber:* utter shrill, piping cries.

[75] *stars with trains of fire:* comets.

[76] *dews of blood:* red dews (a phenomenon caused by insects).

[77] *Disasters in the sun:* ominous signs, perhaps sunspots.

[78] *moist star:* the moon.

[79] *influence:* the moon's influence on the tides.

[80] *Neptune's empire:* i.e., the seas.

[81] *doomsday:* the end of the world.

[82] *sick . . . with eclipse:* almost darkened in a full eclipse. There were two full lunar eclipses and a solar eclipse in 1598.

And even the like precurse[83] of fear'd events,
As harbingers[84] preceding still[85] the fates
And prologue to the omen[86] coming on,
Have heaven and earth together demonstrated
Unto our climatures[87] and countrymen.   125

Re-enter Ghost.

But, soft, behold! Lo, where it comes again!
I'll cross it,[88] though it blast[89] me. Stay, illusion.

                              [*Ghost spreads its arms.*]

If thou hast any sound or use of voice,
Speak to me.
If there be any good thing to be done,   130
That may to thee do ease and grace to me,
Speak to me.
If thou art privy[90] to thy country's fate,
Which happily[91] foreknowing[92] may avoid,
O, speak!   135
Or if thou hast uphoarded[93] in thy life
Extorted[94] treasure in the womb of earth,
For which, they say, you spirits oft walk in death,

                              [*The cock crows.*]

Speak of it. Stay, and speak. Stop it, Marcellus.

---

[83] *precurse*: precursor, foreshadowing.
[84] *harbingers*: persons or signs signaling the approach of something.
[85] *still*: always.
[86] *omen*: calamity, the events portended.
[87] *climatures*: regions of the earth.
[88] *cross it*: confront it, cross its path.
[89] *blast*: wither, smite.
[90] *art privy*: have knowledge of something secret or private.
[91] *happily*: also given as "haply"; perhaps or fortunately.
[92] *foreknowing*: prior knowledge or warning.
[93] *uphoarded*: stored up or hidden.
[94] *Extorted*: obtained by unfair means.

Marcellus. Shall I strike at it with my partisan?[95]   *140*

Horatio. Do, if it will not stand.[96]

Bernardo.   'Tis here!

Horatio.   'Tis here!

Marcellus. 'Tis gone!   [*Exit Ghost.*]

We do it wrong, being so majestical,[97]
To offer it the show of violence;
For it is, as the air, invulnerable,   *145*
And our vain blows malicious mockery.[98]

Bernardo. It was about to speak, when the cock crew.

Horatio. And then it started like a guilty thing
Upon a fearful summons.[99] I have heard
The cock, that is the trumpet[100] to the morn,   *150*
Doth with his lofty and shrill-sounding throat
Awake the god of day;[101] and at his warning,
Whether in sea or fire, in earth or air,
Th' extravagant[102] and erring[103] spirit hies[104]
To his confine;[105] and of the truth herein   *155*
This present object made probation.[106]

---

[95] *partisan*: long-handled spear.

[96] *stand*: stop.

[97] *majestical*: majestic, displaying notable dignity or the appearance of royal power.

[98] *malicious mockery*: a mockery of malice, empty threats. The Ghost is intangible; therefore, their blows fall upon the air.

[99] *a fearful summons*: a call back to the realm of the afterlife.

[100] *trumpet*: trumpeter.

[101] *the god of day*: in classical mythology, Phoebus Apollo, the god of the sun.

[102] *extravagant*: unrestrained, wandering outside proper bounds.

[103] *erring*: wandering.

[104] *hies*: hurries.

[105] *his confine*: the place where his soul is kept after death.

[106] *of the truth . . . probation*: the appearance of the Ghost serves as a proof.

Marcellus. It faded on the crowing of the cock.
  Some say that ever 'gainst that season[107] comes
  Wherein our Saviour's birth is celebrated,
  This bird of dawning[108] singeth all night long;   160
  And then, they say, no spirit dare stir abroad,
  The nights are wholesome,[109] then no planets
    strike,[110]
  No fairy takes,[111] nor witch hath power to charm:
  So hallowed and so gracious[112] is that time.

Horatio. So have I heard, and do in part believe it.   165
  But look, the morn, in russet mantle clad,
  Walks o'er the dew of yon high eastward hill.
  Break we our watch up; and, by my advice,
  Let us impart what we have seen to-night
  Unto young Hamlet; for, upon my life,   170
  This spirit, dumb to us, will speak to him.
  Do you consent we shall acquaint him with it,
  As needful in our loves, fitting our duty?

Marcellus. Let's do't, I pray; and I this morning know
  Where we shall find him most convenient.   175

[*Exeunt.*]

---

[107] *ever 'gainst that season*: in expectation of that time.
[108] *dawning*: the dawn.
[109] *The nights are wholesome*: This was extraordinary (a reflection on its association with Christ), as the night air was proverbially bad for the health at ordinary times.
[110] *strike*: exert an evil influence.
[111] *takes*: bewitches.
[112] *gracious*: full of divine grace.

Scene 2. *Elsinore. The Castle.*

Flourish.[113] *Enter Claudius King of Denmark,
Gertrude the Queen, and Councillors, including
Polonius, his son Laertes, Voltemand, Cornelius,
and Hamlet.*

King. Though yet of Hamlet our dear brother's death
  The memory be green;[114] and that it us befitted
  To bear our hearts in grief, and our whole kingdom
  To be contracted in one brow of woe;[115]
  Yet so far hath discretion fought with nature[116]   5
  That we with wisest sorrow think on him,
  Together with remembrance of ourselves.
  Therefore our sometime sister,[117] now our queen,
  Th' imperial jointress[118] to this warlike state,
  Have we, as 'twere with a defeated[119] joy,   10
  With an auspicious[120] and a dropping[121] eye,
  With mirth in funeral, and with dirge in marriage,
  In equal scale weighing delight and dole,[122]
  Taken to wife; nor have we herein barr'd[123]
  Your better wisdoms,[124] which have freely[125] gone   15
  With this affair along. For all, our thanks.
  Now follows that you know:[126] young Fortinbras,

[113] *Flourish:* fanfare.

[114] *green:* fresh, young, of recent growth.

[115] *contracted . . . woe:* knit together in one mournful brow.

[116] *nature:* i.e., the natural impulse to mourn the death of King Hamlet.

[117] *sometime sister:* former sister-in-law.

[118] *jointress:* widow holding an estate she inherited from her husband; here, asserting that the crown passed with the widow to her second husband.

[119] *defeated:* subdued, overcome.

[120] *auspicious:* cheerful, promising.

[121] *dropping:* mournful.

[122] *dole:* mourning, distress.

[123] *barr'd:* barred; ignored.

[124] *better wisdoms:* cautions, sage advice.

[125] *freely:* fully.

[126] *Now follows that you know:* What will be discussed is something about which you already know.

Holding a weak supposal[127] of our worth,
Or thinking by our late dear brother's death
Our state to be disjoint and out of frame, 20
Co-leagued with this dream of his advantage[128]—
He hath not fail'd to pester us with message
Importing[129] the surrender of those lands
Lost by his father, with all bands of law,[130]
To our most valiant brother. So much for him. 25
Now for ourself, and for this time of meeting,
Thus much the business is: we have here writ
To Norway,[131] uncle of young Fortinbras—
Who, impotent[132] and bed-rid,[133] scarcely hears
Of this his nephew's purpose—to suppress 30
His further gait[134] herein, in that the levies,
The lists, and full proportions,[135] are all made
Out of his subject;[136] and we here dispatch
You, good Cornelius, and you, Voltemand,
For bearers of this greeting to old Norway; 35
Giving to you no further personal power
To business with the King more than the scope
Of these delated[137] articles allow.
Farewell; and let your haste commend[138] your duty.

Cornelius, Voltemand. In that and all things will we
    show our duty. 40

---

[127] *weak supposal*: low estimate.
[128] *Co-leagued . . . his advantage*: allied with dreams of military success.
[129] *Importing*: pertaining to, concerning.
[130] *all bands of law*: legally binding contracts.
[131] *Norway*: i.e., the king of Norway.
[132] *impotent*: helpless.
[133] *bed-rid*: bedridden.
[134] *gait*: proceeding, progress.
[135] *levies . . . full proportions*: the body of enlisted troops and supplies.
[136] *his subject*: his Norwegian subjects. The forces are all Norwegian, not foreign mercenaries.
[137] *delated*: reported, detailed.
[138] *commend*: recommend or demonstrate.

King. We doubt it nothing,[139] heartily farewell.

      [Exeunt Voltemand and Cornelius.]

  And now, Laertes, what's the news with you?
  You told us of some suit;[140] what is't, Laertes?
  You cannot speak of reason to the Dane[141]
  And lose your voice.[142] What wouldst thou beg,
    Laertes,   45
  That shall not be my offer, not thy asking?
  The head is not more native[143] to the heart,
  The hand more instrumental[144] to the mouth,
  Than is the throne of Denmark to thy father.
  What wouldst thou have, Laertes?

Laertes.   My dread[145] lord, 50
  Your leave[146] and favour to return to France;
  From whence though willingly I came to Denmark
  To show my duty in your coronation,
  Yet now, I must confess, that duty done,
  My thoughts and wishes bend again toward France, 55
  And bow them to your gracious leave and pardon.[147]

King. Have you your gracious father's leave?
  What says Polonius?

Polonius. 'A[148] hath, my lord, wrung from me my slow
    leave[149]

---

[139] *nothing:* not at all.
[140] *suit:* petition, request.
[141] *Dane:* king of Denmark (i.e., Claudius).
[142] *You cannot speak . . . And lose your voice:* any reasonable request will not be ignored.
[143] *native:* closely connected.
[144] *instrumental:* serviceable.
[145] *dread:* revered.
[146] *leave:* permission.
[147] *leave and pardon:* As a member of the court, Laertes has an obligation to wait upon the king.
[148] *'A:* he.
[149] *slow leave:* reluctant permission.

By laboursome petition; and at last
Upon his will I seal'd[150] my hard[151] consent.   60
I do beseech you, give him leave to go.

King. Take thy fair hour,[152] Laertes; time be thine,
And thy best graces spend it at thy will![153]
But now, my cousin[154] Hamlet, and my son—

Hamlet. [*Aside*] A little more than kin, and less than
    kind.[155]   65

King. How is it that the clouds still hang on you?

Hamlet. Not so, my lord; I am too much in the sun.[156]

Queen. Good Hamlet, cast thy nighted[157] colour off,
And let thine eye look like a friend on Denmark.[158]
Do not for ever with thy vailed[159] lids   70
Seek for thy noble father in the dust.
Thou know'st 'tis common—all that lives must die,
Passing through nature to eternity.

Hamlet. Ay, madam, it is common.[160]

---

[150] *seal'd*: gave the stamp of approval.

[151] *hard*: reluctant.

[152] *Take thy fair hour*: enjoy youth.

[153] *time be . . . thy will*: Claudius places no limits on the liberty granted to Laertes.

[154] *cousin*: kinsman.

[155] *more than kin . . . kind*: more kin than before (Hamlet was Claudius' nephew and now is his stepson) but less than kind (there is no sincere feeling to support the relationship); perhaps also an attribution of unkindness to Claudius.

[156] *too much in the sun*: too much patronized by (in the sun of) the royal favor; also too much a son (now son and stepson), resenting the name of "son" so used by Claudius; also sun-struck, an allusion and prelude to the feigned madness.

[157] *nighted*: black, as in mourning.

[158] *Denmark*: i.e., the king of Denmark.

[159] *vailed*: downcast.

[160] *common*: a basic condition of humanity, also a cliché, and a sign of cheapness or coarseness.

Queen.   If it be,
  Why seems it so particular[161] with thee?   75

Hamlet. Seems, madam! Nay, it is; I know not seems.
  'Tis not alone my inky cloak, good mother,
  Nor customary suits of solemn black,
  Nor windy suspiration of forc'd breath,[162]
  No, nor the fruitful river in the eye,[163]   80
  Nor the dejected haviour[164] of the visage,[165]
  Together with all forms, moods, shapes of grief,
  That can denote me truly. These, indeed, seem;
  For they are actions that a man might play;
  But I have that within which passes show—   85
  These but the trappings and the suits of woe.[166]

King. 'Tis sweet and commendable in your nature,
    Hamlet,
  To give these mourning duties to your father;
  But you must know your father lost a father;
  That father lost his; and the survivor bound,   90
  In filial obligation, for some term
  To do obsequious[167] sorrow. But to persever[168]
  In obstinate condolement[169] is a course[170]
  Of impious[171] stubbornness; 'tis unmanly grief;
  It shows a will most incorrect[172] to heaven,   95

---

[161] *particular*: personal.

[162] *windy . . . breath*: unrestrained sighs.

[163] *fruitful river in the eye*: stream of tears.

[164] *havior*: behavior or appearance.

[165] *visage*: face, facial expression.

[166] *These . . . woe*: the ornaments, clothes, and actions that are all outward demonstrations of grief.

[167] *obsequious*: excessive, servile; also that which is proper to obsequies (funeral rites).

[168] *persever*: persevere; continue or persist.

[169] *condolement*: grief.

[170] *course*: manner of conduct.

[171] *impious*: showing irreverence or a lack of piety (contrary to the Christian hope and belief that his father is in Heaven).

[172] *incorrect*: rebellious.

A heart unfortified, a mind impatient,
An understanding simple and unschool'd;
For what we know must be, and is as common
As any the most vulgar[173] thing to sense,
Why should we in our peevish opposition   100
Take it to heart? Fie! 'tis a fault to heaven,
A fault against the dead, a fault to nature,
To reason most absurd; whose common theme
Is death of fathers, and who still hath cried,
From the first corse[174] till he that died to-day,   105
"This must be so". We pray you throw to earth
This unprevailing woe, and think of us
As of a father; for let the world take note
You are the most immediate to our throne;[175]
And with no less nobility of love   110
Than that which dearest[176] father bears his son
Do I impart toward you. For your intent
In going back to school in Wittenberg,[177]
It is most retrograde[178] to our desire;
And we beseech you bend you[179] to remain   115
Here, in the cheer and comfort of our eye,
Our chiefest courtier, cousin, and our son.

Queen. Let not thy mother lose[180] her prayers, Hamlet:
I pray thee stay with us; go not to Wittenberg.

Hamlet. I shall in all my best obey you, madam.   120

---

[173] *vulgar*: common or obvious.

[174] *corse*: corpse.

[175] *the most immediate to our throne*: the heir, next in line to the throne.

[176] *dearest*: most affectionate.

[177] *Wittenberg*: university in Germany later named after the Protestant Reformer Martin Luther (1483–1546), where Luther nailed up his *Ninety-Five Theses* (1517); also the university of Christopher Marlowe's fictional character Dr. Faustus.

[178] *retrograde*: contrary or opposite to.

[179] *bend you*: agree or incline yourself.

[180] *lose*: waste.

King. Why, 'tis a loving and a fair[181] reply.
   Be as ourself in Denmark.[182] Madam, come;
   This gentle and unforc'd accord of Hamlet
   Sits smiling to my heart; in grace whereof,
   No jocund[183] health that Denmark drinks to-day   *125*
   But the great cannon to the clouds[184] shall tell,
   And the King's rouse[185] the heaven shall bruit[186]
      again,
   Re-speaking earthly thunder. Come away.

           [*Flourish. Exeunt all but Hamlet.*]

Hamlet. O, that this too too solid[187] flesh would melt,
   Thaw, and resolve[188] itself into a dew!   *130*
   Or that the Everlasting had not fix'd
   His canon[189] 'gainst self-slaughter! O God! God!
   How weary, stale, flat, and unprofitable,
   Seem to me all the uses[190] of this world!
   Fie on't! Ah, fie! 'tis an unweeded garden,   *135*
   That grows to seed; things rank and gross in nature
   Possess it merely.[191] That it should come to this!
   But two months dead! Nay, not so much, not two.
   So excellent a king that was to this
   Hyperion[192] to a satyr;[193] so loving to my mother,   *140*

[181] *fair*: pleasing.
[182] *Be as ourself in Denmark*: enjoy a kingly authority and status in Denmark.
[183] *jocund*: cheerful, lighthearted.
[184] *the great cannon to the clouds*: a large cannon shot into the sky, a demonstration of prestige.
[185] *rouse*: celebratory drinking.
[186] *bruit*: echo; report and spread the news.
[187] *solid*: The Second Quarto has "sallied", which is usually modernized as "sullied", but the First Folio has "solid", which is probably correct because "solid" fits more comfortably with "melt" and "thaw".
[188] *resolve*: dissolve.
[189] *canon*: law (cf. the Fifth Commandment: "Thou shalt not kill").
[190] *uses*: events, practices, customs.
[191] *merely*: completely.
[192] *Hyperion*: in classical mythology, Titan, the god of the sun.
[193] *satyr*: in classical mythology, a male spirit of nature, half-man and half-goat, who was ugly, lecherous, and mischievous.

That he might not beteem[194] the winds of heaven
Visit her face too roughly. Heaven and earth!
Must I remember? Why, she would hang on him
As if increase of appetite had grown
By what it fed on; and yet, within a month—   *145*
Let me not think on't. Frailty, thy name is woman!—
A little month, or ere those shoes were old
With which she followed my poor father's body,
Like Niobe,[195] all tears—why she, even she—
O God! a beast that wants[196] discourse of reason   *150*
Would have mourn'd longer—married with my uncle,
My father's brother; but no more like my father
Than I to Hercules.[197] Within a month,
Ere yet the salt of most unrighteous[198] tears
Had left the flushing[199] in her galled[200] eyes,   *155*
She married. O, most wicked speed, to post[201]
With such dexterity[202] to incestuous[203] sheets!
It is not, nor it cannot come to good.
But break, my heart, for I must hold my tongue.

Enter Horatio, Marcellus, and Bernardo.

Horatio. Hail to your lordship!

Hamlet.   I am glad to see you well.   *160*
      Horatio—or I do forget myself.

---

[194] *beteem*: permit.

[195] *Niobe*: in classical mythology, a figure of absolute grief who wept endlessly after her seven sons and seven daughters were killed by the gods. She eventually turned to stone.

[196] *wants*: lacks.

[197] *Hercules*: in classical mythology, a hero who performed many great deeds and won immortality with the gods.

[198] *unrighteous*: dishonest, insincere.

[199] *flushing*: tears, redness.

[200] *galled*: inflamed.

[201] *post*: hurry.

[202] *dexterity*: ease, readiness.

[203] *incestuous*: referring to an illicit union at too close a blood relationship; here, the marriage between brother and sister-in-law.

Horatio. The same, my lord, and your poor servant ever.

Hamlet. Sir, my good friend. I'll change[204] that name
    with you.
    And what make you from[205] Wittenberg, Horatio?
    Marcellus?   165

Marcellus. My good lord!

Hamlet. I am very glad to see you. [*To Bernardo*] Good
    even, sir.—
    But what, in faith, make you from Wittenberg?

Horatio. A truant disposition, good my lord.

Hamlet. I would not hear your enemy say so;   170
    Nor shall you do my ear that violence,
    To make it truster[206] of your own report
    Against yourself. I know you are no truant.
    But what is your affair in Elsinore?
    We'll teach you to drink deep[207] ere you depart.   175

Horatio. My lord, I came to see your father's funeral.

Hamlet. I prithee[208] do not mock me, fellow student;
    I think it was to see my mother's wedding.

Horatio. Indeed, my lord, it followed hard upon.[209]

Hamlet. Thrift, thrift, Horatio! The funeral
    bak'd-meats[210]   180
    Did coldly[211] furnish forth the marriage tables.
    Would I had met my dearest[212] foe in heaven

---

[204] *change*: exchange (the name of servant).
[205] *what make you from*: what has brought you away from.
[206] *truster*: trustful, trusting.
[207] *deep*: deeply, heavily.
[208] *I prithee*: i.e., I pray you.
[209] *hard upon*: immediately after.
[210] *bak'd-meats*: refreshments.
[211] *coldly*: unfeelingly, or literally as "cold meats".
[212] *dearest*: most hated.

Or ever[213] I had seen that day, Horatio!
My father—methinks I see my father.

Horatio. Where, my lord?

Hamlet.   In my mind's eye, Horatio.   185

Horatio. I saw him once; 'a[214] was a goodly king.

Hamlet. 'A was a man, take him for all in all,
I shall not look upon his like again.

Horatio. My lord, I think I saw him yester-night.

Hamlet. Saw who?   190

Horatio. My lord, the King your father.

Hamlet.   The King my father!

Horatio. Season[215] your admiration[216] for a while
With an attent[217] ear, till I may deliver,[218]
Upon the witness of these gentlemen,[219]
This marvel to you.

Hamlet.   For God's love, let me hear.   195

Horatio. Two nights together had these gentlemen,
Marcellus and Bernardo, on their watch,
In the dead waste[220] and middle of the night,
Been thus encount'red. A figure like your father,
Armed at point exactly,[221] cap-a-pe,[222]   200

---

[213] *Or ever*: before.
[214] *'a*: he.
[215] *Season*: control, keep (as with wood, to dry it until it is fit for use).
[216] *admiration*: wonder, amazement.
[217] *attent*: attentive.
[218] *deliver*: report.
[219] *these gentlemen*: i.e., Marcellus and Bernardo.
[220] *dead waste*: emptiness.
[221] *at point exactly*: exactly like or as if in readiness.
[222] *cap-a-pe*: head to foot.

Appears before them, and with solemn march
Goes slow and stately by them; thrice he walk'd
By their oppress'd[223] and fear-surprised eyes,
Within his truncheon's[224] length; whilst they,
   distill'd[225]
Almost to jelly with the act[226] of fear,   205
Stand dumb and speak not to him. This to me
In dreadful secrecy impart they did;[227]
And I with them the third night kept the watch;
Where, as they had delivered,[228] both in time,
Form of the thing, each word made true and good,   210
The apparition comes. I knew your father;
These hands are not more like.[229]

Hamlet.   But where was this?

Marcellus. My lord, upon the platform where we watch.

Hamlet. Did you not speak to it?

Horatio.   My lord, I did;
But answer made it none; yet once methought   215
It lifted up it[230] head and did address
Itself to motion,[231] like as it would speak;
But even then the morning cock crew loud,
And at the sound it shrunk in haste away
And vanish'd from our sight.

Hamlet.   'Tis very strange.   220

---

[223] *oppress'd*: oppressed, overwhelmed.
[224] *truncheon's*: A truncheon is a ceremonial staff or baton.
[225] *distill'd*: melted.
[226] *act*: action, effect.
[227] *In dreadful secrecy impart they did*: They told as a dreadful secret.
[228] *delivered*: reported.
[229] *These hands are not more like*: As a person's hands are identical to each other, the Ghost is identical to Hamlet's father.
[230] *it*: its.
[231] *address / Itself to motion*: gesture or move as if about to speak.

Horatio. As I do live, my honour'd lord, 'tis true;
  And we did think it writ down in our duty
  To let you know of it.

Hamlet. Indeed, indeed, sirs, but this troubles me.
  Hold you the watch to-night?

All.   We do, my lord.   225

Hamlet. Arm'd, say you?

All.   Arm'd, my lord.

Hamlet. From top to toe?

All.   My lord, from head to foot.

Hamlet. Then saw you not his face?

Horatio. O yes, my lord; he wore his beaver[232] up.

Hamlet. What, look'd he frowningly?   230

Horatio. A countenance more in sorrow than in anger.

Hamlet. Pale or red?

Horatio. Nay, very pale.

Hamlet.   And fix'd his eyes upon you?

Horatio. Most constantly.

Hamlet.   I would I had been there.

Horatio. It would have much amaz'd you.   235

Hamlet. Very like, very like. Stay'd it long?

Horatio. While one with moderate haste might tell[233] a
    hundred.

---

[232] *beaver*: lower part of the helmet, mouthguard.
[233] *tell*: count.

Both. Longer, longer.

Horatio. Not when I saw't.

Hamlet. His beard was grizzl'd[234]—no?

Horatio. It was, as I have seen it in his life,   240
   A sable[235] silver'd.

Hamlet.   I will watch to-night;
   Perchance[236] 'twill walk again.

Horatio.   I warr'nt it will.[237]

Hamlet. If it assume my noble father's person,
   I'll speak to it, though hell itself should gape[238]
   And bid me hold my peace.[239] I pray you all,   245
   If you have hitherto conceal'd this sight,
   Let it be tenable[240] in your silence still;
   And whatsomever[241] else shall hap[242] to-night,
   Give it an understanding, but no tongue;[243]
   I will requite your loves.[244] So, fare you well—   250
   Upon the platform, 'twixt eleven and twelve,
   I'll visit you.

All.   Our duty to your honour.

Hamlet. Your loves, as mine to you; farewell.

                         [*Exeunt all but Hamlet.*]

---

[234] *grizzl'd*: mixed with gray.
[235] *sable*: black.
[236] *Perchance*: perhaps, by some chance.
[237] *I warr'nt it will*: I do not doubt that it will.
[238] *gape*: open wide (often in reference to a mouth; here, the mouth of Hell speaking forth).
[239] *hold my peace*: remain silent.
[240] *tenable*: maintained, defended against attack, held close.
[241] *whatsomever*: whatsoever.
[242] *hap*: happen.
[243] *but no tongue*: an injunction not to speak of it.
[244] *requite your loves*: reciprocate your friendship, or a promise of reward.

My father's spirit in arms! All is not well.
I doubt[245] some foul play. Would the night were come!   255
Till then sit still, my soul. Foul deeds will rise,
Though all the earth o'erwhelm them, to men's eyes.

[*Exit.*]

Scene 3. *Elsinore. The house of Polonius.*

Enter Laertes and Ophelia his sister.

Laertes. My necessaries are embark'd.[246] Farewell.
And, sister, as the winds give benefit
And convoy is assistant, do not sleep,
But let me hear from you.[247]

Ophelia.   Do you doubt that?

Laertes. For Hamlet, and the trifling of his favour,   5
Hold it a fashion and a toy in blood,[248]
A violet[249] in the youth of primy[250] nature,
Forward[251] not permanent, sweet not lasting.
The perfume and suppliance of a minute;[252]
No more.

Ophelia. No more but so?

Laertes.   Think it no more;   10
For nature crescent[253] does not grow alone
In thews[254] and bulk, but as this temple[255] waxes,

---

[245] *doubt*: suspect.
[246] *My necessaries are embark'd*: My personal luggage is aboard the ship.
[247] *as the winds . . . let me hear from you*: soliciting the promise of a letter.
[248] *a toy in blood*: a capricious fancy or idle impulse of desire.
[249] *violet*: representive of a brief or transient existence.
[250] *primy*: primal, springlike, part of an early emotional experience.
[251] *Forward*: of early growth.
[252] *suppliance of a minute*: idle occupation.
[253] *crescent*: increasing, growing.
[254] *thews*: muscles, bodily strength.
[255] *temple*: i.e., the human body.

The inward service of the mind and soul
Grows wide withal.[256] Perhaps he loves you now,
And now no soil[257] nor cautel[258] doth besmirch[259]   15
The virtue of his will; but you must fear,
His greatness weigh'd,[260] his will is not his own;
For he himself is subject to his birth:
He may not, as unvalued[261] persons do,
Carve for himself;[262] for on his choice depends   20
The sanity and health of this whole state;
And therefore must his choice be circumscrib'd
Unto the voice and yielding of that body[263]
Whereof he is the head.[264] Then if he says he loves
    you,
It fits your wisdom so far to believe it   25
As he in his particular act and place
May give his saying deed;[265] which is no further
Than the main voice[266] of Denmark goes withal.[267]
Then weigh what loss your honour may sustain,
If with too credent[268] ear you list[269] his songs,   30
Or lose your heart, or your chaste treasure[270] open
To his unmast'red importunity.[271]

---

[256] *The inward service . . . wide withal*: with the growth of the body, the capabilities of the mind and soul become more vast, more impressive.

[257] *soil*: stain.

[258] *cautel*: deceit.

[259] *besmirch*: smirch, blemish.

[260] *His greatness weigh'd*: taking into consideration his royal status.

[261] *unvalued*: without rank or of low rank.

[262] *Carve for himself*: choose according to his own desires.

[263] *body*: the body politic, i.e., the state of Demark; corresponding to the risk of Ophelia surrendering her body to Hamlet's wooing.

[264] *Whereof he is the head*: Hamlet may someday be king of Denmark; therefore, his marriage is of great significance to the state as a whole.

[265] *As he . . . may give his saying deed*: as his words may be put into effect or action.

[266] *main voice*: general opinion (also voter support).

[267] *goes withal*: accords with.

[268] *credent*: credulous, trusting.

[269] *list*: listen to.

[270] *chaste treasure*: her body or, more crudely, her virginity.

[271] *unmast'red importunity*: unrestrained, thoughtless wooing.

Fear it, Ophelia, fear it, my dear sister;
And keep you in the rear of your affection,[272]
Out of the shot[273] and danger of desire.   35
The chariest[274] maid is prodigal[275] enough
If she unmask her beauty to the moon.[276]
Virtue itself scapes[277] not calumnious strokes;[278]
The canker galls the infants of the spring
Too oft before their buttons be disclos'd;[279]   40
And in the morn and liquid dew[280] of youth
Contagious blastments[281] are most imminent[282]
Be wary, then; best safety lies in fear:
Youth to itself rebels, though none else near.

Ophelia. I shall the effect of this good lesson keep   45
As watchman to my heart. But, good my brother,
Do not, as some ungracious[283] pastors do,
Show me the steep and thorny way to heaven,
Whiles, like a puff'd[284] and reckless libertine,[285]
Himself the primrose path of dalliance[286] treads   50
And recks not his own rede.[287]

---

[272] *keep you in the rear of your affection*: disassociate yourself from your passions.

[273] *shot*: range.

[274] *chariest*: most cautious, most modest.

[275] *prodigal*: extravagant, foolish, careless.

[276] *unmask . . . the moon*: The moon was classically conceived as having influence over female passions.

[277] *scapes*: escapes.

[278] *calumnious strokes*: scandalous gossip or defamatory statements.

[279] *The canker . . . be disclos'd*: the first flowers of spring are often blighted by the canker worm before their buds open.

[280] *liquid dew*: the time when the dew is still wet.

[281] *Contagious blastments*: withering blights.

[282] *imminent*: referring to an overhanging, pending occurrence.

[283] *ungracious*: lacking in divine grace.

[284] *puff'd*: bloated, arrogant.

[285] *libertine*: someone freely indulgent in sensual pleasures.

[286] *dalliance*: casual romantic or sexual relationship.

[287] *recks not his own rede*: hypocritically does not listen to his own advice, heeds not his own rule.

Laertes.   O, fear me not![288]

Enter Polonius.

I stay too long. But here my father comes.
A double blessing is a double grace;
Occasion smiles upon a second leave.

Polonius. Yet here, Laertes! Aboard, aboard, for shame!   55
The wind sits in the shoulder of your sail,[289]
And you are stay'd for.[290] There—my blessing with
     thee!
And these few precepts in thy memory
Look thou character.[291] Give thy thoughts no
     tongue,
Nor any unproportion'd[292] thought his act.   60
Be thou familiar,[293] but by no means vulgar.[294]
Those friends thou hast, and their adoption tried,[295]
Grapple[296] them to thy soul with hoops of steel;
But do not dull thy palm[297] with entertainment[298]
Of each new-hatch'd, unfledg'd[299] courage. Beware   65
Of entrance to a quarrel; but, being in,
Bear't[300] that th' opposed may beware of thee.
Give every man thy ear, but few thy voice;

---

[288] *fear me not!*: fear not for me!

[289] *sail*: the sail on the ship.

[290] *stay'd for*: waited for.

[291] *character*: write or inscribe.

[292] *unproportion'd*: without proportions, extreme, unfitting.

[293] *familiar*: affable and friendly.

[294] *vulgar*: common or coarse.

[295] *their adoption tried*: the choosing of such friends tried and proved by experience.

[296] *Grapple*: hold tight.

[297] *dull thy palm*: make your handshake (and friendship) cheap.

[298] *entertainment*: giving time and attention.

[299] *unfledg'd*: unfledged, immature (as in a bird that lacks the feathers necessary for flight).

[300] *Bear't*: Bear, conduct yourself.

Take[301] each man's censure,[302] but reserve thy
　　judgment.
Costly[303] thy habit[304] as thy purse can buy,   70
But not express'd in fancy;[305] rich, not gaudy;
For the apparel oft proclaims the man;
And they in France of the best rank and station
Are of a most select and generous choice in that.
Neither a borrower nor a lender be;   75
For loan oft loses both itself and friend,
And borrowing dulls the edge of husbandry.[306]
This above all—to thine own self be true,
And it must follow, as the night the day,
Thou canst not then be false to any man.   80
Farewell; my blessing season[307] this in thee!

Laertes. Most humbly do I take my leave, my lord.

Polonius. The time invites[308] you; go, your servants
　　tend.[309]

Laertes. Farewell, Ophelia; and remember well
　　What I have said to you.

Ophelia.　　　　　　　　　　'Tis in my memory lock'd,   85
And you yourself shall keep the key of it.

Laertes. Farewell.   [*Exit.*]

Polonius. What is't, Ophelia, he hath said to you?

Ophelia. So please you, something touching[310] the Lord
　　Hamlet.

---

[301] *Take*: hear or accept.
[302] *censure*: opinion (even criticism).
[303] *Costly*: expensive.
[304] *habit*: clothes.
[305] *fancy*: deliberately overdone, meant to be sexually attractive.
[306] *husbandry*: thrift, also the care and cultivation of crops and animals.
[307] *season*: preserve or mature.
[308] *invites*: presses upon.
[309] *tend*: wait upon you, wait for you.
[310] *touching*: concerning.

Polonius. Marry,[311] well bethought!   90
 'Tis told me he hath very oft of late
 Given private time to you; and you yourself
 Have of your audience[312] been most free and
   bounteous.
 If it be so—as so 'tis put on me,
 And that in way of caution—I must tell you   95
 You do not understand yourself so clearly[313]
 As it behoves[314] my daughter and your honour.
 What is between you? Give me up the truth.

Ophelia. He hath, my lord, of late made many tenders[315]
 Of his affection to me.   100

Polonius. Affection! Pooh! You speak like a green[316] girl,
 Unsifted[317] in such perilous circumstance.
 Do you believe his tenders, as you call them?

Ophelia. I do not know, my lord, what I should think.

Polonius. Marry, I will teach you: think yourself a baby   105
 That you have ta'en these tenders for true pay
 Which are not sterling.[318] Tender yourself more
   dearly;[319]
 Or—not to crack the wind[320] of the poor phrase,
 Running it thus—you'll tender me a fool.[321]

---

[311] *Marry:* indeed.

[312] *audience:* listening, willingness to be in his company.

[313] *so clearly:* as well.

[314] *behoves:* is the obligation or duty of.

[315] *tenders:* formal offers or declarations.

[316] *green:* young, inexperienced.

[317] *Unsifted:* as someone who has not examined such situations carefully or well, untested.

[318] *not sterling:* fraudulent or counterfeit.

[319] *Tender yourself more dearly:* account or assess your worth at a higher price; also, take better care of yourself.

[320] *crack the wind:* "Cracking the wind" of a horse was to cause it to exert itself so vigorously as to cause recurrent airway obstruction (an asthmalike disease).

[321] *you'll tender me a fool:* you'll make me appear a fool; also, you'll present me with an illegitimate grandchild.

Ophelia. My lord, he hath importun'd me with love   110
   In honourable fashion.

Polonius. Ay, fashion[322] you may call it; go to, go to.[323]

Ophelia. And hath given countenance[324] to his speech,
      my lord,
   With almost all the holy vows of heaven.

Polonius. Ay, springes to catch woodcocks![325] I do know,   115
   When the blood burns, how prodigal the soul
   Lends the tongue vows. These blazes,[326] daughter,
   Giving more light than heat—extinct in both,
   Even in their promise, as it is a-making—
   You must not take for fire. From this time   120
   Be something scanter of your maiden presence;
   Set your entreatments at a higher rate
   Than a command to parle. For Lord Hamlet,
   Believe so much in him, that he is young,
   And with a larger tether[327] may he walk   125
   Than may be given you. In few,[328] Ophelia,
   Do not believe his vows; for they are brokers,[329]
   Not of that dye which their investments show,[330]
   But mere implorators of unholy suits,
   Breathing[331] like sanctified and pious bonds,   130
   The better to beguile. This is for all—
   I would not, in plain terms, from this time forth
   Have you so slander any moment leisure[332]

---

[322] *fashion:* pretense, deceit.
[323] *go to, go to:* an expression of contempt.
[324] *countenance:* verification, support, the appearance of truth.
[325] *springes to catch woodcocks:* snares to catch proverbially gullible birds.
[326] *blazes:* passionate declarations of love.
[327] *tether:* rope or chain to restrain or limit walking.
[328] *In few:* in short.
[329] *brokers:* go-betweens.
[330] *Not of that dye . . . show:* not what they seem (referring to garments).
[331] *Breathing:* sounding, endeavoring to persuade.
[332] *slander any moment leisure:* besmear or sully an idle moment.

As to give words or talk with the Lord Hamlet.
Look to't, I charge you. Come your ways.   *135*

Ophelia. I shall obey, my lord.   [*Exeunt.*]

Scene 4. *Elsinore. The guard-platform of the Castle.*

Enter Hamlet, Horatio, and Marcellus.

Hamlet. The air bites shrewdly; it is very cold.

Horatio. It is a nipping[333] and an eager air.

Hamlet. What hour now?

Horatio.   I think it lacks[334] of twelve.

Marcellus. No, it is struck.

Horatio. Indeed? I heard it not. It then draws near the   *5*
    season
Wherein the spirit held his wont to walk.

      [*A flourish of trumpets, and two pieces[335] go off.*]

What does this mean, my lord?

Hamlet. The King doth wake to-night and takes his
    rouse,[336]
Keeps wassail,[337] and the swagg'ring up-spring reels,[338]
And, as he drains his draughts of Rhenish[339] down,   *10*
The kettle-drum and trumpet thus bray[340] out
The triumph of his pledge.[341]

---

[333] *nipping*: cold enough to cause pain.
[334] *it lacks*: it is not yet the hour.
[335] *pieces*: firearms or cannon.
[336] *rouse*: revels.
[337] *wassail*: carousing, also spiced ale or mulled wine.
[338] *reels*: lively folk dances (Irish or Scottish).
[339] *Rhenish*: Rhine wine.
[340] *bray*: call out or declare.
[341] *pledge*: the pledge or toast of his drinking, drunk in a single gulp.

Horatio.   Is it a custom?

Hamlet. Ay, marry, is't;
   But to my mind, though I am native here
   And to the manner born, it is a custom   15
   More honour'd in the breach than the observance.
   This heavy-headed revel east and west
   Makes us traduc'd[342] and tax'd of[343] other nations;
   They clepe[344] us drunkards, and with swinish phrase
   Soil[345] our addition;[346] and, indeed, it takes   20
   From our achievements, though perform'd at
      height,[347]
   The pith[348] and marrow[349] of our attribute.[350]
   So, oft it chances in particular[351] men
   That, for some vicious mole[352] of nature in them,
   As in their birth, wherein they are not guilty,   25
   Since nature cannot choose his origin;
   By the o'ergrowth of some complexion,[353]
   Oft breaking down the pales[354] and forts[355] of
      reason;
   Or by some habit that too much o'er-leavens[356]
   The form of plausive[357] manners—that these men,   30
   Carrying, I say, the stamp[358] of one defect,

---

[342] *traduc'd*: spoken badly of.
[343] *tax'd of*: accused of wrongdoing by.
[344] *clepe*: call or name.
[345] *Soil*: calumniate, seek to discredit or dirty.
[346] *addition*: conquest, gained lands, goods, power.
[347] *at height*: excellently.
[348] *pith*: true nature or essence.
[349] *marrow*: vital parts.
[350] *attribute*: reputation.
[351] *particular*: individual.
[352] *mole*: defect or blemish.
[353] *complexion*: general character.
[354] *pales*: fences.
[355] *forts*: defensive buildings.
[356] *o'er-leavens*: causes to rise, as leaven (yeast) in dough.
[357] *plausive*: pleasing.
[358] *stamp*: impression, mark, or distinctive appearance.

Being nature's livery[359] or fortune's star,[360]
His virtues else,[361] be they as pure as grace,
As infinite as man may undergo,[362]
Shall in the general censure[363] take corruption   35
From that particular fault. The dram[364] of eale[365]
Doth all the noble substance of a doubt
To his own scandal.

Enter Ghost.

Horatio.   Look, my lord, it comes.

Hamlet. Angels and ministers of grace defend us!
Be thou a spirit of health[366] or goblin damn'd,   40
Bring with thee airs from heaven or blasts from hell,
Be thy intents wicked or charitable,
Thou com'st in such a questionable shape
That I will speak to thee. I'll call thee Hamlet,
King, father, royal Dane. O, answer me!   45
Let me not burst in ignorance, but tell
Why thy canoniz'd[367] bones, hearsed[368] in death,
Have burst their cerements;[369] why the sepulchre[370]
Wherein we saw thee quietly enurn'd[371]
Hath op'd his ponderous and marble jaws   50
To cast thee up again. What may this mean

---

[359] *nature's livery*: characteristics with which a man is born.
[360] *fortune's star*: characteristics granted by fortune.
[361] *His virtues else*: his other virtues.
[362] *undergo*: endure or carry.
[363] *general censure*: popular opinion.
[364] *dram*: small drink, dose.
[365] *eale*: evil.
[366] *spirit of health*: wholesome spirit.
[367] *canoniz'd*: canonized; a soul declared by the Church to be in Heaven, buried with rites authorized by the Church.
[368] *hearsed*: entombed.
[369] *cerements*: waxed clothes for wrapping a corpse.
[370] *sepulchre*: tomb, vault.
[371] *enurn'd*: interred.

That thou, dead corse,[372] again in complete steel[373]
Revisits thus the glimpses of the moon,
Making night hideous, and we fools of nature
So horridly to shake our disposition   55
With thoughts beyond the reaches of our souls?
Say, why is this? wherefore? What should we do?

                [*Ghost beckons Hamlet.*]

Horatio. It beckons you to go away with it,
   As if it some impartment[374] did desire
   To you alone.

Marcellus.   Look with what courteous action   60
   It waves you to a more removed[375] ground.
   But do not go with it.

Horatio.   No, by no means.

Hamlet. It will not speak; then I will follow it.

Horatio. Do not, my lord.

Hamlet.   Why, what should be the fear?
   I do not set my life at a pin's fee;[376]   65
   And for my soul, what can it do to that,
   Being a thing immortal as itself?
   It waves me forth again; I'll follow it.

Horatio. What if it tempt you toward the flood, my
     lord,
   Or to the dreadful summit of the cliff   70
   That beetles[377] o'er his base into the sea,

---

[372] *corse*: corpse.
[373] *steel*: armor.
[374] *impartment*: impartation, communication.
[375] *removed*: distant or private.
[376] *fee*: worth, value, price.
[377] *beetles*: hurries, rushes, hangs out over.

And there assume some other horrible form,[378]
Which might deprive your sovereignty of reason[379]
And draw you into madness? Think of it:
The very place puts toys of desperation,[380]   75
Without more motive, into every brain
That looks so many fathoms to the sea
And hears it roar beneath.[381]

Hamlet.   It waves me still.
  Go on; I'll follow thee.

Marcellus. You shall not go, my lord.

Hamlet.   Hold off your hands.   80

Horatio. Be rul'd;[382] you shall not go.

Hamlet.   My fate cries out,
  And makes each petty arture[383] in this body
  As hardy as the Nemean lion's[384] nerve.

                    [*Ghost beckons.*]

Still am I call'd. Unhand me, gentlemen.
By heaven, I'll make a ghost of him that lets[385] me.   85
I say, away! Go on; I'll follow thee.

                    [*Exeunt Ghost and Hamlet.*]

Horatio. He waxes[386] desperate with imagination.

---

[378] *horrible form:* Spirits could assume any shape.
[379] *sovereignty of reason:* the rule of reason over the mind.
[380] *desperation:* i.e., suicide.
[381] i.e., the temptation to suicide.
[382] *rul'd:* ruled, restrained.
[383] *each petty arture:* every tiny ligament (artery).
[384] *Nemean lion's:* In classical mythology, the Nemean lion was a monster killed by Hercules.
[385] *lets:* hinders, tries to stop.
[386] *waxes:* becomes increasingly.

Marcellus. Let's follow; 'tis not fit thus to obey him.

Horatio. Have after. To what issue will this come?

Marcellus. Something is rotten in the state of Denmark.   90

Horatio. Heaven will direct it.

Marcellus.   Nay, let's follow him.

                              [*Exeunt.*]

            Scene 5. *Elsinore. The battlements of the Castle.*

                    Enter Ghost and Hamlet.

Hamlet. Whither wilt thou lead me? Speak. I'll go no
      further.

Ghost. Mark me.

Hamlet.   I will.

Ghost.   My hour is almost come,
      When I to sulph'rous and tormenting flames
      Must render up myself.

Hamlet.   Alas, poor ghost!

Ghost.   Pity me not, but lend thy serious[387] hearing   5
      To what I shall unfold.

Hamlet.   Speak; I am bound to hear.

Ghost. So art thou to revenge, when thou shalt hear.

Hamlet. What?

Ghost. I am thy father's spirit,
      Doom'd for a certain term to walk the night,   10
      And for the day confin'd to fast in fires,

_____

[387] *serious:* close, attentive.

Till the foul crimes done in my days of nature[388]
Are burnt and purg'd away. But that I am forbid
To tell the secrets of my prison-house,
I could a tale unfold whose lightest word   15
Would harrow up thy soul, freeze thy young blood,
Make thy two eyes, like stars, start from their spheres,
Thy knotted and combined locks[389] to part,
And each particular hair to stand an end,
Like quills upon the fretful porpentine.[390]   20
But this eternal blazon[391] must not be
To ears of flesh and blood. List,[392] list, O, list!
If thou didst ever thy dear father love—

Hamlet. O God!

Ghost. Revenge his foul and most unnatural murder.   25

Hamlet. Murder!

Ghost. Murder most foul, as in the best it is;
But this most foul, strange, and unnatural.

Hamlet. Haste me to know't, that I, with wings as swift
As meditation or the thoughts of love,   30
May sweep to my revenge.

Ghost.   I find thee apt;[393]
And duller shouldst thou be than the fat weed
That roots itself in ease on Lethe wharf,[394]
Wouldst thou not stir in this. Now, Hamlet, hear:

[388] *days of nature*: life on earth.

[389] *locks*: locks of hair.

[390] *porpentine*: porcupine; a large rodent with defensive quills on its body and tail.

[391] *blazon*: heraldry or the revelation of eternal things.

[392] *List*: listen.

[393] *apt*: quick to learn.

[394] *the fat weed . . . Lethe wharf*: in classical mythology, the reeds in the river Lethe, the river of the dead (of the realm of Hades), the water of which, when drunk, causes dead souls to forget their lives on earth.

'Tis given out that, sleeping in my orchard,   35
A serpent stung me; so the whole ear of Denmark
Is by a forged process[395] of my death
Rankly abus'd;[396] but know, thou noble youth,
The serpent that did sting thy father's life
Now wears his crown.

Hamlet.   O my prophetic soul!   40
My uncle!

Ghost. Ay, that incestuous, that adulterate[397] beast,
With witchcraft of his wits, with traitorous gifts—
O wicked wit and gifts that have the power
So to seduce!—won to his shameful lust   45
The will of my most seeming[398] virtuous queen.
O Hamlet, what a falling off was there,
From me, whose love was of that dignity
That it went hand in hand even with the vow
I made to her in marriage; and to decline[399]   50
Upon a wretch whose natural gifts were poor
To those of mine!
But virtue, as it never will be moved,
Though lewdness court it in a shape of heaven,[400]
So lust, though to a radiant angel link'd,   55
Will sate[401] itself in a celestial bed
And prey on garbage.
But soft! methinks I scent[402] the morning air.
Brief let me be. Sleeping within my orchard,
My custom always of the afternoon,   60
Upon my secure[403] hour thy uncle stole,

[395] *forged process*: false account.
[396] *abus'd*: deceived.
[397] *adulterate*: adulterous.
[398] *seeming*: appearing.
[399] *decline*: move downward; descend.
[400] *shape of heaven*: heavenly form.
[401] *sate*: satiate.
[402] *scent*: smell.
[403] *secure*: unsuspicious.

With juice of cursed hebona[404] in a vial,
And in the porches of my ears did pour
The leperous distilment;[405] whose effect
Holds such an enmity with blood of man   65
That swift as quicksilver[406] it courses through
The natural gates and alleys of the body;
And with a sudden vigour it doth posset
And curd,[407] like eager[408] droppings into milk,
The thin and wholesome blood. So did it mine;   70
And a most instant tetter[409] bark'd[410] about,
Most lazar-like,[411] with vile and loathsome crust,
All my smooth body.
Thus was I, sleeping, by a brother's hand
Of life, of crown, of queen, at once dispatch'd; 75
Cut off even in the blossoms of my sin,[412]
Unhous'led,[413] disappointed,[414] unanel'd;[415]
No reck'ning made, but sent to my account[416]
With all my imperfections on my head.
O, horrible! O, horrible! most horrible!   80
If thou hast nature[417] in thee, bear it not;
Let not the royal bed of Denmark be
A couch for luxury[418] and damned incest.
But, howsomever thou pursuest this act,

[404] hebona: a poison.

[405] distilment: a liquid, i.e., the poison.

[406] quicksilver: liquid mercury, signifying rapid, unpredictable movement.

[407] posset / And curd: coagulate and curdle.

[408] eager: sour, acidic.

[409] tetter: covering of scabs.

[410] bark'd: formed a rough covering, like bark on a tree.

[411] lazar-like: like a leper, with biblical connotations concerning the story of the leper Lazarus and moral warnings coming from the dead to the living (c.f. Luke 16:19–31).

[412] in the blossoms of my sin: without benefit of the final sacraments.

[413] Unhous'led: without receiving the sacraments.

[414] disappointed: without spiritual preparation.

[415] unanel'd: unaneled; unanointed, without the sacrament of extreme unction.

[416] account: particular judgment.

[417] nature: natural feelings (of a son to his father).

[418] luxury: lust.

Taint not thy mind, nor let thy soul contrive   85
Against thy mother aught; leave her to heaven,
And to those thorns that in her bosom lodge
To prick and sting her. Fare thee well at once.
The glowworm[419] shows the matin[420] to be near,
And gins[421] to pale his uneffectual fire.   90
Adieu, adieu, adieu! Remember me.   [*Exit.*]

Hamlet. O all you host of heaven! O earth! What else?
  And shall I couple hell?[422] O, fie! Hold, hold, my
      heart;
  And you, my sinews, grow not instant old,
  But bear me stiffly up. Remember thee!   95
  Ay, thou poor ghost, whiles memory holds a seat
  In this distracted globe.[423] Remember thee!
  Yea, from the table of my memory
  I'll wipe away all trivial fond records,
  All saws[424] of books, all forms, all pressures past,   100
  That youth and observation copied there,
  And thy commandment all alone shall live
  Within the book and volume of my brain,
  Unmix'd with baser matter. Yes, by heaven!
  O most pernicious woman!   105
  O villain, villain, smiling, damned villain!
  My tables—meet it is I set it down
  That one may smile, and smile, and be a villain;
  At least I am sure it may be so in Denmark.

                              [*Writing.*]

[419] *glowworm*: soft-bodied beetle, the female of which uses light to attract
males.
[420] *matin*: early morning or predawn, referencing the offices of night prayer
(Matins) and of early prayer (now Lauds, but originally Matins).
[421] *gins*: begins.
[422] *couple Hell*: join (as in marriage) to Hell, or add to the ranks of damned
souls.
[423] *globe*: his head, brain.
[424] *saws*: wise sayings.

So, uncle, there you are. Now to my word: *110*
It is "Adieu, adieu! Remember me".
I have sworn't.

Horatio. [*Within*] My lord, my lord!

Enter Horatio and Marcellus.

Marcellus. Lord Hamlet!

Horatio. Heavens secure him!

Hamlet. So be it!

Marcellus. Illo, ho, ho, my lord!   *115*

Hamlet. Hillo, ho, ho, boy! Come, bird, come.[425]

Marcellus. How is't, my noble lord?

Horatio.   What news, my lord?

Hamlet. O, wonderful!

Horatio. Good my lord, tell it.

Hamlet.   No; you will reveal it.

Horatio. Not I, my lord, by heaven!

Marcellus.   Nor I, my lord.   *120*

Hamlet. How say you, then; would heart of man once
     think it?
     But you'll be secret?

Both.   Ay, by heaven, my lord!

Hamlet. There's never a villain dwelling in all Denmark
     But he's an arrant knave.[426]

---

[425] *Come, bird, come*: a falconer's cry.
[426] *arrant knave*: dishonorable, unscrupulous man.

Horatio. There needs no ghost, my lord, come from the
    grave   *125*
  To tell us this.

Hamlet. Why, right; you are in the right;
  And so, without more circumstance[427] at all,
  I hold it fit that we shake hands and part;
  You, as your business and desire shall point you—
  For every man hath business and desire,
  Such as it is; and for my own poor part,   *130*
  Look you, I will go pray.

Horatio. These are but wild and whirling words, my lord.

Hamlet. I am sorry they offend you, heartily;
  Yes, faith, heartily.

Horatio.   There's no offence, my lord.   *135*

Hamlet. Yes, by Saint Patrick,[428] but there is, Horatio,
  And much offence too. Touching this vision here—
  It is an honest ghost, that let me tell you.
  For your desire to know what is between us,
  O'ermaster't[429] as you may. And now, good friends,   *140*
  As you are friends, scholars, and soldiers,
  Give me one poor request.

Horatio.   What is't, my lord? We will.

Hamlet. Never make known what you have seen to-night.

Both. My lord, we will not.

Hamlet.   Nay, but swear't.

Horatio.   In faith,   *145*
  My lord, not I.

---

[427] *circumstance:* ceremony.
[428] *Saint Patrick:* Saint Patrick (387–c. 493), an apostle of Ireland, was considered the keeper of Purgatory.
[429] *O'ermaster't:* overmaster, overcome, control, repress it.

Marcellus. Nor I, my lord, in faith.

Hamlet. Upon my sword.⁴³⁰

Marcellus. We have sworn, my lord, already.

Hamlet. Indeed, upon my sword, indeed.

Ghost. [*Cries under the stage.*] Swear.

Hamlet. Ha, ha, boy! say'st thou so? Art thou there,   *150*
    truepenny?⁴³¹
  Come on. You hear this fellow in the cellarage:⁴³²
  Consent to swear.

Horatio.   Propose the oath, my lord.

Hamlet. Never to speak of this that you have seen,
  Swear by my sword.

Ghost. [*Beneath*] Swear.   *155*

Hamlet. Hic et ubique?⁴³³ Then we'll shift our ground.
  Come hither, gentlemen,
  And lay your hands again upon my sword.
  Swear by my sword
  Never to speak of this that you have heard.   *160*

Ghost. [*Beneath*] Swear, by his sword.

Hamlet. Well said, old mole!⁴³⁴ Canst work i' th' earth
    so fast?
  A worthy pioneer! Once more remove, good friends.

Horatio. O day and night, but this is wondrous strange!

---

⁴³⁰ *Upon my sword*: on the cross formed by the hilt of the sword.
⁴³¹ *truepenny*: trusty fellow.
⁴³² *cellerage*: cellars, collectively.
⁴³³ *Hic et ubique*: here and everywhere (Latin).
⁴³⁴ *mole*: a mammal that burrows into the ground, referring to the direction from which the voice of the Ghost is heard.

Hamlet. And therefore as a stranger give it welcome.   165
  There are more things in heaven and earth, Horatio,
  Than are dreamt of in your philosophy.
  But come.
  Here, as before, never, so help you mercy,
  How strange or odd some'er I bear myself—   170
  As I perchance hereafter shall think meet
  To put an antic disposition[435] on—
  That you, at such times, seeing me, never shall,
  With arms encumb'red[436] thus, or this head-shake,
  Or by pronouncing of some doubtful phrase,   175
  As "Well, well, we know" or "We could, an if we
    would"
  Or "If we list[437] to speak" or "There be, an if they
    might"
  Or such ambiguous giving out,[438] to note
  That you know aught[439] of me—this do swear,
  So grace and mercy at your most need help you.   180

Ghost. [*Beneath*] Swear.

Hamlet. Rest, rest, perturbed spirit! So, gentlemen,
  With all my love I do commend me to you;
  And what so poor a man as Hamlet is   185
  May do t'express his love and friending[440] to you,
  God willing, shall not lack. Let us go in together;
  And still your fingers on your lips, I pray.
  The time is out of joint. O cursed spite,
  That ever I was born to set it right!   190
  Nay, come, let's go together.   [*Exeunt.*]

---

[435] *antic disposition*: pretense of insanity.
[436] *encumb'red*: crossed or folded.
[437] *list*: cared or were disposed.
[438] *giving out*: making of a sign.
[439] *aught*: anything.
[440] *friending*: friendship.

ACT 2

Scene 1. *Elsinore. The house of Polonius.*

Enter Polonius and Reynaldo.

Polonius. Give him this money and these notes,
  Reynaldo.

Reynaldo. I will, my lord.

Polonius. You shall do marvellous[1] wisely, good Reynaldo,
  Before you visit him, to make inquire
  Of his behaviour.

Reynaldo.   My lord, I did intend it.   5

Polonius. Marry, well said; very well said. Look you, sir,
  Enquire me first what Danskers[2] are in Paris;
  And how, and who, what means, and where they keep,
  What company, at what expense; and finding
  By this encompassment[3] and drift of question   10
  That they do know my son, come you more nearer
  Than your particular demands will touch it.
  Take you, as 'twere, some distant knowledge of him;
  As thus: "I know his father and his friends,
  And in part him". Do you mark this, Reynaldo?   15

Reynaldo. Ay, very well, my lord.

Polonius. "And in part him—but" you may say "not well;
  But if't be he I mean, he's very wild;
  Addicted so and so"; and there put on him
  What forgeries[4] you please; marry, none so rank   20
  As may dishonour him; take heed of that;

---

[1] *marvellous:* marvelously.
[2] *Danskers:* i.e., Danes.
[3] *encompassment:* roundabout method of questioning.
[4] *forgeries:* lies or stories concocted.

But, sir, such wanton,[5] wild, and usual slips
As are companions noted and most known
To youth and liberty.

Reynaldo.   As gaming, my lord.

Polonius. Ay, or drinking, fencing, swearing, quarrelling,   25
Drabbing[6]—you may go so far.

Reynaldo. My lord, that would dishonour him.

Polonius. Faith, no; as you may season it in the charge.
You must not put another scandal on him,
That he is open to incontinency;[7]   30
That's not my meaning. But breathe his faults so
    quaintly[8]
That they may seem the taints of liberty;
The flash and outbreak of a fiery mind,
A savageness in unreclaimed[9] blood,
Of general assault.[10]

Reynaldo.   But, my good lord—   35

Polonius. Wherefore should you do this?

Reynaldo.   Ay, my lord,
I would know that.

Polonius.   Marry, sir, here's my drift,
And I believe it is a fetch of warrant:[11]
You laying these slight sullies[12] on my son,

---

[5] *wanton*: irresponsible, sportive.

[6] *Drabbing*: patronizing prostitutes.

[7] *incontinency*: utter lack of self-restraint.

[8] *quaintly*: artfully, delicately.

[9] *unreclaimed*: untamed.

[10] *Of general assault*: to which young men are generally subject.

[11] *fetch of warrant*: authorization allowing something (here, gossip about the character of Laertes).

[12] *sullies*: imputations of evil or immoral actions.

As 'twere a thing a little soil'd wi' th' working,[13]   40
Mark you,
Your party in converse,[14] him you would sound,
Having ever seen in the prenominate[15] crimes
The youth you breathe of guilty, be assur'd
He closes[16] with you in this consequence—   45
"Good sir" or so, or "friend" or "gentleman"
According to the phrase or the addition
Of man and country.

Reynaldo.   Very good, my lord.

Polonius. And then, sir, does 'a[17] this—'a does—
What was I about to say? By the mass,[18]   50
I was about to say something; where did I leave?

Reynaldo. At "closes in the consequence", at "friend or
      so" and "gentleman".

Polonius. At "closes in the consequence"—ay, marry,
He closes thus: "I know the gentleman;   55
I saw him yesterday, or t'other day,
Or then, or then; with such, or such; and, as you say,
There was 'a gaming; there o'ertook in's[19] rouse;
There falling out at tennis"; or perchance
"I saw him enter such a house of sale"   60
Videlicet,[20] a brothel,[21] or so forth. See you now
Your bait of falsehood take this carp[22] of truth;
And thus do we of wisdom and of reach,[23]

[13] *soil'd wi' th' working*: shopworn, overused.
[14] *converse*: conversation.
[15] *prenominate*: aforementioned.
[16] *closes*: falls in.
[17] *'a*: he.
[18] *By the mass*: a colloquial exclamation.
[19] *in's*: in his.
[20] *Videlicet*: namely (Latin).
[21] *brothel*: house of ill repute.
[22] *carp*: i.e., fish.
[23] *reach*: grasp, capacity, understanding.

With windlasses[24] and with assays of bias,[25]   65
By indirections find directions out;
So, by my former lecture and advice,
Shall you my son. You have[26] me, have you not?

Reynaldo. My lord, I have.

Polonius.   God buy ye;[27] fare ye well.

Reynaldo. Good my lord!   70

Polonius. Observe his inclination in[28] yourself.

Reynaldo. I shall, my lord.

Polonius. And let him ply his music.[29]

Reynaldo.   Well, my lord.

Polonius. Farewell!   [*Exit Reynaldo.*]

Enter Ophelia.

How now, Ophelia! What's the matter?

Ophelia. O my lord, my lord, I have been so affrighted![30]   75

Polonius. With what, i' th' name of God?

Ophelia. My lord, as I was sewing in my closet,[31]
Lord Hamlet, with his doublet[32] all unbrac'd,[33]
No hat upon his head, his stockings fouled,[34]

---

[24] *windlasses*: winches or methods of drawing something (or someone) in.
[25] *assays of bias*: indirect approaches.
[26] *have*: understand.
[27] *God buy ye*: God be with you, a form of farewell (an early form of "good-bye").
[28] *in*: for.
[29] *ply his music*: continue his study and practice of music.
[30] *affrighted*: frightened.
[31] *closet*: private room.
[32] *doublet*: close-fitting jacket.
[33] *unbrac'd*: unfastened or loose, unlaced.
[34] *fouled*: dirtied.

Ungart'red³⁵ and down-gyved³⁶ to his ankle;   80
Pale as his shirt, his knees knocking each other,
And with a look so piteous in purport
As if he had been loosed out of hell
To speak of horrors—he comes before me.

Polonius. Mad for thy love?

Ophelia.   My lord, I do not know,   85
But truly I do fear it.

Polonius.   What said he?

Ophelia. He took me by the wrist, and held me hard;
Then goes he to the length of all his arm,
And, with his other hand thus o'er his brow,
He falls to such perusal of my face   90
As 'a would draw it. Long stay'd he so.
At last, a little shaking of mine arm,
And thrice his head thus waving up and down,
He rais'd a sigh so piteous and profound
As it did seem to shatter all his bulk³⁷   95
And end his being. That done, he lets me go,
And, with his head over his shoulder turn'd,
He seem'd to find his way without his eyes;
For out adoors he went without their helps
And to the last bended their light on me.   100

Polonius. Come, go with me. I will go seek the King.
This is the very ecstasy³⁸ of love,
Whose violent property fordoes³⁹ itself,
And leads the will to desperate undertakings
As oft as any passion under heaven   105

---

³⁵ *ungart'red*: loose.
³⁶ *down-gyved*: hanging down, as in the fetters (gyves) on a prisoner's legs.
³⁷ *all his bulk*: his entire body.
³⁸ *ecstasy*: madness.
³⁹ *fordoes*: destroys.

That does afflict our natures. I am sorry—
What, have you given him any hard words of late?

Ophelia. No, my good lord; but, as you did command,
I did repel his letters, and denied
His access to me.

Polonius.   That hath made him mad.   *110*
I am sorry that with better heed and judgment
I had not quoted[40] him. I fear'd he did but trifle,
And meant to wreck[41] thee; but beshrew my
     jealousy![42]
By heaven, it is as proper to our age
To cast beyond ourselves[43] in our opinions   *115*
As it is common for the younger sort
To lack discretion. Come, go we to the King.
This must be known; which, being kept close, might
     move
More grief to hide than hate to utter love.
Come.   [*Exeunt.*] *120*

Scene 2. *Elsinore. The Castle.*

*Flourish. Enter King, Queen, Rosencrantz,
Guildenstern, and Attendants.*

King. Welcome, dear Rosencrantz and Guildenstern!
Moreover that we much did long to see you,
The need we have to use you did provoke
Our hasty sending. Something have you heard
Of Hamlet's transformation; so I call it,   *5*
Sith nor[44] th' exterior nor the inward man

---

[40] *quoted:* observed.
[41] *wreck:* dishonor.
[42] *beshrew my jealousy:* a curse against Polonius' suspicions.
[43] *cast beyond ourselves:* overcast or overestimate.
[44] *Sith nor:* since neither.

Resembles that it was. What it should be,
More than his father's death, that thus hath put him
So much from th' understanding of himself,   10
I cannot deem of. I entreat you both
That, being of so young days[45] brought up with him,
And sith[46] so neighboured[47] to his youth and
      haviour,[48]
That you vouchsafe your rest[49] here in our court
Some little time; so by your companies
To draw him on to pleasures, and to gather,   15
So much as from occasion you may glean,
Whether aught to us unknown afflicts him thus
That, open'd, lies within our remedy.

Queen. Good gentlemen, he hath much talk'd of you;
      And sure I am two men there is not living   20
      To whom he more adheres.[50] If it will please you
      To show us so much gentry[51] and good will
      As to expend your time with us awhile
      For the supply and profit of our hope,
      Your visitation shall receive such thanks   25
      As fits a king's remembrance.[52]

Rosencrantz.   Both your Majesties
      Might, by the sovereign power you have of us,
      Put your dread pleasures more into command
      Than to entreaty.

Guildenstern.   But we both obey,
      And here give up ourselves, in the full bent,[53]   30

---

[45] of so young days: since youth or childhood.
[46] sith: since.
[47] so neighboured: so closely related, as friends.
[48] havior: behavior.
[49] vouchsafe your rest: agree to stay.
[50] adheres: believes in, or sticks to (as a friend).
[51] gentry: courtesy.
[52] remembrance: gratitude.
[53] in the full bent: bending all faculties and strength to the task.

To lay our service freely at your feet,
To be commanded.

King. Thanks, Rosencrantz and gentle Guildenstern.

Queen. Thanks, Guildenstern and gentle Rosencrantz.
And I beseech you instantly to visit   35
My too much changed son. Go, some of you,
And bring these gentlemen where Hamlet is.

Guildenstern. Heavens make our presence and our
        practices
Pleasant and helpful to him!

Queen.   Aye amen!

[*Exeunt Rosencrantz, Guildenstern, and some Attendants.*]

Enter Polonius.

Polonius. Th' ambassadors from Norway, my good lord,   40
Are joyfully return'd.

King. Thou still hast been the father of good news.

Polonius. Have I, my lord? I assure you, my good liege,
I hold my duty, as I hold my soul,
Both to my God and to my gracious King;   45
And I do think—or else this brain of mine
Hunts not the trail of policy⁵⁴ so sure
As it hath us'd to do—that I have found
The very cause of Hamlet's lunacy.

King. O, speak of that; that do I long to hear.   50

Polonius. Give first admittance to th' ambassadors;
My news shall be the fruit to that great feast.

---

⁵⁴*policy:* investigation or procedure.

King. Thyself do grace to them, and bring them in.

[*Exit Polonius.*]

He tells me, my dear Gertrude, he hath found
The head and source of all your son's distemper.[55]   55

Queen. I doubt it is no other but the main,[56]
His father's death and our o'erhasty marriage.

King. Well, we shall sift him.

Re-enter Polonius, with Voltemand and Cornelius.

Welcome, my good friends!

Say, Voltemand; what from our brother Norway?

Voltemand. Most fair return of greetings and desires.   60
Upon our first, he sent out to suppress
His nephew's levies;[57] which to him appear'd
To be a preparation 'gainst the Polack;
But, better look'd into, he truly found
It was against your Highness. Whereat griev'd,   65
That so his sickness, age, and impotence,
Was falsely borne in hand, sends out arrests
On Fortinbras; which he, in brief, obeys;
Receives rebuke from Norway; and, in fine,
Makes vow before his uncle never more   70
To give th' assay of arms[58] against your Majesty.
Whereon old Norway, overcome with joy,
Gives him threescore thousand crowns in annual fee,
And his commission to employ those soldiers,
So levied as before, against the Polack;   75
With an entreaty, herein further shown,

[*Gives a paper.*]

[55] *distemper*: disorder, illness.
[56] *main*: primary or most obvious cause.
[57] *levies*: body of enlisted troops.
[58] *assay of arms*: test or attempt of military force.

That it might please you to give quiet pass
Through your dominions for this enterprise,
On such regards of safety and allowance
As therein are set down.

King.   It likes us well;   80
And at our more considered time we'll read,
Answer, and think upon this business.
Meantime we thank you for your well-took labour.
Go to your rest; at night we'll feast together.
Most welcome home!

          [*Exeunt Ambassadors and Attendants.*]

Polonius.   This business is well ended.   85
My liege, and madam, to expostulate[59]
What majesty should be, what duty is,
Why day is day, night is night, and time is time,
Were nothing, but to waste night, day, and time.
Therefore, since brevity is the soul of wit,   90
And tediousness the limbs and outward flourishes,
I will be brief. Your noble son is mad.
Mad call I it; for, to define true madness,
What is't but to be nothing else but mad?
But let that go.

Queen.   More matter with less art.[60]   95

Polonius. Madam, I swear I use no art at all.
That he's mad, 'tis true: 'tis true 'tis pity;
And pity 'tis 'tis true. A foolish figure!
But farewell it, for I will use no art.
Mad let us grant him, then; and now remains   100
That we find out the cause of this effect;
Or rather say the cause of this defect,
For this effect defective comes by cause.

---

[59] *expostulate*: express strong disapproval.
[60] *art*: rhetorical display.

Thus it remains, and the remainder thus.
Perpend.[61]   *105*
I have a daughter—have while she is mine[62]—
Who in her duty and obedience, mark,
Hath given me this. Now gather, and surmise.[63]

> [*Reads.*]

"To the celestial, and my soul's idol, the most
beautified Ophelia." That's an ill phrase, a vile phrase;
"beautified" is a vile phrase. But you shall hear. Thus:
[*Reads.*] "In her excellent white bosom, these, etc."

Queen. Came this from Hamlet to her?

Polonius. Good madam, stay awhile; I will be faithful.   *115*
> [*Reads.*]
>> "Doubt thou the stars are fire;
>> Doubt that the sun doth move;
>> Doubt truth to be a liar;
>> But never doubt I love.

O dear Ophelia, I am ill at these numbers.
I have not art to reckon my groans; but that I   *120*
love thee best, O most best, believe it. Adieu.

> Thine evermore, most dear lady, whilst this
> machine is to him, Hamlet."

This, in obedience, hath my daughter shown me;
And more above, hath his solicitings,[64]   *125*
As they fell out by time, by means, and place,
All given to mine ear.

King.   But how hath she
Receiv'd his love?

---

[61] *Perpend:* attend or ponder.
[62] *while she is mine:* until she is married.
[63] *surmise:* form a supposition from what is heard.
[64] *solicitings:* wooing letters, solicitations for her favor.

Polonius.   What do you think of me?

King. As of a man faithful and honourable.

Polonius. I would fain prove so. But what might you
    think,   130
  When I had seen this hot love on the wing,
  As I perceiv'd it, I must tell you that,
  Before my daughter told me—what might you,
  Or my dear Majesty your queen here, think,
  If I had play'd the desk or table-book;   135
  Or given my heart a winking, mute and dumb;
  Or look'd upon this love with idle sight—
  What might you think? No, I went round to work,
  And my young mistress thus I did bespeak:
  "Lord Hamlet is a prince out of thy star;[65]   140
  This must not be". And then I prescripts[66] gave her,
  That she should lock herself from his resort,
  Admit no messengers, receive no tokens.
  Which done, she took the fruits of my advice;
  And he repelled, a short tale to make,   145
  Fell into a sadness, then into a fast,
  Thence to a watch, thence into a weakness,
  Thence to a lightness, and, by this declension,
  Into the madness wherein now he raves
  And all we mourn for.   150

King.   Do you think 'tis this?

Queen. It may be, very like.

Polonius. Hath there been such a time—I would fain
    know that—
  That I have positively said " 'Tis so",
  When it prov'd otherwise?

King.   Not that I know.

---

[65] *star*: social sphere.
[66] *prescripts*: orders.

Polonius. Take this from this, if this be otherwise.   *155*
   If circumstances lead me, I will find
   Where truth is hid, though it were hid indeed
   Within the centre.[67]

King.   How may we try it further?

Polonius. You know sometimes he walks four hours
      together,
   Here in the lobby.

Queen.   So he does, indeed.   *160*

Polonius. At such a time I'll loose[68] my daughter to him.
   Be you and I behind an arras[69] then;
   Mark the encounter: if he love her not,
   And be not from his reason fall'n thereon,
   Let me be no assistant for a state,   *165*
   But keep a farm and carters.[70]

King.   We will try it.

Enter Hamlet, reading on a book.

Queen. But look where sadly the poor wretch comes
      reading.

Polonius. Away, I do beseech you, both away:
   I'll board[71] him presently. O, give me leave.

                        [*Exeunt King and Queen.*]

   How does my good Lord Hamlet?   *170*

Hamlet. Well, God-a-mercy.[72]

---

[67] *centre*: center of the earth, believed to be the center of the universe until proved otherwise by Nicolaus Copernicus (1473–1543).

[68] *loose*: release or allow to walk freely (to meet with Hamlet).

[69] *arras*: tapestry wall hanging.

[70] *carters*: laborers who work with carts.

[71] *board*: accost or speak to.

[72] *God-a-mercy*: thank you.

Polonius. Do you know me, my lord?

Hamlet. Excellent well; you are a fish-monger.[73]

Polonius. Not I, my lord.

Hamlet. Then I would you were so honest a man. 175

Polonius. Honest, my lord!

Hamlet. Ay, sir; to be honest, as this world goes, is to be one man pick'd out of ten thousand.

Polonius. That's very true, my lord. 179

Hamlet. For if the sun breed maggots in a dead dog, being a good kissing carrion[74]—Have you a daughter?

Polonius. I have, my lord.

Hamlet. Let her not walk i' th' sun.[75] Conception is a blessing. But as your daughter may conceive[76]— friend, look to't.

Polonius. How say you by that? [*Aside*] Still harping on my daughter. Yet he knew me not at first; 'a[77] said I was a fishmonger. 'A is far gone, far gone. And truly in my youth I suff'red much extremity for love. Very near this. I'll speak to him again.—What do you read, my lord? 190

Hamlet. Words, words, words.

Polonius. What is the matter, my lord?

---

[73] *fish-monger*: seller of fish in the marketplace or a bawd.

[74] *carrion*: decaying flesh of dead animals.

[75] *walk i' th' sun*: walk where it may ruin her complexion; also, spend too much time with Hamlet (the sun) and lay herself open to impregnation (this meaning is also derived from classical myths of women being impregnated by the rays of the sun).

[76] *conceive*: i.e., an illegitimate child.

[77] *'a*: he.

Hamlet. Between who?

Polonius. I mean, the matter that you read, my lord.   194

Hamlet. Slanders, sir; for the satirical rogue says here
that old men have grey beards; that their faces are
wrinkled; their eyes purging thick amber and
plum-tree gum; and that they have a plentiful lack
of wit, together with most weak hams—all which,
sir, though I most powerfully and potently believe,
yet I hold it not honesty to have it thus set
down;[78] for you yourself, sir, shall grow old as I
am, if, like a crab, you could go backward.[79]

Polonius. [*Aside*] Though this be madness, yet there is
method in't.—Will you walk out of the air, my
lord?   205

Hamlet. Into my grave?

Polonius. Indeed, that's out of the air. [*Aside*] How
pregnant[80] sometimes his replies are! a happiness
that often madness hits on, which reason and
sanity could not so prosperously be delivered of. I
will leave him, and suddenly contrive the means
of meeting between him and my daughter.—My
lord, I will take my leave of you.   213

Hamlet. You cannot, sir, take from me anything that I
will more willingly part withal—except my life,
except my life, except my life.   216

Enter Rosencrantz and Guildenstern.

Polonius. Fare you well, my lord.

---

[78] *set down*: in print.
[79] *crab . . . backward*: crabs walk sideways.
[80] *pregnant*: full of meaning.

Hamlet. These tedious old fools!

Polonius. You go to seek the Lord Hamlet; there he is.

Rosencrantz. [*To Polonius*] God save you, sir!   220

          [*Exit Polonius.*]

Guildenstern. My honour'd lord!

Rosencrantz. My most dear lord!

Hamlet. My excellent good friends! How dost thou,
  Guildenstern? Ah, Rosencrantz! Good lads, how
  do you both?   225

Rosencrantz. As the indifferent children of the earth.[81]

Guildenstern. Happy in that we are not over-happy;
  On fortune's cap we are not the very button.[82]

Hamlet. Nor the soles of her shoe?

Rosencrantz. Neither, my lord.   230

Hamlet. Then you live about her waist, or in the
  middle of her favours?

Guildenstern. Faith, her privates we.

Hamlet. In the secret parts of Fortune? O, most true;
  she is a strumpet.[83] What news?

Rosencrantz. None, my lord, but that the world's grown
  honest.   236

Hamlet. Then is doomsday near. But your news is not
  true. Let me question more in particular. What

---

[81] *children of the earth*: lower-class or average people.

[82] *button*: summit.

[83] *strumpet*: whore, following the bawdy exploration of the body of personified Fortune.

have you, my good friends, deserved at the hands
of Fortune, that she sends you to prison hither?   *240*

Guildenstern. Prison, my lord!

Hamlet. Denmark's a prison.

Rosencrantz. Then is the world one.

Hamlet. A goodly one; in which there are many
confines, wards, and dungeons, Denmark being
one o' th' worst.   *246*

Rosencrantz. We think not so, my lord.

Hamlet. Why, then, 'tis none to you; for there is
nothing either good or bad, but thinking makes it
so. To me it is a prison.

Rosencrantz. Why, then your ambition makes it one; 'tis
too narrow for your mind.   *252*

Hamlet. O God, I could be bounded in a nutshell and
count myself a king of infinite space, were it not
that I have bad dreams.

Guildenstern. Which dreams indeed are ambition; for
the very substance of the ambitious is merely the
shadow of a dream.   *258*

Hamlet. A dream itself is but a shadow.

Rosencrantz. Truly, and I hold ambition of so airy and
light a quality that it is but a shadow's shadow.   *261*

Hamlet. Then are our beggars bodies, and our monarchs
and outstretch'd heroes the beggars' shadows.
Shall we to th' court? for, by my fay,[84] I cannot
reason.[85]

---

[84] *fay*: faith.
[85] *reason*: speak reasonably.

Both. We'll wait upon you.[86]   265

Hamlet. No such matter. I will not sort you with the
    rest of my servants; for, to speak to you like an
    honest man, I am most dreadfully attended. But,
    in the beaten way[87] of friendship, what make you
    at Elsinore?

Rosencrantz. To visit you, my lord; no other occasion.   270

Hamlet. Beggar that I am, I am even poor in thanks;
    but I thank you; and sure, dear friends, my thanks
    are too dear[88] a half-penny. Were you not sent
    for? Is it your own inclining? Is it a free visitation?
    Come, come, deal justly with me. Come, come;
    nay, speak.   275

Guildenstern. What should we say, my lord?

Hamlet. Why any thing. But to th' purpose: you were
    sent for; and there is a kind of confession in your
    looks, which your modesties have not craft
    enough to colour; I know the good King and
    Queen have sent for you.   280

Rosencrantz. To what end, my lord?

Hamlet. That you must teach me. But let me conjure[89]
    you by the rights of our fellowship, by the
    consonancy[90] of our youth, by the obligation of
    our ever-preserved love, and by what more dear a
    better proposer can charge you withal, be even
    and direct with me, whether you were sent for or
    no?

[86] *wait upon you:* await you or (as follows) work as servants.
[87] *beaten way:* well-tried, long-trodden path.
[88] *too dear:* not worth.
[89] *conjure:* implore.
[90] *consonancy:* agreement, compatibility, harmony.

Rosencrantz. [*Aside to Guildenstern*] What say you?

Hamlet. [*Aside*] Nay, then, I have an eye of you.—If
    you love me, hold not off.   290

Guildenstern. My lord, we were sent for.

Hamlet. I will tell you why; so shall my anticipation
    prevent your discovery,[91] and your secrecy to the
    King and Queen moult no feather. I have of
    late—but wherefore I know not—lost all my
    mirth, forgone all custom of exercises; and indeed
    it goes so heavily with my disposition that this
    goodly frame, the earth, seems to me a sterile
    promontory;[92] this most excellent canopy the air,
    look you, this brave o'er-hanging firmament, this
    majestical roof fretted[93] with golden fire—why, it
    appeareth no other thing to me than a foul and
    pestilent congregation of vapours.[94] What a piece
    of work is a man! How noble in reason! how
    infinite in faculties! in form and moving, how
    express[95] and admirable! in action, how like an
    angel! in apprehension, how like a god! the
    beauty of the world! the paragon of animals! And
    yet, to me, what is this quintessence of dust? Man
    delights not me—no, nor woman neither, though
    by your smiling you seem to say so.   309

Rosencrantz. My lord, there was no such stuff in my
    thoughts.

Hamlet. Why did ye laugh, then, when I said "Man
    delights not me"?

---

[91] *prevent your discovery*: forestall the disclosure.
[92] *promontory*: point of high land jutting out into a body of water.
[93] *fretted*: decorated, adorned.
[94] *vapours*: substances suspended in air.
[95] *express*: exact.

Rosencrantz. To think, my lord, if you delight not in
    man, what lenten[96] entertainment the players
    shall receive from you. We coted[97] them on the
    way; and hither are they coming to offer you
    service.   316

Hamlet. He that plays the king shall be welcome—his
    Majesty shall have tribute on me; the adventur-
    ous knight shall use his foil[98] and target;[99] the
    lover shall not sigh gratis; the humorous man[100]
    shall end his part in peace; the clown shall make
    those laugh whose lungs are tickle a' th' sere;[101]
    and the lady shall say her mind freely, or the
    blank verse shall halt for't.[102] What players are
    they?   323

Rosencrantz. Even those you were wont to take such
    delight in—the tragedians of the city.

Hamlet. How chances it they travel? Their residence,
    both in reputation and profit, was better both ways.

Rosencrantz. I think their inhibition[103] comes by the
    means of the late innovation.[104]   329

Hamlet. Do they hold the same estimation they did
    when I was in the city? Are they so followed?

Rosencrantz. No, indeed, are they not.

Hamlet. How comes it? Do they grow rusty?   333

---

[96] *lenten*: meager.
[97] *coted*: overtook, met.
[98] *foil*: blunt sword.
[99] *target*: shield.
[100] *humorous man*: man with an odd trait, a stock character in the theater.
[101] *sere*: hair trigger.
[102] *for't*: for it.
[103] *inhibition*: hindrance (to their success).
[104] *innovation*: changing of ideas (afterward described).

Rosencrantz. Nay, their endeavour keeps in the wonted
    pace; but there is, sir, an eyrie[105] of children, little
    eyases,[106] that cry out on the top of question, and
    are most tyrannically[107] clapp'd for't. These are
    now the fashion, and so berattle[108] the common
    stages[109]—so they call them—that many wearing
    rapiers[110] are afraid of goose quills[111] and dare
    scarce come thither.   340

Hamlet. What, are they children? Who maintains 'em?
    How are they escoted?[112] Will they pursue the qual-
    ity[113] no longer than they can sing? Will they not
    say afterwards, if they should grow themselves to
    common players—as it is most like, if their means
    are no better—their writers do them wrong to make
    them exclaim against their own succession?[114]   347

Rosencrantz. Faith, there has been much to-do on both
    sides; and the nation holds it no sin to tarre[115]
    them to controversy. There was for a while no
    money bid for argument,[116] unless the poet and
    the player went to cuffs[117] in the question.   352

Hamlet. Is't possible?

Guildenstern. O, there has been much throwing about
    of brains.   355

---

[105] *eyrie*: nest where young birds of prey live.
[106] *eyases*: trained young hawks that cry out shrilly.
[107] *tyrannically*: loudly, violently, or unfairly.
[108] *berattle*: cry down, decry.
[109] *common stages*: where adult actors performed.
[110] *rapiers*: light, thin swords used for thrusting.
[111] *goose quills*: pens (of satirists and critics).
[112] *escoted*: supported financially.
[113] *quality*: acting profession.
[114] *succession*: future success or adult career.
[115] *tarre*: incite.
[116] *argument*: plot of a play.
[117] *cuffs*: fisticuffs; blows.

Hamlet. Do the boys carry it away?

Rosencrantz. Ay, that they do, my lord—Hercules and his load[118] too.

Hamlet. It is not very strange; for my uncle is King of Denmark, and those that would make mows at him while my father lived give twenty, forty, fifty, a hundred ducats apiece for his picture in little.[119] 'Sblood,[120] there is something in this more than natural, if philosophy could find it out.

[*A flourish.*]

Guildenstern. There are the players. 365

Hamlet. Gentlemen, you are welcome to Elsinore. Your hands, come then; th' appurtenance[121] of welcome is fashion and ceremony. Let me comply with you in this garb;[122] lest my extent[123] to the players, which, I tell you, must show fairly outwards, should more appear like entertainment than yours. You are welcome. But my uncle-father and aunt-mother are deceived. 372

Guildenstern. In what, my dear lord?

Hamlet. I am but mad north-north-west;[124] when the wind is southerly I know a hawk[125] from a handsaw.[126] 375

Re-enter Polonius.

---

[118] *Hercules and his load*: reference to the Globe theater, in the front of which was a sign with the mythical hero Hercules bearing the globe on his back.

[119] *picture in little*: miniature portrait.

[120] *'Sblood*: by God's blood, a colloquial exclamation.

[121] *appurtenance*: accessory, trappings.

[122] *garb*: clothing or outward guise.

[123] *extent*: behavior; the size or scale of his welcome.

[124] *north-north-west*: on one compass point.

[125] *hawk*: bird of prey, also a kind of pickax.

[126] *handsaw*: carpenter's tool, also a pun on "hernshaw" (heron).

Polonius. Well be with you, gentlemen!

Hamlet. Hark you, Guildenstern, and you too—at each
ear a hearer: that great baby you see there is not
yet out of his swaddling clouts.[127]

Rosencrantz. Happily he is the second time come to
them; for they say an old man is twice a child.   381

Hamlet. I will prophesy he comes to tell me of the
players; mark it. You say right, sir: a Monday
morning; 'twas then indeed.

Polonius. My lord, I have news to tell you.   385

Hamlet. My lord, I have news to tell you. When
Roscius[128] was an actor in Rome—

Polonius. The actors are come hither, my lord.

Hamlet. Buzz, buzz!

Polonius. Upon my honour—   390

Hamlet. Then came each actor on his ass—

Polonius. The best actors in the world, either for
tragedy, comedy, history, pastoral, pastoral-comical,
historical-pastoral, tragical-historical,
tragical-comical-historical-pastoral, scene
individable,[129] or poem unlimited.[130] Seneca[131]
cannot be too heavy nor Plautus[132] too light. For
the law of writ and the liberty,[133] these are the
only men.   397

---

[127] *swaddling clouts:* swaddling clothes, as in the clothes of an infant.

[128] *Roscius:* Quintus Roscius Gallus (c.126–62 B.C.), Roman actor.

[129] *scene individable:* observing the unities of time, place, and action.

[130] *poem unlimited:* not restricted by the tenets of criticism.

[131] *Seneca:* Lucius Annaeus Seneca (c. 4 B.C.–A.D. 65), Roman Stoic philosopher and dramatist.

[132] *Plautus:* Titus Maccius Plautus (c. 254–184 B.C.), Roman dramatist, writer of comedies.

[133] *the law of writ and the liberty:* the letter of the text and improvisation.

Hamlet. O Jephthah, judge of Israel,[134] what a treasure
    hadst thou!

Polonius. What a treasure had he, my lord?

Hamlet. Why—   401

    "One fair daughter, and no more,
    The which he loved passing well".

Polonius. [*Aside*] Still on my daughter.

Hamlet. Am I not i' th' right, old Jephthah?

Polonius. If you call me Jephthah, my lord, I have a
    daughter that I love passing well.

Hamlet. Nay, that follows not.

Polonius. What follows then, my lord?

Hamlet. Why—   410

    "As by lot, God wot"

and then, you know,

    "It came to pass, as most like it was".

The first row of the pious chanson[135] will show you
more; for look where my abridgement[136] comes.   415

Enter the Players.

You are welcome, masters; welcome, all.—I am glad
    to see thee well.—Welcome, good friends.—O, my
    old friend! Why thy face is valanc'd[137] since I saw
    thee last; com'st thou to beard me in Denmark?—

---

[134] *O Jephthah, judge of Israel*: "O Jephthah, Judge of Israel", a ballad of which
no copies are extant and from which the subsequent quotations are probably
taken. Jephthah was a judge of Israel obliged by a vow to sacrifice his only daughter (Judges 11:30–40).

[135] *chanson*: spiritual song (French).

[136] *abridgement*: curtailment or interrupter (entertainer who abridges the time).

[137] *valanc'd*: A valance is decorative drapery (here, a beard); female characters were performed by young men.

What, my young lady and mistress! By'r lady, your
ladyship is nearer to heaven than when I saw you
last by the altitude of a chopine.[138] Pray God,
your voice, like a piece of uncurrent gold, be not
crack'd within the ring.[139]—Masters, you are all
welcome. We'll e'en to't like French falconers, fly
at anything we see. We'll have a speech straight.
Come, give us a taste of your quality; come, a
passionate speech.

1 Player. What speech, my good lord?   427

Hamlet. I heard thee speak me a speech once, but it
was never acted; or, if it was, not above once; for
the play, I remember, pleas'd not the million; 'twas
caviary to the general.[140] But it was—as I
received it, and others whose judgments in such
matters cried in the top of[141] mine—an excellent
play, well digested in the scenes, set down with as
much modesty as cunning. I remember one said
there were no sallets[142] in the lines to make the
matter savoury,[143] nor no matter in the phrase
that might indict the author of affectation;[144] but
call'd it an honest method, as wholesome as sweet,
and very much more handsome than fine. One
speech in it I chiefly lov'd: 'twas Aeneas'[145] tale
to Dido;[146] and thereabout of it especially where

---

[138] *chopine:* thick-soled shoe.

[139] *like a piece . . . within the ring:* Coins were not legally fit tender if they bore
a crack extending into the circle around the monarch's head. Hamlet is also
referring musically to the changes of a young man's voice.

[140] *caviary to the general:* too choice for the multitude.

[141] *in the top of:* louder than or overcoming, overtopping.

[142] *sallets:* salads, i.e., spicy jests.

[143] *savoury:* morally wholesome.

[144] *affectation:* pretense of feeling or emotion.

[145] *Aeneas':* In classical mythology, Aeneas was a Trojan prince and ancestor
of the founders of Rome.

[146] *Dido:* in classical mythology, queen of Carthage and Aeneas' deserted lover.

he speaks of Priam's[147] slaughter. If it live in your
memory, begin at this line—let me see, let me see: *443*

"The rugged Pyrrhus,[148] like th' Hyrcanian
beast,"[149]

'Tis not so; it begins with Pyrrhus.

"The rugged Pyrrhus, he whose sable[150] arms,   *445*
Black as his purpose, did the night resemble
When he lay couched in the ominous horse,[151]
Hath now this dread and black complexion smear'd
With heraldry[152] more dismal;[153] head to foot   *450*
Now is he total gules,[154] horridly trick'd[155]
With blood of fathers, mothers, daughters, sons,
Bak'd and impasted[156] with the parching streets,
That lend a tyrannous and damned light
To their lord's murder. Roasted in wrath and fire,   *455*
And thus o'er-sized with coagulate gore,
With eyes like carbuncles, the hellish Pyrrhus
Old grandsire Priam seeks."

So proceed you.

Polonius. For God, my lord, well spoken, with good
accent and good discretion.   *461*

1 Player. "Anon he finds him
Striking too short at Greeks; his antique sword,

---

[147] *Priam's*: In classical mythology, Priam was king of Troy.
[148] *Pyrrhus*: in classical mythology, a warrior, the son of Achilles. Pyrrhus slaughtered members of the Trojan royal family.
[149] *Hyrcanian beast*: tiger.
[150] *sable*: black.
[151] *horse*: i.e., the Trojan horse.
[152] *heraldry*: armorial bearings.
[153] *dismal*: ill-omened.
[154] *gules*: red (here, a heraldic tincture).
[155] *trick'd*: adorned, pasted.
[156] *impasted*: encrusted.

Rebellious to his arm, lies where it falls,
Repugnant[157] to command. Unequal match'd,   465
Pyrrhus at Priam drives, in rage strikes wide;
But with the whiff and wind of his fell sword
Th' unnerved father falls. Then senseless Ilium,[158]
Seeming to feel this blow, with flaming top
Stoops to his base,[159] and with a hideous crash   470
Takes prisoner Pyrrhus' ear. For, lo! his sword,
Which was declining on the milky head
Of reverend Priam, seem'd i' th' air to stick.
So, as a painted tyrant,[160] Pyrrhus stood
And, like a neutral to his will and matter,   475
Did nothing.
But as we often see, against some storm,
A silence in the heavens, the rack[161] stand still,
The bold winds speechless, and the orb below
As hush as death, anon the dreadful thunder   480
Doth rend the region; so, after Pyrrhus' pause,
A roused vengeance sets him new a-work;
And never did the Cyclops'[162] hammers fall
On Mars's armour,[163] forg'd for proof eterne,[164]
With less remorse than Pyrrhus' bleeding sword   485
Now falls on Priam.
Out, out, thou strumpet, Fortune! All you gods,
In general synod,[165] take away her power;
Break all the spokes and fellies[166] from her wheel,

---

[157] *Repugnant*: disobedient.
[158] *Ilium*: besieged city of Troy.
[159] *Stoops to his base*: collapses.
[160] *a painted tyrant*: a tyrant in a picture.
[161] *rack*: clouds.
[162] *Cyclops'*: In classical mythology, the Cyclops were mighty one-armed giants.
[163] *Mars's armour*: in classical mythology, the armor of Achilles, forged by the gods and passed to Achilles' son.
[164] *proof eterne*: endurance through eternity.
[165] *synod*: council.
[166] *fellies*: rims.

And bowl the round nave[167] down the hill of heaven,   *490*
As low as to the fiends."

Polonius. This is too long.

Hamlet. It shall to the barber's, with your beard.
      Prithee say on. He's for a jig, or a tale of bawdry,
      or he sleeps. Say on; come to Hecuba.[168]   *495*

1 Player. "But who, ah, who had seen the mobled[169]
      queen—"

Hamlet. "The mobled queen"?

Polonius. That's good; "mobled queen" is good.

1 Player. "Run barefoot up and down, threatening the
      flames
      With bisson rheum;[170] a clout[171] upon that head   *500*
      Where late the diadem stood, and for a robe,
      About her lank and all o'er-teemed[172] loins,
      A blanket, in the alarm of fear caught up—
      Who this had seen, with tongue in venom steep'd,
      'Gainst Fortune's state would treason have pronounc'd.   *505*
      But if the gods themselves did see her then,
      When she saw Pyrrhus make malicious sport
      In mincing[173] with his sword her husband's limbs,
      The instant burst of clamour that she made—
      Unless things mortal move them not at all—   *510*
      Would have made milch[174] the burning eyes of
      heaven,
      And passion in the gods."

---

[167] *nave*: hub.
[168] *Hecuba*: in classical mythology, the queen of Troy and wife of Priam.
[169] *mobled*: muffled or robed.
[170] *bisson rheum*: blinding tears.
[171] *clout*: mourning veil, rag.
[172] *o'er-teemed*: exhausted by childbearing.
[173] *mincing*: cutting up or shredding into very tiny pieces.
[174] *milch*: moist, milk-giving (tearful).

Polonius. Look whe'er[175] he has not turn'd his colour, and has tears in 's eyes. Prithee no more. *514*

Hamlet. 'Tis well; I'll have thee speak out the rest of this soon.—Good my lord, will you see the players well bestowed?[176] Do you hear: let them be well used;[177] for they are the abstract and brief chronicles of the time; after your death you were better have a bad epitaph than their ill report while you live. *520*

Polonius. My lord, I will use them according to their desert.

Hamlet. God's bodykins,[178] man, much better. Use every man after his desert, and who shall scape whipping? Use them after your own honour and dignity: the less they deserve, the more merit is in your bounty. Take them in. *527*

Polonius. Come, sirs.

Hamlet. Follow him, friends. We'll hear a play to-morrow. Dost thou hear me, old friend; can you play "The Murder of Gonzago"?[179]

1 Player. Ay, my lord. *533*

Hamlet. We'll ha't to-morrow night. You could, for a need, study a speech of some dozen or sixteen lines which I would set down and insert in't, could you not?

1 Player. Ay, my lord. *537*

---

[175] *whe'er*: whether.
[176] *bestowed*: housed and fed.
[177] *well used*: taken good care of.
[178] *God's bodykins*: God's little body, a colloquial exclamation.
[179] *"The Murder of Gonzago"*: perhaps referencing an actual murder. Luigi Gonzaga supposedly murdered Francesco Maria I, Duke of Urbino (1538).

Hamlet. Very well. Follow that lord; and look you mock
    him not. [*Exeunt Polonius and Players.*] My good
    friends, I'll leave you till night. You are welcome
    to Elsinore. 540

Rosencrantz. Good my lord!

        [*Exeunt Rosencrantz and Guildenstern.*]

Hamlet. Ay, so God buy to you! Now I am alone.
    O, what a rogue and peasant slave am I!
    Is it not monstrous that this player here,
    But in a fiction, in a dream of passion, 545
    Could force his soul so to his own conceit[180]
    That from her working all his visage wann'd;[181]
    Tears in his eyes, distraction in's aspect,
    A broken voice, and his whole function[182] suiting
    With forms[183] to his conceit? And all for nothing! 550
    For Hecuba!
    What's Hecuba to him or he to Hecuba,
    That he should weep for her? What would he do,
    Had he the motive and the cue for passion
    That I have? He would drown the stage with tears, 555
    And cleave[184] the general ear with horrid speech;
    Make mad the guilty, and appal[185] the free,[186]
    Confound the ignorant, and amaze indeed
    The very faculties of eyes and ears.
    Yet I, 560
    A dull and muddy-mettl'd[187] rascal, peak,

---

[180] *conceit:* imagination.
[181] *wann'd:* turned pale.
[182] *function:* action.
[183] *forms:* bodily expressions.
[184] *cleave:* split, assail.
[185] *appal:* appall.
[186] *free:* guiltless.
[187] *muddy-mettl'd:* weak-spirited, wanting in resilience.

Like John-a-dreams,[188] unpregnant[189] of my cause,
And can say nothing; no, not for a king
Upon whose property and most dear life
A damn'd defeat was made. Am I a coward?   565
Who calls me villain, breaks my pate across,
Plucks off my beard and blows it in my face,
Tweaks me by the nose, gives me the lie i' th' throat[190]
As deep as to the lungs? Who does me this?
Ha!   570
'Swounds,[191] I should take it; for it cannot be
But I am pigeon-liver'd[192] and lack gall
To make oppression bitter, or ere this
I should 'a fatted all the region kites[193]
With this slave's offal. Bloody, bawdy villain!   575
Remorseless, treacherous, lecherous, kindless[194]
    villain!
O, vengeance!
Why, what an ass am I! This is most brave,
That I, the son of a dear father murder'd,
Prompted to my revenge by heaven and hell,   580
Must, like a whore, unpack my heart with words,
And fall a-cursing like a very drab,[195]
A scullion![196] Fie upon't! foh!
About,[197] my brains. Hum—I have heard
That guilty creatures, sitting at a play,   585
Have by the very cunning of the scene

[188] *John-a-dreams*: a moping, idle fellow.
[189] *unpregnant*: unquickened, without meaning or purpose.
[190] *gives me the lie i' th' throat*: a common expression referring to a deliberate or particularly heinous lie; when "given", it signifies the casting back or confrontation of such a lie.
[191] *'Swounds*: by God's wounds, a colloquial exclamation.
[192] *pigeon-liver'd*: gentle as a dove or cowardly.
[193] *kites*: scavenger birds.
[194] *kindless*: unnatural.
[195] *drab*: prostitute.
[196] *scullion*: servant assigned the most menial kitchen tasks; also, given as "stallion" (male prostitute).
[197] *About*: to work (an imperative statement).

Been struck so to the soul that presently
They have proclaim'd their malefactions;
For murder, though it have no tongue, will speak
With most miraculous organ. I'll have these players   590
Play something like the murder of my father
Before mine uncle. I'll observe his looks;
I'll tent[198] him to the quick. If 'a do blench,[199]
I know my course. The spirit that I have seen
May be a devil; and the devil hath power   595
T' assume a pleasing shape; yea, and perhaps
Out of my weakness and my melancholy,
As he is very potent with such spirits,
Abuses me to damn me. I'll have grounds
More relative[200] than this. The play's the thing   600
Wherein I'll catch the conscience of the King.

[*Exit.*]

---

[198] *tent*: probe.
[199] *blench*: flinch, turn pale.
[200] *relative*: pertinent, plausible.

ACT 3

Scene 1. *Elsinore. The Castle.*

Enter King, Queen, Polonius, Ophelia,
Rosencrantz, and Guildenstern.

King. And can you by no drift of conference[1]
  Get from him why he puts on this confusion,[2]
  Grating so harshly all his days of quiet
  With turbulent and dangerous lunacy?

Rosencrantz. He does confess he feels himself distracted,   5
  But from what cause 'a will by no means speak.

Guildenstern. Nor do we find him forward to be sounded;[3]
  But, with a crafty madness, keeps aloof
  When we would bring him on to some confession
  Of his true state.

Queen.   Did he receive you well?   10

Rosencrantz. Most like a gentleman.

Guildenstern. But with much forcing of his disposition.[4]

Rosencrantz. Niggard[5] of question; but of our demands
  Most free in his reply.

Queen.   Did you assay[6] him
  To any pastime?   15

Rosencrantz. Madam, it so fell out that certain players
  We o'er-raught[7] on the way. Of these we told him;

---

[1] *drift of conference*: management of conversation.
[2] *confusion*: madness.
[3] *forward to be sounded*: willing to be interrogated.
[4] *much forcing of his disposition*: effort.
[5] *Niggard*: miserly, disinclined to speak.
[6] *assay*: tempt, lure.
[7] *o'er-raught*: overcame, came upon.

And there did seem in him a kind of joy
To hear of it. They are here about the court,
And, as I think, they have already order   20
This night to play before him.

Polonius.   'Tis most true;
And he beseech'd me to entreat your Majesties
To hear and see the matter.

King. With all my heart; and it doth much content me
To hear him so inclin'd.   25
Good gentlemen, give him a further edge,
And drive his purpose into these delights.

Rosencrantz. We shall, my lord.

[*Exeunt Rosencrantz and Guildenstern.*]

King.   Sweet Gertrude, leave us too;
For we have closely⁸ sent for Hamlet hither,
That he, as 'twere by accident, may here   30
Affront⁹ Ophelia.
Her father and myself—lawful espials¹⁰—
Will so bestow ourselves that, seeing unseen,
We may of their encounter frankly judge,
And gather by him, as he is behav'd,   35
If't be th' affliction of his love or no
That thus he suffers for.

Queen.   I shall obey you;
And for your part, Ophelia, I do wish
That your good beauties be the happy cause
Of Hamlet's wildness; so shall I hope your virtues   40
Will bring him to his wonted¹¹ way again,
To both your honours.

---

⁸ *closely:* secretly.
⁹ *Affront:* meet face-to-face.
¹⁰ *espials:* spies.
¹¹ *wonted:* usual.

Ophelia.   Madam, I wish it may.

                                                    [*Exit Queen.*]

Polonius. Ophelia, walk you here.—Gracious, so please
     you,
     We will bestow ourselves.—Read on this book;[12]
     That show of such an exercise may colour[13]   45
     Your loneliness.—We are oft to blame in this:
     'Tis too much prov'd, that with devotion's visage
     And pious action we do sugar o'er
     The devil himself.

King. [*Aside*] O, 'tis too true!
     How smart a lash that speech doth give my
          conscience!   50
     The harlot's cheek, beautied with plast'ring art,[14]
     Is not more ugly to the thing that helps it
     Than is my deed[15] to my most painted word.[16]
     O heavy burden!

Polonius. I hear him coming; let's withdraw, my lord.   55

                              [*Exeunt King and Polonius.*]

Enter Hamlet.

Hamlet. To be, or not to be—that is the question;
     Whether 'tis nobler in the mind to suffer
     The slings and arrows of outrageous fortune,
     Or to take arms against a sea of troubles,
     And by opposing end them? To die, to sleep—   60
     No more; and by a sleep to say we end
     The heart-ache and the thousand natural shocks

[12] *book*: presumably a devotional work.
[13] *colour*: give a plausible hue (it would have been inappropriate or unlikely
that she would have been alone under other circumstances).
[14] *plast'ring art*: makeup.
[15] *my deed*: i.e., the murder of his brother.
[16] *most painted word*: the most grievous lies he has told.

That flesh is heir to. 'Tis a consummation
Devoutly to be wish'd. To die, to sleep;
To sleep, perchance to dream. Ay, there's the rub;[17]   65
For in that sleep of death what dreams may come,
When we have shuffled off this mortal coil,[18]
Must give us pause. There's the respect[19]
That makes calamity of so long life;
For who would bear the whips and scorns of time,   70
Th' oppressor's wrong, the proud man's contumely,[20]
The pangs of despis'd love, the law's delay,
The insolence of office, and the spurns
That patient merit of th' unworthy takes,
When he himself might his quietus[21] make   75
With a bare bodkin?[22] Who would these fardels[23]
    bear,
To grunt and sweat under a weary life,
But that the dread of something after death—
The undiscover'd country, from whose bourn[24]
No traveller returns—puzzles the will,   80
And makes us rather bear those ills we have
Than fly to others that we know not of?
Thus conscience[25] does make cowards of us all;
And thus the native hue of resolution
Is sicklied o'er with the pale cast[26] of thought,   85
And enterprises of great pitch and moment,
With this regard,[27] their currents turn awry
And lose the name of action.—Soft you now!

---

[17] *rub*: central difficulty, impediment.
[18] *coil*: turmoil or a ring of rope (here, the soul encircling, enclosing the body).
[19] *respect*: consideration.
[20] *contumely*: insulting language.
[21] *quietus*: full discharge (a legal term).
[22] *bodkin*: dagger with a thin blade.
[23] *fardels*: burdens.
[24] *bourn*: boundaries.
[25] *conscience*: self-consciousness, introspection.
[26] *cast*: color.
[27] *regard*: thought, consideration.

The fair Ophelia.—Nymph,[28] in thy orisons[29]
Be all my sins rememb'red.

Ophelia.   Good my lord,   90
How does your honour for this many a day?

Hamlet. I humbly thank you; well, well, well.

Ophelia. My lord, I have remembrances of yours
That I have longed long to re-deliver.
I pray you now receive them.

Hamlet.   No, not I;   95
I never gave you aught.

Ophelia. My honour'd lord, you know right well you did,
And with them words of so sweet breath compos'd
As made the things more rich; their perfume lost,
Take these again; for to the noble mind   100
Rich gifts wax poor when givers prove unkind.
There, my lord.

Hamlet.   Ha, ha! Are you honest?[30]

Ophelia. My lord?

Hamlet. Are you fair?   105

Ophelia. What means your lordship?

Hamlet. That if you be honest and fair, your honesty
should admit no discourse to your beauty.[31]

Ophelia. Could beauty, my lord, have better commerce
than with honesty?   110

---

[28] *Nymph:* in classical mythology, a spirit of nature appearing as a beautiful young woman; here, simply a beautiful young woman.

[29] *orisons:* prayers.

[30] *honest:* truthful or chaste.

[31] *your honesty . . . to your beauty:* your chastity should not allow you to listen to overtures of love.

Hamlet. Ay, truly; for the power of beauty will sooner
transform honesty from what it is to a bawd[32]
than the force of honesty can translate beauty
into his likeness. This was sometime a paradox,
but now the time gives it proof. I did love you
once.   115

Ophelia. Indeed, my lord, you made me believe so.

Hamlet. You should not have believ'd me; for virtue
cannot so inoculate[33] our old stock but we shall
relish of it. I loved you not.

Ophelia. I was the more deceived.   120

Hamlet. Get thee to a nunnery. Why wouldst thou be a
breeder of sinners? I am myself indifferent
honest,[34] but yet I could accuse me of such things
that it were better my mother had not borne me: I
am very proud, revengeful, ambitious; with more
offences at my beck[35] than I have thoughts to put
them in, imagination to give them shape, or time
to act them in. What should such fellows as I do
crawling between earth and heaven? We are
arrant knaves, all; believe none of us. Go thy ways
to a nunnery. Where's your father?   130

Ophelia. At home, my lord.

Hamlet. Let the doors be shut upon him, that he may
play the fool nowhere but in's own house. Farewell.

Ophelia. O, help him, you sweet heavens!   134

Hamlet. If thou dost marry, I'll give thee this plague for
thy dowry: be thou as chaste as ice, as pure as

---

[32] *bawd:* procurer.
[33] *inoculate:* graft.
[34] *indifferent honest:* moderately virtuous.
[35] *beck:* call.

snow, thou shalt not escape calumny.[36] Get thee
to a nunnery, go, farewell. Or, if thou wilt needs
marry, marry a fool; for wise men know well
enough what monsters[37] you make of them. To a
nunnery, go; and quickly too. Farewell.   *140*

Ophelia. O heavenly powers, restore him!

Hamlet. I have heard of your paintings[38] too, well
enough; God hath given you one face, and you
make yourselves another. You jig and amble, and
you lisp, and nickname God's creatures, and make
your wantonness your ignorance.[39] Go to, I'll no
more on't; it hath made me mad. I say we will
have no moe[40] marriage: those that are married
already, all but one, shall live; the rest shall keep
as they are. To a nunnery, go.   [*Exit.*]

Ophelia. O, what a noble mind is here o'er-thrown!   *150*
The courtier's, soldier's, scholar's, eye, tongue, sword;
Th' expectancy and rose[41] of the fair state,
The glass[42] of fashion and the mould of form,[43]
Th' observ'd of all observers—quite, quite down!
And I, of ladies most deject and wretched,   *155*
That suck'd the honey of his music vows,
Now see that noble and most sovereign reason,
Like sweet bells jangled, out of time and harsh;
That unmatch'd form and feature of blown[44] youth

---

[36] *calumny*: scandalous rumors or defamatory statements.
[37] *monsters*: beasts, horned beasts, cuckolds.
[38] *paintings*: makeup.
[39] *make your wantonness your ignorance*: excuse wantonness because of pretended naïveté.
[40] *moe*: more.
[41] *expectancy and rose*: cheerful expectations or fair hopes.
[42] *glass*: mirror.
[43] *mould of form*: patterns of (excellent) behavior.
[44] *blown*: blooming.

Blasted with ecstasy.[45] O, woe is me   *160*
T' have seen what I have seen, see what I see!

Re-enter King and Polonius.

King. Love! His affections[46] do not that way tend;
Nor what he spake, though it lack'd form a little,
Was not like madness. There's something in his soul
O'er which his melancholy sits on brood;   *165*
And I do doubt[47] the hatch[48] and the disclose
Will be some danger; which to prevent
I have in quick determination
Thus set it down: he shall with speed to England
For the demand of our neglected tribute.   *170*
Haply the seas and countries different,
With variable objects, shall expel
This something-settled[49] matter in his heart
Whereon his brains still beating puts him thus
From fashion of himself. What think you on't?   *175*

Polonius. It shall do well. But yet do I believe
The origin and commencement of his grief
Sprung from neglected love. How now, Ophelia!
You need not tell us what Lord Hamlet said;
We heard it all. My lord, do as you please;   *180*
But if you hold it fit, after the play
Let his queen mother all alone entreat him
To show his grief. Let her be round[50] with him;
And I'll be plac'd, so please you, in the ear
Of all their conference. If she find him not,[51]   *185*

---

[45] *ecstasy*: madness.
[46] *affections*: inclinations.
[47] *doubt*: fear.
[48] *hatch*: birth (continuing the metaphor of the bird's nest).
[49] *something-settled*: partly or imperfectly settled.
[50] *round*: blunt, direct.
[51] *find him not*: does not discover the source of his current character.

To England send him; or confine him where
Your wisdom best shall think.

King.   It shall be so:
Madness in great ones must not unwatch'd go.

                                    [*Exeunt.*]

Scene 2. *Elsinore. The Castle.*

Enter Hamlet and three of the Players.

Hamlet. Speak the speech, I pray you, as I pronounc'd
it to you, trippingly on the tongue; but if you
mouth it, as many of our players do, I had as lief[52]
the town-crier spoke my lines. Nor do not saw the
air too much with your hand, thus, but use all
gently; for in the very torrent, tempest, and, as I
may say, whirlwind of your passion, you must
acquire and beget a temperance that may give it
smoothness. O, it offends me to the soul to hear a
robustious[53] periwig-pated[54] fellow tear a passion
to tatters,[55] to very rags, to split the ears of the
groundlings,[56] who, for the most part, are capable
of nothing[57] but inexplicable dumb shows[58] and
noise. I would have such a fellow whipp'd for
o'erdoing Termagant;[59] it out-herods Herod.[60]
Pray you avoid it.   14

[52] *had as lief*: would rather.

[53] *robustious*: boisterous.

[54] *periwig-pated*: wearing a wig upon his head (pate).

[55] *tear a passion to tatters*: so poorly perform a passionate speech as to destroy
the meaning and sense.

[56] *groundlings*: theatergoers who pay the lowest price and stand in the pit before
the stage.

[57] *capable of nothing*: capable of understanding nothing.

[58] *dumb shows*: miming.

[59] *Termagant*: a mythical Muslim god (conceived by Westerners); a boisterous
character in old mystery plays.

[60] *Herod*: King Herod (73–4 B.C.); a boisterous character in old mystery plays.

1 Player. I warrant your honour.[61]

Hamlet. Be not too tame neither, but let your own
    discretion be your tutor. Suit the action to the
    word, the word to the action; with this special
    observance, that you o'er-step not the modesty of
    nature; for any-thing so o'erdone is from[62] the
    purpose of playing, whose end, both at the first
    and now, was and is to hold, as 'twere, the mirror
    up to nature; to show virtue her own feature,
    scorn her own image, and the very age and body
    of the time his form and pressure.[63] Now, this
    overdone or come tardy off, though it makes the
    unskilful laugh, cannot but make the judicious
    grieve; the censure of the which one must, in your
    allowance, o'erweigh a whole theatre of others. O,
    there be players that I have seen play—and heard
    others praise, and that highly—not to speak it
    profanely, that, neither having th' accent of
    Christians, nor the gait of Christian, pagan, nor
    man, have so strutted and bellowed that I have
    thought some of Nature's journeymen[64] had made
    men, and not made them well, they imitated
    humanity so abominably.   *34*

1 Player. I hope we have reform'd that indifferently[65]
    with us, sir.

Hamlet. O, reform it altogether. And let those that play
    your clowns speak no more than is set down for
    them; for there be of them that will themselves
    laugh, to set on some quantity of barren spectators
    to laugh too, though in the meantime some

---

[61] *I warrant your honour:* I do not doubt you.
[62] *from:* contrary to.
[63] *pressure:* image (impress).
[64] *journeymen:* laborers (perhaps not reliable) employed by another.
[65] *indifferently:* to a degree, tolerably.

necessary question of the play be then to be
considered. That's villainous, and shows a most
pitiful ambition in the fool that uses it. Go, make
you ready.   [*Exeunt Players.*]

Enter Polonius, Rosencrantz, and Guildenstern.

How now, my lord! Will the King hear this piece of
work?   45

Polonius. And the Queen too, and that presently.

Hamlet. Bid the players make haste.

[*Exit Polonius.*]

Will you two help to hasten them?

Rosencrantz. Ay, my lord.   [*Exeunt they two.*]

Hamlet. What, ho, Horatio!   50

Enter Horatio.

Horatio. Here, sweet lord, at your service.

Hamlet. Horatio, thou art e'en as just a man
As e'er my conversation cop'd withal.[66]

Horatio. O my dear lord!

Hamlet.   Nay, do not think I flatter;
For what advancement[67] may I hope from thee,   55
That no revenue[68] hast but thy good spirits
To feed and clothe thee? Why should the poor be
    flatter'd?
No, let the candied[69] tongue lick absurd pomp,
And crook the pregnant[70] hinges of the knee

---

[66] *cop'd withal*: met with.
[67] *advancement*: promotion (signifying an ulterior motive).
[68] *revenue*: financial return.
[69] *candied*: flattering, sugared.
[70] *pregnant*: pliant or full of promise.

Where thrift[71] may follow fawning.[72] Dost thou hear?   60
Since my dear soul was mistress of her choice
And could of men distinguish her election,
Sh'hath seal'd[73] thee for herself; for thou hast been
As one in suff'ring all, that suffers nothing;
A man that Fortune's buffets and rewards   65
Hast ta'en with equal thanks; and blest are those
Whose blood[74] and judgment are so well comeddled[75]
That they are not a pipe for Fortune's finger
To sound what stop she please. Give me that man
That is not passion's slave, and I will wear him   70
In my heart's core, ay, in my heart of heart,
As I do thee. Something too much of this.
There is a play to-night before the King;
One scene of it comes near the circumstance
Which I have told thee of my father's death.   75
I prithee, when thou seest that act afoot,
Even with the very comment[76] of thy soul
Observe my uncle. If his occulted[77] guilt
Do not itself unkennel[78] in one speech,
It is a damned ghost that we have seen,   80
And my imaginations are as foul
As Vulcan's stithy.[79] Give him heedful note;
For I mine eyes will rivet to his face;
And, after, we will both our judgments join
In censure of his seeming.[80]

---

[71] *thrift*: profit.

[72] *fawning*: flattery.

[73] *Sh'hath seal'd*: she has set a mark (upon the soul).

[74] *blood*: passion.

[75] *comeddled*: mixed, blended.

[76] *very comment*: deepest wisdom.

[77] *occulted*: hidden.

[78] *unkennel*: reveal itself.

[79] *Vulcan's stithy*: the smithy or blacksmith's shop of the classical mythological god of fire, Vulcan.

[80] *his seeming*: Claudius' false appearance of integrity.

Horatio.   Well, my lord.   85
  If 'a steal[81] aught the whilst this play is playing,
  And scape[82] detecting, I will pay the theft.[83]

Enter trumpets and kettledrums. Danish march. Sound a
  flourish. Enter King, Queen, Polonius, Ophelia,
  Rosencrantz, Guildenstern, and other Lords
  attendant, with the Guard carrying torches.

Hamlet. They are coming to the play; I must be idle.[84]
  Get you a place.

King. How fares our cousin Hamlet?   90

Hamlet. Excellent, i' faith; of the chameleon's dish.[85] I
  eat the air, promise-cramm'd; you cannot feed
  capons[86] so.

King. I have nothing with this answer, Hamlet; these
  words are not mine.   94

Hamlet. No, nor mine now. [*To Polonius*] My lord, you
  play'd once i' th' university, you say?

Polonius. That did I, my lord, and was accounted a
  good actor.

Hamlet. What did you enact?   99

Polonius. I did enact Julius Caesar; I was kill'd i' th'
  Capitol; Brutus[87] kill'd me.

Hamlet. It was a brute part of him to kill so capital a
  calf there. Be the players ready?

[81] *steal:* sneak.
[82] *scape:* escape.
[83] *pay the theft:* take full responsibility.
[84] *be idle:* put on a pretense of madness.
[85] *chameleon's dish:* the food on which chameleons were supposed to survive.
[86] *capons:* castrated domestic roosters fattened for eating.
[87] *Brutus:* Marcus Junius Brutus (85–42 B.C.) was a Roman senator and complicit in the assassination of Julius Caesar.

Rosencrantz. Ay, my lord; they stay upon your patience.

Queen. Come hither, my dear Hamlet, sit by me.   105

Hamlet. No, good mother; here's metal more
      attractive.[88]

Polonius. [*To the King*] O, ho! do you mark that?

Hamlet. Lady, shall I lie in your lap?

            [*Lying down at Ophelia's feet.*]

Ophelia. No, my lord.

Hamlet. I mean, my head upon your lap?   110

Ophelia. Ay, my lord.

Hamlet. Do you think I meant country matters?[89]

Ophelia. I think nothing, my lord.

Hamlet. That's a fair thought to lie between maids' legs.

Ophelia. What is, my lord?   115

Hamlet. Nothing.

Ophelia. You are merry, my lord.

Hamlet. Who, I?

Ophelia. Ay, my lord.   119

Hamlet. O God, your only jig-maker![90] What should a
      man do but be merry? For look you how cheerfully
      my mother looks, and my father died within's two
      hours.

Ophelia. Nay, 'tis twice two months, my lord.   123

[88] *attractive:* magnetic.
[89] *country matters:* rustic doings, also a vulgar pun.
[90] *jig-maker:* composer of songs and dances (often a fool).

Hamlet. So long? Nay then, let the devil wear black,
    for I'll have a suit of sables.[91] O heavens! die two
    months ago, and not forgotten yet? Then there's
    hope a great man's memory may outlive his life
    half a year; but, by'r lady,[92] 'a must build
    churches, then; or else shall 'a suffer not thinking
    on, with the hobby-horse,[93] whose epitaph is "For
    O, for O, the hobby-horse is forgot!"   130

The trumpet sounds. Hautboys[94] play. The Dumb Show
    enters.

Enter a King and a Queen, very lovingly; the Queen
    embracing him and he her. She kneels, and makes
    show of protestation unto him. He takes her up, and
    declines his head upon her neck. He lies him down
    upon a bank of flowers; she, seeing him asleep, leaves
    him. Anon comes in a Fellow, takes off his crown,
    kisses it, pours poison in the sleeper's ears, and leaves
    him. The Queen returns; finds the King dead, and
    makes passionate action. The Poisoner, with some two
    or three Mutes, comes in again, seeming to condole
    with her. The dead body is carried away. The
    Poisoner woos the Queen with gifts; she seems harsh
    awhile, but in the end accepts his love. [*Exeunt.*]

Ophelia. What means this, my lord?

Hamlet. Marry, this is miching mallecho;[95] it means
    mischief.

Ophelia. Belike this show imports the argument[96] of
    the play.   135

---

[91] *suit of sables*: black mourning garments. Also, sables are luxurious furs.
[92] *by'r lady*: by our Lady, a colloquial exclamation.
[93] *hobby-horse*: mock horse worn by performer in a folk (morris) dance.
[94] *Hautboys*: oboes.
[95] *miching mallecho*: sneaking mischief.
[96] *argument*: plot.

Enter Prologue.

Hamlet. We shall know by this fellow: the players
    cannot keep counsel; they'll tell all.

Ophelia. Will 'a tell us what this show meant?   138

Hamlet. Ay, or any show that you will show him. Be
    not you asham'd to show, he'll not shame to tell
    you what it means.   141

Ophelia. You are naught,[97] you are naught. I'll mark
    the play.

Prologue. For us, and for our tragedy,
    Here stooping to your clemency,   145
    We beg your hearing patiently.   [*Exit.*]

Hamlet. Is this a prologue, or the posy[98] of a ring?

Ophelia. 'Tis brief, my lord.

Hamlet. As woman's love.

Enter the Player King and Queen.

Player King. Full thirty times hath Phoebus' cart[99] *gone*
    round   150
Neptune's[100] *salt wash*[101] *and Tellus'*[102] *orbed ground,*
And thirty dozen moons with borrowed sheen
About the world have times twelve thirties been,
Since love our hearts and Hymen[103] *did our hands*
Unit[104] *comutual in most sacred bands.*   155

---

[97] *naught*: wicked, improper.

[98] *posy*: motto inscribed on a ring.

[99] *Phoebus' cart*: in classical mythology, the sun chariot of Phoebus Apollo.

[100] *Neptune's*: In classical mythology, Neptune was the god of the sea.

[101] *salt wash*: i.e., the sea.

[102] *Tellus'*: In classical mythology, Tellus Mater was the goddess of the earth.

[103] *Hymen*: in classical mythology, the god of marriage.

[104] *Unit*: unite.

Player Queen. So many journeys may the sun and moon
   Make us again count o'er ere love be done!
   But, woe is me, you are so sick of late,
   So far from cheer and from your former state,
   That I distrust[105] you. Yet, though I distrust,   160
   Discomfort you, my lord, it nothing must;
   For women fear too much even as they love,
   And women's fear and love hold quantity,
   In neither aught, or in extremity.
   Now, what my love is, proof hath made you know;
   And as my love is siz'd, my fear is so.   165
   Where love is great, the littlest doubts are fear;
   Where little fears grow great, great love grows there.

Player King. Faith, I must leave thee, love, and shortly too: 168
   My operant powers their functions leave to do;
   And thou shalt live in this fair world behind,
   Honour'd, belov'd; and haply one as kind
   For husband shalt thou—

Player Queen.   O, confound the rest!
   Such love must needs be treason in my breast.
   In second husband let me be accurst!
   None wed the second but who kill'd the first.   175

Hamlet. That's wormwood,[106] wormwood.

Player Queen. The instances[107] that second marriage
   move[108]
   Are base respects of thrift,[109] but none of love.
   A second time I kill my husband dead,
   When second husband kisses me in bed.   180

---

[105] *distrust:* am anxious about.
[106] *wormwood:* a very bitter herb (or bitterness generally).
[107] *instances:* motives.
[108] *move:* induce.
[109] *respects of thrift:* considerations of profit.

Player King. I do believe you think what now you speak;
　　But what we do determine oft we break.
　　Purpose is but the slave to memory,
　　Of violent birth, but poor validity;[110]
　　Which now, the fruit unripe, sticks on the tree;   185
　　But fall unshaken when they mellow be.
　　Most necessary 'tis that we forget
　　To pay ourselves what to ourselves is debt.
　　What to ourselves in passion we propose,
　　The passion ending, doth the purpose lose.   190
　　The violence of either grief or joy
　　Their own enactures[111] with themselves destroy.
　　Where joy most revels grief doth most lament;
　　Grief joys, joy grieves, on slender accident.
　　This world is not for aye; nor 'tis not strange   195
　　That even our loves should with our fortunes change;
　　For 'tis a question left us yet to prove,
　　Whether love lead fortune or else fortune love.
　　The great man down, you mark his favourite flies;
　　The poor advanc'd makes friends of enemies.   200
　　And hitherto doth love on fortune tend;
　　For who not needs shall never lack a friend,
　　And who in want a hollow friend doth try,
　　Directly seasons[112] him his enemy.
　　But, orderly to end where I begun,   205
　　Our wills and fates do so contrary run
　　That our devices still are overthrown;
　　Our thoughts are ours, their ends none of our own.
　　So think thou wilt no second husband wed;
　　But die thy thoughts when thy first lord is dead.   210

Player Queen. Nor earth to me give food, nor heaven light,
　　Sport and repose lock from me day and night,
　　To desperation turn my trust and hope,

---

[110] *validity:* force.
[111] *enactures:* acts.
[112] *seasons:* ripens, forms.

An anchor's[113] cheer in prison be my scope,
Each opposite that blanks[114] the face of joy   215
Meet what I would have well, and it destroy,
Both here and hence pursue me lasting strife,
If, once a widow, ever I be wife!

Hamlet. If she should break it now!

Player King. 'Tis deeply sworn. Sweet, leave me here awhile; 220
My spirits grow dull, and fain I would beguile
The tedious day with sleep.

                                        [*Sleeps.*]

Player Queen.   Sleep rock thy brain,
And never come mischance between us twain!

                                        [*Exit.*]

Hamlet. Madam, how like you this play?

Queen. The lady doth protest too much, methinks.   225

Hamlet. O, but she'll keep her word.

King. Have you heard the argument?[115] Is there no
    offence in't?   230

Hamlet. No, no; they do but jest, poison in jest; no
    offence i' th' world.

King. What do you call the play?

Hamlet. "The Mouse-trap." Marry, how? Tropically.[116]
    This play is the image of a murder done in
    Vienna: Gonzago is the duke's name; his wife,
    Baptista. You shall see anon. 'Tis a knavish piece
    of work; but what of that? Your Majesty, and we

---

[113] *anchor's*: referring to an anchorite, a religious recluse.
[114] *blanks*: blanches.
[115] *argument*: central argument, plot.
[116] *Tropically*: figuratively, also a pun on "trap".

that have free[117] souls, it touches us not. Let the
galled jade[118] wince, our withers are unwrung.

Enter Lucianus.

This is one Lucianus, nephew to the King.

Ophelia. You are as good as a chorus,[119] my lord.

Hamlet. I could interpret between you and your love, if   239
I could see the puppets dallying.

Ophelia. You are keen,[120] my lord, you are keen.

Hamlet. It would cost you a groaning to take off mine
edge.

Ophelia. Still better, and worse.   245

Hamlet. So you mis-take[121] your husbands.—Begin,
murderer; pox,[122] leave thy damnable faces and
begin. Come; the croaking raven doth bellow for
revenge.

Lucianus.   *Thoughts black, hands apt, drugs fit, and time*
agreeing;
Confederate season,[123] *else no creature seeing;*   250
Thou mixture rank, of midnight weeds collected,
With Hecat's ban[124] *thrice blasted, thrice infected,*
Thy natural magic and dire property[125]
On wholesome life usurps immediately.   254

[*Pours the poison in his ears.*]

---

[117] *free*: innocent, free from sin.
[118] *galled jade*: sore-backed horse.
[119] *chorus*: character in a play who explains the action.
[120] *keen*: perceptive, with a secondary connotation of sexual arousal.
[121] *mis-take*: err in taking.
[122] *pox*: viral disease leaving blemishes on the face.
[123] *Confederate season*: opportunity allied to interests.
[124] *Hecat's ban*: curse of the goddess of sorcery.
[125] *property*: nature.

Hamlet. 'A poisons him i' th' garden for his estate. His
    name's Gonzago. The story is extant, and written
    in very choice Italian. You shall see anon how the
    murderer gets the love of Gonzago's wife.

Ophelia. The King rises.

Hamlet. What, frighted with false fire![126]   260

Queen. How fares my lord?

Polonius. Give o'er the play.

King. Give me some light. Away!

Polonius. Lights, lights, lights!

    [*Exeunt all but Hamlet and Horatio.*]

Hamlet. Why, let the strucken deer go weep,   265
        The hart ungalled play;
    For some must watch, while some must sleep;
        Thus runs the world away.
    Would not this, sir, and a forest of feathers—if the
        rest of my fortunes turn Turk[127] with me—with
        two Provincial roses[128] on my raz'd[129] shoes, get
        me a fellowship in a cry[130] of players, sir?

Horatio. Half a share.

Hamlet. A whole one, I.   274

---

[126] *false fire*: blank discharge of firearms.
[127] *turn Turk*: turn renegade, as a Christian converting to Islam.
[128] *Provincial roses*: rosettes.
[129] *raz'd*: ornamented with sashes.
[130] *cry*: company.

For thou dost know, O Damon[131] dear,
   This realm dismantled was
Of Jove[132] himself; and now reigns here
A very, very—paiock.[133]

Horatio. You might have rhym'd.[134]

Hamlet. O good Horatio, I'll take the ghost's word for a
   thousand pound. Didst perceive?   281

Horatio. Very well, my lord.

Hamlet. Upon the talk of the poisoning.

Horatio. I did very well note him.

Hamlet. Ah, ha! Come, some music. Come, the
   recorders.[135]   286
For if the King like not the comedy,
Why, then, belike he likes it not, perdy.[136]
Come, some music.

Re-enter Rosencrantz and Guildenstern.

Guildenstern. Good my lord, vouchsafe me a word with
   you.   290

Hamlet. Sir, a whole history.

Guildenstern. The King, sir—

Hamlet. Ay, sir, what of him?

Guildenstern. Is, in his retirement, marvellous
   distemp'red.

Hamlet. With drink, sir?   295

---

[131] *Damon:* conventional name for a shepherd.
[132] *Jove:* in classical mythology, king of the gods.
[133] *paiock:* peacock.
[134] *rhym'd:* i.e., rhymed "was" with "ass".
[135] *recorders:* flutelike instruments.
[136] *perdy:* by God (taken from the French, "par Dieu").

Guildenstern. No, my lord, rather with choler.[137]

Hamlet. Your wisdom should show itself more richer to
signify this to his doctor; for for me to put him to
his purgation would perhaps plunge him into far
more choler.

Guildenstern. Good my lord, put your discourse into
some frame,[138] and start not so wildly from my
affair.   *301*

Hamlet. I am tame, sir. Pronounce.

Guildenstern. The Queen, your mother, in most great
affliction of spirit, hath sent me to you.

Hamlet. You are welcome.   *305*

Guildenstern. Nay, good my lord, this courtesy is not of
the right breed. If it shall please you to make me a
wholesome[139] answer, I will do your mother's
commandment; if not, your pardon and my return
shall be the end of my business.   *310*

Hamlet. Sir, I cannot.

Rosencrantz. What, my lord?

Hamlet. Make you a wholesome answer; my wit's
diseas'd. But, sir, such answer as I can make, you
shall command; or rather, as you say, my mother.
Therefore no more, but to the matter: my mother,
you say—   *316*

Rosencrantz. Then thus she says: your behaviour hath
struck her into amazement and admiration.[140]

---

[137] *choler:* anger or biliousness.
[138] *frame:* order, control.
[139] *wholesome:* sane.
[140] *admiration:* wonder.

Hamlet. O wonderful son, that can so stonish[141] a
mother! But is there no sequel at the heels of this
mother's admiration? Impart.[142]   *321*

Rosencrantz. She desires to speak with you in her closet
ere you go to bed.

Hamlet. We shall obey, were she ten times our mother.
Have you any further trade with us?   *325*

Rosencrantz. My lord, you once did love me.

Hamlet. And do still, by these pickers and stealers.[143]

Rosencrantz. Good my lord, what is your cause of
distemper? You do surely bar the door upon your
own liberty, if you deny your griefs to your friend.   *330*

Hamlet. Sir, I lack advancement.

Rosencrantz. How can that be, when you have the
voice of the King himself for your succession in
Denmark?   *333*

Hamlet. Ay, sir, but "While the grass grows"[144]—the
proverb is something musty.

Re-enter the Players, with recorders.

O, the recorders! Let me see one. To withdraw[145]
with you—why do you go about to recover the
wind[146] of me, as if you would drive me into a
toil?[147]

---

[141] *stonish*: astonish.
[142] *Impart*: explain, tell.
[143] *pickers and stealers*: hands.
[144] *While the grass grows*: a proverb: "While the grass groweth, the horse
starveth."
[145] *withdraw*: speak privately.
[146] *recover the wind*: move to the windward side.
[147] *toil*: snare.

Guildenstern. O my lord, if my duty be too bold, my
    love is too unmannerly.[148]   340

Hamlet. I do not well understand that. Will you play
    upon this pipe?

Guildenstern. My lord, I cannot.

Hamlet. I pray you.

Guildenstern. Believe me, I cannot.   345

Hamlet. I do beseech you.

Guildenstern. I know no touch of it, my lord.

Hamlet. It is as easy as lying: govern these ventages[149]
    with your fingers and thumb, give it breath with
    your mouth, and it will discourse most eloquent
    music. Look you, these are the stops.   351

Guildenstern. But these cannot I command to any
    utterance of harmony; I have not the skill.   353

Hamlet. Why, look you now, how unworthy a thing you
    make of me! You would play upon me; you would
    seem to know my stops; you would pluck out the
    heart of my mystery; you would sound me from
    my lowest note to the top of my compass;[150] and
    there is much music, excellent voice, in this little
    organ,[151] yet cannot you make it speak.
    'Sblood,[152] do you think I am easier to be play'd
    on than a pipe? Call me what instrument you will,
    though you can fret[153] me, yet you cannot play
    upon me.

[148] *if my duty . . . too unmannerly:* if the questions appear rude, my love for
you leads me beyond good manners.
[149] *ventages:* open holes (stops) on a recorder.
[150] *compass:* range of voice.
[151] *organ:* i.e., the recorder.
[152] *'Sblood:* by God's blood, a colloquial exclamation.
[153] *fret:* vex, referencing also the ridges (frets) that guide fingering on some
instruments.

Re-enter Polonius.

God bless you, sir!

Polonius. My lord, the Queen would speak with you,
    and presently.   365

Hamlet. Do you see yonder cloud that's almost in shape
    of a camel?

Polonius. By th' mass, and 'tis like a camel indeed.

Hamlet. Methinks it is like a weasel.

Polonius. It is back'd like a weasel.   370

Hamlet. Or like a whale?

Polonius. Very like a whale.

Hamlet. Then I will come to my mother by and by.
    [*Aside*] They fool me to the top of my
    bendt.[154]—I will come by and by.[155]   375

Polonius. I will say so.   [*Exit Polonius.*]

Hamlet. "By and by" is easily said. Leave me, friends.

                [*Exeunt all but Hamlet.*]

'Tis now the very witching time of night,
When churchyards yawn, and hell itself breathes out
Contagion to this world. Now could I drink hot
    blood,   380
And do such bitter business as the day
Would quake to look on. Soft! now to my mother.
O heart, lose not thy nature; let not ever
The soul of Nero[156] enter this firm bosom.
Let me be cruel, not unnatural: 385

---

[154] *fool me . . . my bendt:* compel me to play the fool to the limit of my capacity.
[155] *by and by:* soon.
[156] *Nero:* Nero Claudius Caesar Augustus Germanicus (A.D. 37–68), Roman
emperor who ordered the murder of his mother, Agrippina.

I will speak daggers to her, but use none.
My tongue and soul in this be hypocrites—
How in my words somever she be shent,[157]
To give them seals[158] never, my soul, consent!

[Exit.]

Scene 3. Elsinore. The Castle.

Enter King, Rosencrantz, and Guildenstern.

King. I like him not; nor stands it safe with us.
To let his madness range. Therefore prepare you;
I your commission will forthwith dispatch,
And he to England shall along with you.
The terms of our estate may not endure   5
Hazard so near's[159] as doth hourly grow
Out of his brows.

Guildenstern. We will ourselves provide.
Most holy and religious fear it is
To keep those many many bodies safe
That live and feed upon your Majesty.   10

Rosencrantz. The single and peculiar[160] life is bound
With all the strength and armour of the mind
To keep itself from noyance;[161] but much more
That spirit upon whose weal depends and rests
The lives of many. The cease[162] of majesty   15
Dies not alone, but like a gulf[163] doth draw
What's near it with it. It is a massy wheel,

---

[157] *shent*: rebuked.
[158] *give them seals*: confirm them with deeds.
[159] *near's*: near us.
[160] *peculiar*: individual.
[161] *noyance*: annoyance.
[162] *cease*: also given as "cess", cessation or death.
[163] *gulf*: whirlpool.

Fix'd on the summit of the highest mount,
To whose huge spokes ten thousand lesser things
Are mortis'd and adjoin'd; which when it falls,   20
Each small annexment, petty consequence,
Attends[164] the boist'rous ruin. Never alone
Did the king sigh, but with a general groan.

King. Arm[165] you, I pray you, to this speedy voyage;
For we will fetters put about this fear,   25
Which now goes too free-footed.

Rosencrantz.   We will haste us.

> [*Exeunt Rosencrantz and Guildenstern.*]

Enter Polonius.

Polonius. My lord, he's going to his mother's closet.
Behind the arras[166] I'll convey myself
To hear the process.[167] I'll warrant she'll tax him
     home;[168]
And, as you said, and wisely was it said,   30
'Tis meet that some more audience than a mother,
Since nature makes them partial, should o'erhear
The speech, of vantage.[169] Fare you well, my liege.
I'll call upon you ere you go to bed,
And tell you what I know.

King.   Thanks, dear my lord.   35

> [*Exit Polonius.*]

O, my offence is rank, it smells to heaven;
It hath the primal eldest curse[170] upon't—

---

[164] *Attends:* participates in.
[165] *Arm:* prepare.
[166] *arras:* tapestry wall hanging.
[167] *process:* proceedings.
[168] *tax him home:* censure him sharply.
[169] *vantage:* a place of advantage.
[170] *primal eldest curse:* the curse of Cain, who killed his brother Abel.

A brother's murder! Pray can I not,
Though inclination be as sharp as will.
My stronger guilt defeats my strong intent,   40
And, like a man to double business bound,
I stand in pause where I shall first begin,
And both neglect. What if this cursed hand
Were thicker than itself with brother's blood,
Is there not rain enough in the sweet heavens   45
To wash it white as snow? Whereto serves mercy
But to confront the visage of offence?
And what's in prayer but this twofold force,
To be forestalled ere we come to fall,
Or pardon'd being down? Then I'll look up;   50
My fault is past. But, O, what form of prayer
Can serve my turn? "Forgive me my foul murder"!
That cannot be; since I am still possess'd
Of those effects[171] for which I did the murder—
My crown, mine own ambition, and my queen.   55
May one be pardon'd and retain th' offence?
In the corrupted currents of this world
Offence's gilded hand may shove by justice;
And oft 'tis seen the wicked prize itself
Buys out the law. But 'tis not so above: 60
There is no shuffling;[172] there the action lies
In his true nature; and we ourselves compell'd,
Even to the teeth and forehead of our faults,
To give in evidence. What then? What rests?[173]
Try what repentance can. What can it not?   65
Yet what can it when one can not repent?
O wretched state! O bosom black as death!
O limed[174] soul, that, struggling to be free,

---

[171] *effects*: things gained.
[172] *shuffling*: trickery.
[173] *rests*: remains.
[174] *limed*: caught (birdlime is a sticky substance spread on boughs to ensnare birds).

Art more engag'd! Help, angels. Make assay:[175]
Bow, stubborn knees; and, heart, with strings of steel,   70
Be soft as sinews of the new-born babe.
All may be well.

                          [Retires and kneels.]

Enter Hamlet.

Hamlet. Now might I do it pat, now 'a is a-praying;
    And now I'll do't—and so 'a goes to heaven,
    And so am I reveng'd. That would be scann'd:[176]   75
    A villain kills my father; and for that,
    I, his sole son, do this same villain send
    To heaven.
    Why, this is hire and salary, not revenge.
    'A took my father grossly, full of bread,[177]   80
    With all his crimes broad blown,[178] as flush[179] as May;
    And how his audit[180] stands who knows save heaven?
    But in our circumstance and course of thought
    'Tis heavy with him; and am I then reveng'd
    To take him in the purging[181] of his soul,   85
    When he is fit and season'd for his passage?
    No.
    Up, sword, and know thou a more horrid hent.[182]
    When he is drunk asleep, or in his rage;
    Or in th' incestuous pleasure of his bed;   90
    At game, a-swearing, or about some act
    That has no relish of salvation in't—
    Then trip him, that his heels may kick at heaven,
    And that his soul may be as damn'd and black

---

[175] *assay*: attempt.
[176] *scann'd*: looked into.
[177] *bread*: i.e., worldly gratification.
[178] *broad blown*: in full bloom.
[179] *flush*: vigorous.
[180] *audit*: account.
[181] *purging*: confession and cleansing.
[182] *hent*: grasp (here, occasion for seizing).

As hell, whereto it goes. My mother stays.   95
This physic[183] but prolongs thy sickly days.

                                        [*Exit.*]

King. [*Rising*] My words fly up, my thoughts remain
    below.
Words without thoughts never to heaven go.

                                        [*Exit.*]

                Scene 4. *The Queen's closet.*

                Enter Queen and Polonius.

Polonius. 'A will come straight. Look you lay home[184]
    to him;
    Tell him his pranks have been too broad[185] to bear
        with,
    And that your Grace hath screened and stood between
    Much heat and him. I'll silence me even here.
    Pray you be round with him.

Hamlet. [*Within*] Mother, mother, mother!

Queen. I'll warrant you. Fear me not.

    Withdraw, I hear him coming.

                    [*Polonius goes behind the arras.*[186]]

Enter Hamlet.

Hamlet. Now, mother, what's the matter?

Queen. Hamlet, thou hast thy father much offended.

___

[183] *physic*: i.e., Claudius' purgation by prayer.
[184] *lay home*: rebuke him sharply; also, descriptive of a sword thrust.
[185] *broad*: unrestrained.
[186] *arras*: tapestry wall hanging.

Hamlet. Mother, you have my father much offended. 10

Queen. Come, come, you answer with an idle[187] tongue.

Hamlet. Go, go, you question with a wicked tongue.

Queen. Why, how now, Hamlet!

Hamlet. What's the matter now?

Queen. Have you forgot me?

Hamlet. No, by the rood,[188] not so:
You are the Queen, your husband's brother's wife; 15
And—would it were not so!—you are my mother.

Queen. Nay then, I'll set those to you that can speak.

Hamlet. Come, come, and sit you down; you shall not
budge.
You go not till I set you up a glass[189]
Where you may see the inmost part of you. 20

Queen. What wilt thou do? Thou wilt not murder me?
Help, help, ho!

Polonius. [*Behind*] What, ho! help, help, help!

Hamlet. [*Draws.*] How now! a rat?
Dead, for a ducat,[190] dead! [*Kills Polonius with a
pass through the arras.*]

Polonius. [*Behind*] O, I am slain!

Queen. O me, what hast thou done?

Hamlet. Nay, I know not: 25
Is it the King?

---

187 *idle*: foolish.
188 *by the rood*: by the Cross of Christ, a colloquial expression.
189 *glass*: mirror.
190 *ducat*: gold coin.

Queen. O, what a rash and bloody deed is this!

Hamlet. A bloody deed!—almost as bad, good mother,
  As kill a king and marry with his brother.

Queen. As kill a king!

Hamlet.   Ay, lady, it was my word.   30

                       [*Parting the arras.*]

  Thou wretched, rash, intruding fool, farewell!
  I took thee for thy better. Take thy fortune;
  Thou find'st to be too busy is some danger.
  Leave wringing of your hands. Peace; sit you down,
  And let me wring your heart; for so I shall,   35
  If it be made of penetrable stuff;
  If damned custom have not braz'd[191] it so
  That it be proof[192] and bulwark[193] against sense.

Queen. What have I done that thou dar'st wag thy tongue
  In noise so rude against me?   40

Hamlet.   Such an act
  That blurs the grace and blush of modesty;
  Calls virtue hypocrite; takes off the rose
  From the fair forehead of an innocent love,
  And sets a blister there; makes marriage-vows
  As false as dicers' oaths. O, such a deed   45
  As from the body of contraction[194] plucks
  The very soul, and sweet religion makes
  A rhapsody of words. Heaven's face does glow
  O'er this solidity and compound mass
  With heated visage, as against the doom[195]—   50
  Is thought-sick at the act.

---

[191] *braz'd*: hardened, like brass.
[192] *proof*: armor.
[193] *bulwark*: defensive wall.
[194] *contraction*: making contracts, as in a marriage contract.
[195] *doom*: Judgment Day.

Queen.   Ay me, what act,
   That roars so loud and thunders in the index?[196]

Hamlet. Look here upon this picture and on this,
   The counterfeit presentment[197] of two brothers.
   See what a grace was seated on this brow;   55
   Hyperion's[198] curls; the front of Jove[199] himself;
   An eye like Mars,[200] to threaten and command;
   A station[201] like the herald Mercury[202]
   New lighted on a heaven-kissing hill—
   A combination and a form indeed   60
   Where every god did seem to set his seal,
   To give the world assurance of a man.
   This was your husband. Look you now what follows:
   Here is your husband, like a mildew'd ear
   Blasting his wholesome brother. Have you eyes?   65
   Could you on this fair mountain leave to feed,
   And batten[203] on this moor? Ha! have you eyes?
   You cannot call it love; for at your age
   The heyday[204] in the blood is tame, it's humble,
   And waits upon the judgment; and what judgment   70
   Would step from this to this? Sense, sure, you have,
   Else could you not have motion; but sure that sense
   Is apoplex'd;[205] for madness would not err,
   Nor sense to ecstasy[206] was ne'er so thrall'd
   But it reserv'd some quantity of choice   75
   To serve in such a difference. What devil was't

---

[196] *index*: prologue.
[197] *presentment*: represented image.
[198] *Hyperion's*: In classical mythology, Hyperion was a Titan, the god of the sun.
[199] *Jove*: in classical mythology, the king of the gods.
[200] *Mars*: in classical mythology, the god of war.
[201] *station*: bearing.
[202] *Mercury*: in classical mythology, the messenger god.
[203] *batten*: feed to excess.
[204] *heyday*: excitement.
[205] *apoplex'd*: paralyzed.
[206] *ecstasy*: madness.

That thus hath cozen'd[207] you at hoodman-blind?[208]
Eyes without feeling, feeling without sight,
Ears without hands or eyes, smelling sans[209] all,
Or but a sickly part of one true sense   80
Could not so mope. O shame! where is thy blush?
Rebellious hell,
If thou canst mutine in a matron's bones,
To flaming youth let virtue be as wax
And melt in her own fire; proclaim no shame   85
When the compulsive ardour[210] gives the charge,
Since frost itself as actively doth burn,
And reason panders will.[211]

Queen.   O Hamlet, speak no more!
Thou turn'st my eyes into my very soul;
And there I see such black and grained[212] spots   90
As will not leave their tinct.[213]

Hamlet.   Nay, but to live
In the rank sweat of an enseamed[214] bed,
Stew'd in corruption, honeying and making love
Over the nasty sty!

Queen.   O, speak to me no more!
These words like daggers enter in my ears;   95
No more, sweet Hamlet.

Hamlet.   A murderer and a villain!
A slave that is not twentieth part the tithe[215]

---

[207] *cozen'd*: cheated.
[208] *hoodman-blind*: blindman's bluff.
[209] *sans*: without (French).
[210] *compulsive ardour*: compelling passion.
[211] *reason panders will*: reason acts as a procurer for desire.
[212] *grained*: fast dyed.
[213] *tinct*: color.
[214] *enseamed*: greasy, much wrinkled.
[215] *tithe*: a tenth part.

Of your precedent lord;[216] a vice[217] of kings;
A cutpurse of the empire and the rule,
That from a shelf the precious diadem stole   *100*
And put it in his pocket!

Queen. No more!

Enter Ghost.

Hamlet. A king of shreds and patches—
Save me, and hover o'er me with your wings,
You heavenly guards! What would your gracious
    figure?

Queen. Alas, he's mad!   *105*

Hamlet. Do you not come your tardy son to chide,
That, laps'd in time and passion, lets go by
Th' important acting of your dread command?
O, say!

Ghost. Do not forget; this visitation   *110*
Is but to whet[218] thy almost blunted purpose.
But look, amazement on thy mother sits.
O, step between her and her fighting soul!
Conceit[219] in weakest bodies strongest works.
Speak to her, Hamlet.   *115*

Hamlet. How is it with you, lady?

Queen.   Alas, how is't with you,
That you do bend your eye on vacancy,
And with th' incorporal[220] air do hold discourse?
Forth at your eyes your spirits wildly peep;
And, as the sleeping soldiers in th' alarm,

---

[216] *precedent lord*: i.e., the dead king, her former husband.
[217] *vice*: Vice, a fool and mischief maker in the old morality plays.
[218] *whet*: sharpen.
[219] *Conceit*: imagination.
[220] *incorporal*: bodiless.

Your bedded hairs[221] like life in excrements[222]
Start up and stand an[223] end. O gentle son,
Upon the heat and flame of thy distemper
Sprinkle cool patience! Whereon do you look?

Hamlet. On him, on him! Look you how pale he glares.   *125*
His form and cause conjoin'd, preaching to stones,
Would make them capable.[224]—Do not look upon me,
Lest with this piteous action you convert
My stern effects;[225] then what I have to do
Will want true colour—tears perchance for blood.   *130*

Queen. To whom do you speak this?

Hamlet. Do you see nothing there?

Queen. Nothing at all; yet all that is I see.

Hamlet. Nor did you nothing hear?

Queen. No, nothing but ourselves.

Hamlet. Why, look you there. Look how it steals away.
My father, in his habit[226] as he liv'd!   *135*
Look where he goes even now out at the portal.

                         [*Exit Ghost.*]

Queen. This is the very coinage of your brain.
This bodiless creation ecstasy
Is very cunning in.

Hamlet.   Ecstasy!
My pulse as yours doth temperately keep time,   *140*
And makes as healthful music. It is not madness

---

[221] *bedded hairs*: flattened hairs.
[222] *excrements*: outgrowths (here, the hair).
[223] *an*: on.
[224] *capable*: receptive, sensible.
[225] *effects*: deeds.
[226] *habit*: clothes (called a "nightgown", a dressing gown, in some sources).

That I have utt'red. Bring me to the test,
And I the matter will re-word which madness
Would gambol[227] from. Mother, for love of grace,
Lay not that flattering unction[228] to your soul,   145
That not your trespass but my madness speaks:
It will but skin and film the ulcerous place,
Whiles rank corruption, mining[229] all within,
Infects unseen. Confess yourself to heaven;
Repent what's past; avoid what is to come;   150
And do not spread the compost[230] on the weeds,
To make them ranker. Forgive me this my virtue;
For in the fatness of these pursy[231] times
Virtue itself of vice must pardon beg,
Yea, curb and woo for leave to do him good.   155

Queen. O Hamlet, thou hast cleft my heart in twain.

Hamlet. O, throw away the worser part of it,
And live the purer with the other half.
Good night—but go not to my uncle's bed;
Assume a virtue, if you have it not.   160
That monster custom, who all sense doth eat,
Of habits devil, is angel yet in this,
That to the use[232] of actions fair and good
He likewise gives a frock or livery
That aptly is put on. Refrain to-night;   165
And that shall lend a kind of easiness
To the next abstinence; the next more easy;
For use almost can change the stamp of nature,
And either curb[233] the devil, or throw him out,
With wondrous potency. Once more, good night;   170

---

[227] *gambol*: frolic or leap forth.
[228] *unction*: ointment.
[229] *mining*: undermining.
[230] *compost*: fertilizing substance.
[231] *pursy*: bloated.
[232] *use*: practice.
[233] *curb*: bow low.

And when you are desirous to be blest,
I'll blessing beg of you. For this same lord
I do repent; but Heaven hath pleas'd it so,
To punish me with this, and this with me,
That I must be their[234] scourge and minister.   *175*
I will bestow[235] him, and will answer well
The death I gave him. So, again, good night.
I must be cruel only to be kind;
Thus bad begins and worse remains behind.
One word more, good lady.

Queen.   What shall I do?   *180*

Hamlet. Not this, by no means, that I bid you do:
Let the bloat King tempt you again to bed;
Pinch wanton on your cheek; call you his mouse;
And let him, for a pair of reechy[236] kisses,
Or paddling in your neck with his damn'd fingers,   *185*
Make you to ravel[237] all this matter out,
That I essentially am not in madness,
But mad in craft. 'Twere good you let him know;
For who that's but a queen, fair, sober, wise,
Would from a paddock,[238] from a bat, a gib,[239]   *190*
Such dear concernings hide? Who would do so?
No, in despite of sense and secrecy,
Unpeg the basket on the house's top,
Let the birds fly, and, like the famous ape,
To try conclusions, in the basket creep   *195*
And break your own neck down.

Queen. Be thou assur'd, if words be made of breath
And breath of life, I have no life to breathe
What thou hast said to me.

---

[234] *their*: i.e., the heavens'.
[235] *bestow*: stow.
[236] *reechy*: foul.
[237] *ravel*: unravel, reveal.
[238] *paddock*: toad.
[239] *gib*: tomcat.

Hamlet. I must to England; you know that?

Queen.   Alack,   *200*
   I had forgot. 'Tis so concluded on.

Hamlet. There's letters seal'd; and my two school-fellows,
   Whom I will trust as I will adders fang'd—
   They bear the mandate; they must sweep my way
   And marshal me to knavery. Let it work;   *205*
   For 'tis the sport to have the engineer
   Hoist with his own petar;[240] and't shall go hard
   But I will delve one yard below their mines
   And blow them at the moon. O, 'tis most sweet
   When in one line two crafts[241] directly meet.   *210*
   This man shall set me packing.
   I'll lug the guts into the neighbour room.
   Mother, good night. Indeed, this counsellor
   Is now most still, most secret, and most grave,
   Who was in life a foolish prating knave.   *215*
   Come, sir, to draw toward an end with you.
   Good night, mother.

              [*Exeunt severally; Hamlet tugging in Polonius.*]

---

[240] *petar:* grenadelike bomb.
[241] *crafts:* ships or crafty schemes.

ACT 4

Scene 1. *Elsinore.*[1] *The Castle.*

Enter King, Queen, Rosencrantz, and Guildenstern.

King. There's matter in these sighs, these profound
    heaves,
  You must translate; 'tis fit we understand them.
  Where is your son?

Queen. Bestow this place on us[2] a little while.

                [*Exeunt Rosencrantz and Guildenstern.*]

  Ah, mine own lord, what have I seen to-night!   5

King. What, Gertrude? How does Hamlet?

Queen. Mad as the sea and wind, when both contend
  Which is the mightier. In his lawless fit,
  Behind the arras hearing something stir,
  Whips out his rapier, cries "A rat, a rat!"   10
  And in this brainish[3] apprehension kills
  The unseen good old man.

King.   O heavy deed!
  It had been so with us had we been there.
  His liberty is full of threats to all—
  To you yourself, to us, to every one.   15
  Alas, how shall this bloody deed be answer'd?
  It will be laid to us, whose providence[4]
  Should have kept short, restrain'd, and out of haunt,[5]
  This mad young man. But so much was our love,

---

[1] *Elsinore:* In some early versions, the act break does not occur here; Gertrude remains onstage.

[2] *Bestow this place on us:* Grant us privacy.

[3] *brainish:* deluded, mad.

[4] *providence:* foresight.

[5] *short . . . out of haunt:* restrained, away from association with others.

119

We would not understand what was most fit; 20
But, like the owner of a foul disease,
To keep it from divulging,[6] let it feed
Even on the pith[7] of life. Where is he gone?

Queen. To draw apart the body he hath kill'd;
O'er whom his very madness, like some ore[8] 25
Among a mineral of metals base,
Shows itself pure: 'a weeps for what is done.

King. O Gertrude, come away!
The sun no sooner shall the mountains touch
But we will ship him hence; and this vile deed 30
We must with all our majesty and skill
Both countenance and excuse. Ho, Guildenstern!

Re-enter Rosencrantz and Guildenstern.

Friends, both go join you with some further aid:
Hamlet in madness hath Polonius slain,
And from his mother's closet hath he dragg'd him; 35
Go seek him out; speak fair, and bring the body
Into the chapel. I pray you haste in this.

[*Exeunt Rosencrantz and Guildenstern.*]

Come, Gertrude, we'll call up our wisest friends
And let them know both what we mean to do
And what's untimely done; so haply slander[9]— 40
Whose whisper o'er the world's diameter,
As level as the cannon to his blank,[10]
Transports his pois'ned shot—may miss our name,

---

[6] *divulging*: being made known.

[7] *pith*: true nature or essence.

[8] *ore*: vein of gold.

[9] *so haply slander*: This phrase does not appear in the text of the First Folio, etc., but it is suggested as the missing piece (to finish out the required number of accents in the line) by the Shakespearean critic Edward Capell (1713–1781) and is usually printed; another suggestion is "so envious slander".

[10] *blank*: white central point of a target.

And hit the woundless[11] air. O, come away!
My soul is full of discord and dismay.   [*Exeunt.*]   45

Scene 2. *Elsinore. The Castle.*

Enter Hamlet.

Hamlet. Safely stow'd.

Gentlemen. [*Within*] Hamlet! Lord Hamlet!

Hamlet. But soft! What noise? Who calls on Hamlet?
    O, here they come!

Enter Rosencrantz and Guildenstern.

Rosencrantz. What have you done, my lord, with the
    dead body?   5

Hamlet. Compounded it with dust, whereto 'tis kin.[12]

Rosencrantz. Tell us where 'tis, that we may take it
    thence
And bear it to the chapel.

Hamlet. Do not believe it.

Rosencrantz. Believe what?   10

Hamlet. That I can keep your counsel, and not mine
    own. Besides, to be demanded of[13] a
    sponge—what replication[14] should be made by
    the son of a king?   13

Rosencrantz. Take you me for a sponge, my lord?

---

[11] *woundless:* invulnerable.
[12] *dust . . . kin:* cf. Genesis 3:19: "[T]ill you return to the ground, for out of it
you were taken; you are dust, and to dust you shall return."
[13] *demanded of:* interrogated by.
[14] *replication:* reply.

Hamlet. Ay, sir; that soaks up the King's
countenance,[15] his rewards, his authorities. But
such officers do the King best service in the end:
he keeps them, like an ape an apple in the corner
of his jaw; first mouth'd, to be last swallowed;
when he needs what you have glean'd, it is but
squeezing you and, sponge, you shall be dry again.   20

Rosencrantz. I understand you not, my lord.

Hamlet. I am glad of it; a knavish speech sleeps[16] in a
foolish ear.

Rosencrantz. My lord, you must tell us where the body
is, and go with us to the King.   25

Hamlet. The body is with the King, but the King is not
with the body. The King is a thing—

Guildenstern.   A thing, my lord!

Hamlet. Of nothing.[17] Bring me to him.
Hide fox, and all after.[18]   [*Exeunt.*]   30

Scene 3. *Elsinore. The Castle.*

Enter King, attended.

King. I have sent to seek him, and to find the body.
How dangerous is it that this man goes loose!
Yet must not we put the strong law on him:
He's lov'd of the distracted[19] multitude,
Who like not in their judgment but their eyes;   5

---

[15] *countenance:* favor.

[16] *sleeps:* means nothing.

[17] *Of nothing:* cf. Psalm 144:4: "Man is like a breath [a thing of naught], his
days are like a passing shadow" (read in the Anglican Book of Common Prayer).

[18] *Hide fox, and all after:* a cry in a game such as hide-and-seek.

[19] *distracted:* deluded, confused.

And where 'tis so, th' offender's scourge[20] is weigh'd,
But never the offence. To bear all smooth and even,
This sudden sending him away must seem
Deliberate pause.[21] Diseases desperate grown
By desperate appliance[22] are reliev'd,   10
Or not at all.

Enter Rosencrantz.

           How now! what hath befall'n?

Rosencrantz. Where the dead body is bestow'd, my lord,
We cannot get from him.

King.   But where is he?

Rosencrantz. Without, my lord; guarded, to know your
pleasure.

King. Bring him before us.   15

Rosencrantz. Ho, Guildenstern! bring in the lord.

Enter Hamlet and Guildenstern.

King. Now, Hamlet, where's Polonius?

Hamlet. At supper.

King. At supper! Where?   19

Hamlet. Not where he eats, but where 'a is eaten; a
certain convocation of politic[23] worms are e'en at
him. Your worm is your only emperor for diet:[24]
we fat[25] all creatures else to fat us, and we fat

---

[20] *scourge*: punishment.
[21] *pause*: planning, decision.
[22] *appliance*: treatment.
[23] *politic*: shrewd, or statesmanlike.
[24] *diet*: perhaps an indirect reference to Charles V's Diet (council) of Worms (1521), before which Martin Luther appeared.
[25] *fat*: fatten.

ourselves for maggots; your fat king and your lean
beggar is but variable service²⁶—two dishes, but
to one table. That's the end.   *25*

King. Alas, alas!

Hamlet. A man may fish with the worm that hath eat
of a king, and eat of the fish that hath fed of that
worm.

King. What dost thou mean by this?

Hamlet. Nothing but to show you how a king may go a
progress²⁷ through the guts of a beggar.   *31*

King. Where is Polonius?

Hamlet. In heaven; send thither to see; if your
messenger find him not there, seek him i' th'
other place yourself. But if, indeed, you find him
not within this month, you shall nose him as you
go up the stairs into the lobby.   *37*

King. [*To Attendants*] Go seek him there.

Hamlet. 'A will stay till you come.

                              [*Exeunt Attendants.*]

King. Hamlet, this deed, for thine especial safety—   *40*
    Which we do tender,²⁸ as we dearly grieve
    For that which thou hast done—must send thee
        hence
    With fiery quickness. Therefore prepare thyself;
    The bark²⁹ is ready, and the wind at help,

---

²⁶ *variable service*: different servings, courses.
²⁷ *progress*: state journey.
²⁸ *tender*: hold dear.
²⁹ *bark*: ship.

Th' associates tend,[30] and everything is bent   45
For England.

Hamlet.   For England!

King.   Ay, Hamlet.

Hamlet.   Good!

King. So is it, if thou knew'st our purposes.

Hamlet. I see a cherub[31] that sees them.
    But, come; for England! Farewell, dear mother,

King. Thy loving father, Hamlet.   50

Hamlet. My mother: father and mother is man and
    wife; man and wife is one flesh; and so, my
    mother. Come, for England.   [Exit.]

King.   Follow him at foot;[32] tempt him with speed
    aboard;
    Delay it not; I'll have him hence to-night.   55
    Away! for everything is seal'd and done
    That else leans on[33] th' affair. Pray you make haste.

[Exeunt all but the King.]

And, England,[34] if my love thou hold'st at aught[35]—
As my great power thereof may give thee sense,
Since yet thy cicatrice[36] looks raw and red   60
After the Danish sword, and thy free awe[37]

[30] tend: await you.
[31] cherub: one of the second-highest order of angels (cherubim), associated with knowledge.
[32] at foot: closely.
[33] leans on: is connected with.
[34] England: i.e., the king of England.
[35] at aught: as having any value.
[36] cicatrice: scar.
[37] free awe: voluntary respect.

Pays homage to us—thou mayst not coldly set[38]
Our sovereign process;[39] which imports at full,
By letters congruing[40] to that effect,
The present[41] death of Hamlet. Do it, England: 65
For like the hectic[42] in my blood he rages,
And thou must cure me. Till I know 'tis done,
Howe'er my haps,[43] my joys were ne'er begun.

                                                        [*Exit.*]

Scene 4. *A plain in Denmark.*

Enter Fortinbras with his Army over the stage.

Fortinbras. Go, Captain, from me greet the Danish
    king.
Tell him that by his licence Fortinbras
Craves the conveyance[44] of a promis'd[45] march
Over his kingdom. You know the rendezvous.
If that his Majesty would aught with us,   5
We shall express our duty in his eye;[46]
And let him know so.

Captain.   I will do't, my lord.

Fortinbras. Go softly[47] on.

                            [*Exeunt all but the Captain.*]

[38] *set*: respect.
[39] *sovereign process*: royal command.
[40] *congruing*: agreeing.
[41] *present*: immediate.
[42] *hectic*: continuous fever.
[43] *haps*: fortunes.
[44] *conveyance*: escort.
[45] *promis'd*: negotiated by diplomats.
[46] *eye*: presence.
[47] *softly*: slowly.

Enter Hamlet, Rosencrantz, Guildenstern, and Others.

Hamlet. Good sir, whose powers[48] are these?

Captain. They are of Norway, sir.   10

Hamlet. How purpos'd, sir, I pray you?

Captain. Against some part of Poland.

Hamlet. Who commands them, sir?

Captain. The nephew to old Norway, Fortinbras.

Hamlet. Goes it against the main[49] of Poland, sir,   15
Or for some frontier?

Captain. Truly to speak, and with no addition,[50]
We go to gain a little patch of ground
That hath in it no profit but the name.
To pay[51] five ducats, five, I would not farm it;   20
Nor will it yield to Norway or the Pole
A ranker[52] rate should it be sold in fee.[53]

Hamlet. Why, then the Polack never will defend it.

Captain. Yes, it is already garrison'd.[54]

Hamlet. Two thousand souls and twenty thousand ducats   25
Will not debate[55] the question of this straw.
This is th' imposthume[56] of much wealth and peace,
That inward breaks, and shows no cause without
Why the man dies. I humbly thank you, sir.   28

---

[48] *powers:* forces.
[49] *main:* main body, region.
[50] *addition:* exaggeration.
[51] *pay:* i.e., as rent.
[52] *ranker:* higher.
[53] *in fee:* outright.
[54] *garrison'd:* defended by soldiers.
[55] *debate:* settle.
[56] *imposthume:* abscess.

Captain. God buy you, sir.   [*Exit.*]

Rosencrantz.   Will't please you go, my lord?   30

Hamlet. I'll be with you straight. Go a little before.

[*Exeunt all but Hamlet.*]

How all occasions do inform against me,
And spur my dull revenge! What is a man,
If his chief good and market[57] of his time
Be but to sleep and feed? A beast, no more!   35
Sure he that made us with such large discourse,[58]
Looking before and after, gave us not
That capability and godlike reason
To fust[59] in us unus'd. Now, whether it be
Bestial oblivion,[60] or some craven scruple   40
Of thinking too precisely on th' event[61]—
A thought which, quarter'd, hath but one part wisdom
And ever three parts coward—I do not know
Why yet I live to say "This thing's to do",
Sith[62] I have cause, and will, and strength, and means,   45
To do't. Examples gross[63] as earth exhort me:
Witness this army, of such mass and charge,[64]
Led by a delicate and tender prince,
Whose spirit, with divine ambition puff'd,
Makes mouths[65] at the invisible event,   50
Exposing what is mortal and unsure
To all that fortune, death, and danger, dare,
Even for an egg-shell. Rightly to be great
Is not to stir without great argument,

[57] *market*: profit, compensation.
[58] *discourse*: powers of understanding.
[59] *fust*: mold.
[60] *oblivion*: forgetfulness.
[61] *event*: outcome.
[62] *Sith*: since.
[63] *gross*: large, evident.
[64] *charge*: expense.
[65] *Makes mouths*: makes scornful faces (is contemptuous of).

But greatly to find quarrel in a straw,[66]   55
When honour's at the stake. How stand I, then,
That have a father kill'd, a mother stain'd,
Excitements of my reason and my blood,
And let all sleep, while to my shame I see
The imminent death of twenty thousand men   60
That, for a fantasy and trick of fame,[67]
Go to their graves like beds, fight for a plot
Whereon the numbers cannot try the cause,
Which is not tomb enough and continent
To hide the slain? O, from this time forth,
My thoughts be bloody, or be nothing worth!

                               [*Exit.*]

Scene 5. *Elsinore. The Castle.*

Enter Queen, Horatio, and a Gentleman.

Queen. I will not speak with her.

Gentleman. She is importunate, indeed distract.
   Her mood will needs be pitied.

Queen.   What would she have?

Gentleman. She speaks much of her father; says she hears
   There's tricks i' th' world, and hems, and beats her
      heart;   5
   Spurns enviously at straws;[68] speaks things in doubt,
   That carry but half sense. Her speech is nothing,
   Yet the unshaped use of it doth move
   The hearers to collection;[69] they yawn[70] at it,

---

[66] *greatly . . . in a straw*: to see the greater argument in even the slightest matters.
[67] *fantasy and trick of fame*: fanciful illusion and negligible detail of reputation.
[68] *Spurns . . . at straws*: takes offense at trifles.
[69] *collection*: an attempt to make sense of her incoherent speech.
[70] *yawn*: also given in some versions as "aim".

And botch[71] the words up fit to their own thoughts;   10
Which, as her winks and nods and gestures yield them,
Indeed would make one think there might be thought,
Though nothing sure, yet much unhappily.

Horatio. 'Twere good she were spoken with; for she may
      strew
Dangerous conjectures in ill-breeding minds.   15

Queen. Let her come in.   [*Exit Gentleman.*]

[*Aside*] To my sick soul, as sin's true nature is,
      Each toy[72] seems prologue to some great amiss.[73]
So full of artless jealousy[74] is guilt,
      It spills[75] itself in fearing to be spilt.   20

Enter Ophelia distracted.

Ophelia. Where is the beautous Majesty of Denmark?

Queen. How now, Ophelia!

Ophelia. [*Sings.*] How should I your true love know
                        From another one?
                  By his cockle hat[76] and staff,   25
                        And his sandal shoon.[77]

Queen. Alas, sweet lady, what imports this song?

Ophelia. Say you? Nay, pray you mark.

---

[71] *botch*: patch.
[72] *toy*: trifle.
[73] *amiss*: misfortune or misdeed.
[74] *artless jealousy*: ill-managed suspicion.
[75] *spills*: destroys.
[76] *cockle hat*: hat with a cockleshell in it, the sign of a pilgrim who had jour-
neyed to overseas shrines (here drawing on an old association of lovers and
pilgrims).
[77] *shoon*: shoes.

[*Sings.*] He is dead and gone, lady,
   He is dead and gone;   30
  At his head a grass-green turf,
   At his heels a stone.

O, ho!

Queen. Nay, but, Ophelia—

Ophelia.   Pray you mark.

[*Sings.*] White his shroud as the mountain snow—

Enter King.

Queen. Alas, look here, my lord.   35

Ophelia. Larded[78] with sweet flowers;
 Which bewept to the grave did not go
 With true-love showers.

King. How do you, pretty lady?   39

Ophelia. Well, God dild[79] you! They say the owl was a
  baker's daughter.[80] Lord, we know what we are, but
  know not what we may be. God be at your table!

King. Conceit[81] upon her father.

Ophelia. Pray let's have no words of this; but when they
  ask you what it means, say you this: 45

[*Sings.*] To-morrow is Saint Valentine's day,[82]
   All in the morning betime,
  And I a maid at your window,
   To be your Valentine.

---

[78] *Larded*: adorned.

[79] *God dild*: a colloquial form of "God yield", signifying a repayment or reward.

[80] *owl . . . baker's daughter*: According to a folktale, a baker's daughter was transformed into an owl because she begrudged bread to Christ.

[81] *Conceit*: brooding fantasies.

[82] *Saint Valentine's day*: February 14, the day on which a bachelor would be the true love of the first girl he saw.

Then up he rose, and donn'd his clothes,   50
And dupp'd[83] the chamber-door;
Let in the maid, that out a maid
Never departed more.

King. Pretty Ophelia!

Ophelia. Indeed, la, without an oath, I'll make an end
    on't.   55

[*Sings.*] By Gis[84] and by Saint Charity,
      Alack, and fie for shame!
    Young men will do't, if they come to't;
      By Cock,[85] they are to blame.
    Quoth she "Before you tumbled me,   60
      You promis'd me to wed".

He answers:

"So would I 'a done, by yonder sun,
An thou hadst not come to my bed".

King. How long hath she been thus?   65

Ophelia. I hope all will be well. We must be patient;
    but I cannot choose but weep to think they would
    lay him i' th' cold ground. My brother shall know
    of it; and so I thank you for your good counsel.
    Come, my coach! Good night, ladies; good night,
    sweet ladies, good night, good night.   [*Exit.*]

King. Follow her close; give her good watch, I pray you.

            [*Exeunt Horatio and Gentleman.*]

O, this is the poison of deep grief; it springs
All from her father's death. And now behold—
O Gertrude, Gertrude!

---

[83] *dupp'd*: opened.
[84] *Gis*: Jesus (a contraction).
[85] *Cock*: colloquial corruption of "God", perhaps also a vulgar reference.

When sorrows come, they come not single spies,[86]   75
But in battalions! First, her father slain;
Next, your son gone, and he most violent author
Of his own just remove;[87] the people muddied,[88]
Thick and unwholesome in their thoughts and
     whispers
For good Polonius' death; and we have done but
     greenly[89]   80
In hugger-mugger[90] to inter him; poor Ophelia
Divided from herself and her fair judgment,
Without the which we are pictures,[91] or mere beasts;
Last, and as much containing as all these,
Her brother is in secret come from France;   85
Feeds on his wonder, keeps himself in clouds,
And wants not buzzers[92] to infect his ear
With pestilent speeches of his father's death;
Wherein necessity, of matter beggar'd,[93]
Will nothing stick[94] our person to arraign[95]   90
In ear and ear. O my dear Gertrude, this,
Like to a murd'ring piece,[96] in many places
Gives me superfluous death.

                                  [A noise within.]

Queen. Alack, what noise is this?

King. Attend!

---

[86] *spies*: scouts.

[87] *most violent . . . remove*: Because of his violence, he is the cause of his own removal.

[88] *muddied*: muddled, confused.

[89] *greenly*: foolishly.

[90] *In hugger-mugger*: disorderedly, secretly.

[91] *pictures*: soulless matter or forms.

[92] *buzzers*: gossips, rumor bearers.

[93] *beggar'd*: uninformed, not provided with facts.

[94] *Will nothing stick*: will not hesitate.

[95] *arraign*: accuse, charge with the crime (that of Polonius' death).

[96] *murd'ring piece*: cannon that fired a scattered shot, like shrapnel.

Enter a Gentleman.

Where are my Switzers?[97] Let them guard the door.
What is the matter?

Gentleman.   Save yourself, my lord: 95
The ocean, overpeering[98] of his list,[99]
Eats not the flats with more impitious[100] haste
Than young Laertes, in a riotous head,[101]
O'erbears your officers. The rabble call him lord;
And, as the world were now but to begin,   100
Antiquity forgot, custom not known,
The ratifiers and props of every word,
They cry "Choose we; Laertes shall be king".
Caps, hands, and tongues, applaud it to the clouds,
"Laertes shall be king, Laertes king".   105

Queen. How cheerfully on the false trail they cry!

[*Noise within.*]

O, this is counter,[102] you false Danish dogs!

King. The doors are broke.

Enter Laertes, with Others, in arms.

Laertes. Where is this king?—Sirs, stand you all without.

All. No, let's come in.

Laertes.   I pray you give me leave.   110

All. We will, we will.   [*Exeunt.*]

[97] *Switzers*: Swiss guards, mercenaries.
[98] *overpeering*: flooding out.
[99] *list*: shore (boundaries).
[100] *impitious*: violent.
[101] *riotous head*: armed, rebellious force.
[102] *counter*: backward, as a hound runs counter when he follows the scent backward from the prey.

Laertes. I thank you. Keep the door.—O thou vile king,
　Give me my father!

Queen.　　　　　　Calmly, good Laertes.

Laertes. That drop of blood that's calm proclaims me
　　bastard;
　Cries cuckold[103] to my father; brands the harlot   *115*
　Even here, between the chaste unsmirched brow
　Of my true mother.

King.　　　　　What is the cause, Laertes,
　That thy rebellion looks so giant-like?[104]
　Let him go, Gertrude; do not fear[105] our person:
　There's such divinity doth hedge a king[106]   *120*
　That treason can but peep to[107] what it would,
　Acts little of his will. Tell me, Laertes,
　Why thou art thus incens'd. Let him go, Gertrude.
　Speak, man.

Laertes. Where is my father?

King.　　　　　　Dead.

Queen.　　　　　　But not by him.   *125*

King. Let him demand his fill.

Laertes. How came he dead? I'll not be juggled[108] with.
　To hell, allegiance! Vows, to the blackest devil!
　Conscience and grace, to the profoundest pit!
　I dare damnation. To this point I stand,   *130*

---

[103] *cuckold*: man dishonored by an unfaithful wife.

[104] *giant-like*: referring to the war the giants waged against Mount Olympus in classical mythology.

[105] *fear*: fear for.

[106] *divinity doth hedge a king*: referencing the theory of the divine right of kings, that the king's authority comes directly from God.

[107] *peep to*: look at, from a distance or through a barrier.

[108] *juggled*: toyed.

That both the worlds I give to negligence,[109]
Let come what comes; only I'll be reveng'd
Most throughly for my father.

King. Who shall stay you?

Laertes.   My will, not all the world's.
And for my means, I'll husband[110] them so well   135
They shall go far with little.

King.   Good Laertes,
   If you desire to know the certainty
   Of dear father, is't writ in your revenge
   That, swoopstake,[111] you will draw both friend and
      foe,
   Winner and loser?

Laertes.   None but his enemies.   140

King. Will you know them, then?

Laertes. To his good friends thus wide I'll ope my arms
   And, like the kind life-rend'ring pelican,[112]
   Repast them with my blood.

King.   Why, now you speak
   Like a good child and a true gentleman.   145
   That I am guiltless of your father's death,
   And am most sensibly[113] in grief for it,
   It shall as level to your judgment 'pear
   As day does to your eye.

               [*A noise within:* "Let her come in."]

---

[109] *That both . . . negligence:* disregarding what may happen in this world and the next.
[110] *husband:* use economically.
[111] *swoopstake:* indiscriminately, in a clean sweep.
[112] *pelican:* a bird that feeds her young with her own blood if nothing else can be found.
[113] *sensibly:* feelingly.

Laertes. How now! What noise is that!   150

Re-enter Ophelia.

> O, heat dry up my brains! tears seven times salt
> Burn out the sense and virtue[114] of mine eye!
> By heaven, thy madness shall be paid with weight
> Till our scale turn the beam.[115] O rose of May!
> Dear maid, kind sister, sweet Ophelia!   155
> O heavens! is't possible a young maid's wits
> Should be as mortal as an old man's life?
> Nature is fine in love; and where 'tis fine[116]
> It sends some precious instance of itself
> After the thing it loves.   160

Ophelia. [*Sings.*] They bore him barefac'd on the bier;
> Hey non nonny, nonny, hey nonny;
> And in his grave rain'd many a tear—

Fare you well, my dove!

Laertes. Hadst thou thy wits, and didst persuade revenge,   165
It could not move thus.

Ophelia. You must sing "A-down, a-down, an you call
   him a-down-a". O, how the wheel[117] becomes it!
   It is the false steward, that stole his master's
   daughter.   170

Laertes. This nothing's more than matter.[118]

Ophelia. There's rosemary, that's for remembrance; pray
   you, love, remember. And there is pansies, that's
   for thoughts.   174

---

[114] *virtue*: power.
[115] *beam*: bar of a balance.
[116] *fine*: refined, delicate.
[117] *wheel*: a turn in a dance or the refrain of the song; sometimes mistaken as a reference to the "wheel of Fortune".
[118] *This nothing's more than matter*: this nonsense is more meaningful than sane speech.

Laertes. A document in madness—thoughts and
    remembrance fitted.

Ophelia. There's fennel[119] for you, and columbines.
    There's rue for you; and here's some for me. We
    may call it herb of grace a Sundays. O, you must
    wear your rue with a difference. There's a daisy. I
    would give you some violets, but they wither'd all
    when my father died. They say 'a made a good end.   *182*

[*Sings.*] For bonny sweet Robin is all my joy.

Laertes. Thought and affliction, passion, hell itself,
    She turns to favour[120] and to prettiness.   *185*

Ophelia. [*Sings.*] And will 'a not come again?
                    And will 'a not come again?
                        No, no, he is dead,
                        Go to thy death-bed,
                    He never will come again.   *190*
                    His beard was as white as snow,
                    All flaxen was his poll;[121]
                        He is gone, he is gone,
                        And we cast away moan:
                    God-a-mercy on his soul!   *195*

And of all Christian souls, I pray God. God buy you.[122]
                                            [*Exit.*]

Laertes. Do you see this, O God?

King. Laertes, I must commune with your grief,
    Or you deny me right. Go but apart,

---

[119] *fennel* . . . : The symbolic meanings of the flowers that Ophelia mentions
are disputed. One possible set of meanings is as follows: fennel—flattery or deceit;
columbines—infidelity; rue—regret (sorrow for Ophelia and repentance for the
queen); daisy—dissembling; and violets—faithfulness.
[120] *favour:* charm.
[121] *poll:* hair.
[122] *God buy you:* a form of farewell ("Good-bye").

Make choice of whom your wisest friends you will,   *200*
And they shall hear and judge 'twixt you and me.
If by direct or by collateral[123] hand
They find us touch'd,[124] we will our kingdom give,
Our crown, our life, and all that we call ours,
To you in satisfaction; but if not,   *205*
Be you content to lend your patience to us,
And we shall jointly labour with your soul
To give it due content.

Laertes.   Let this be so.
His means of death, his obscure funeral—
No trophy,[125] sword, nor hatchment,[126] o'er his
    bones,   *210*
No noble rite nor formal ostentation[127]—
Cry to be heard, as 'twere from heaven to earth,
That I must call't in question.

King.   So you shall;
And where th' offence is, let the great axe fall.
I pray you go with me.   [*Exeunt.*] *215*

Scene 6. *Elsinore. The Castle.*

Enter Horatio with an Attendant.

Horatio. What are they that would speak with me?

Attendant.   Sea-faring men, sir; they say they have
    letters for you.

Horatio. Let them come in.   [*Exit Attendant.*]

---

[123] *collateral*: indirect.
[124] *touch'd*: concerned with or implicated in (the crime).
[125] *trophy*: memorial.
[126] *hatchment*: tablet bearing a coat of arms.
[127] *ostentation*: ceremony.

I do not know from what part of the world
I should be greeted, if not from Lord Hamlet.   5

Enter Sailors.

Sailor. God bless you, sir.

Horatio. Let Him bless thee too.

Sailor. 'A shall, sir, an't please Him. There's a letter for
   you, sir; it came from th' ambassador that was
   bound for England—if your name be Horatio, as I
   am let to know it is.   11

Horatio. [*Reads.*] "Horatio, when thou shalt have
   overlook'd[128] this, give these fellows some
   means[129] to the King: they have letters for him.
   Ere we were two days old at sea, a pirate of very
   warlike appointment[130] gave us chase. Finding
   ourselves too slow of sail, we put on a compelled
   valour; and in the grapple I boarded them. On the
   instant they got clear of our ship; so I alone
   became their prisoner. They have dealt with me
   like thieves of mercy;[131] but they knew what they
   did: I am to do a good turn for them. Let the
   King have the letters I have sent; and repair thou
   to me with as much speed as thou wouldest fly
   death. I have words to speak in thine ear will
   make thee dumb; yet are they much too light for
   the bore[132] of the matter. These good fellows will
   bring thee where I am. Rosencrantz and
   Guildenstern hold their course for England; of
   them I have much to tell thee. Farewell.   25
   He that thou knowest thine, Hamlet."

---

[128] *overlook'd*: read, surveyed.
[129] *means*: access.
[130] *appointment*: equipment.
[131] *thieves of mercy*: merciful thieves.
[132] *bore*: caliber (here, importance).

Come, I will give you way for these your letters,
And do't the speedier that you may direct me
To him from whom you brought them.   [*Exeunt.*]

Scene 7. *Elsinore. The Castle.*

Enter King and Laertes.

King. Now must your conscience my acquittance seal,
    And you must put me in your heart for friend,
    Sith[133] you have heard, and with a knowing ear,
    That he which hath your noble father slain
    Pursu'd my life.

Laertes. It well appears. But tell me   5
    Why you proceeded not against these feats,
    So crimeful and so capital[134] in nature,
    As by your safety, wisdom, all things else,
    You mainly[135] were stirr'd up.

King.   O, for two special reasons,
    Which may to you, perhaps, seem much unsinew'd,[136]   10
    But yet to me th'are strong. The Queen his mother
    Lives almost by his looks; and for myself,
    My virtue or my plague, be it either which—
    She is so conjunctive[137] to my life and soul
    That, as the star moves not but in his sphere,   15
    I could not but by her. The other motive,
    Why to a public count[138] I might not go,
    Is the great love the general gender[139] bear him;
    Who, dipping all his faults in their affection,

[133] *Sith*: since.
[134] *capital*: punishable by death.
[135] *mainly*: powerfully.
[136] *unsinew'd*: weak.
[137] *conjunctive*: closely united.
[138] *count*: trial, reckoning.
[139] *general gender*: common people.

Work like the spring that turneth wood to stone,[140]   20
Convert his gyves[141] to graces; so that my arrows,
Too slightly timber'd[142] for so loud a wind,
Would have reverted to my bow again,
But not where I have aim'd them.

Laertes. And so have I a noble father lost;   25
A sister driven into desp'rate terms,[143]
Whose worth, if praises may go back again,[144]
Stood challenger on mount of all the age
For her perfections. But my revenge will come.

King. Break not your sleeps for that. You must not think   30
That we are made of stuff so flat and dull
That we can let our beard be shook with danger,
And think it pastime. You shortly shall hear more.
I lov'd your father, and we love our self;
And that, I hope, will teach you to imagine—   35

Enter a Messenger with letters.

How now! What news?

Messenger. Letters, my lord, from Hamlet:
These to your Majesty; this to the Queen.

King. From Hamlet! Who brought them?

Messenger. Sailors, my lord, they say; I saw them not.
They were given me by Claudio; he receiv'd them   40
Of him that brought them.

King.   Laertes, you shall hear them.
Leave us.   [*Exit Messenger.*]

---

[140] *spring . . . stone:* There was a spring in Shakespeare's county so charged
with lime that it would petrify the wood placed in it.

[141] *gyves:* fetters, chains.

[142] *timber'd:* shafted.

[143] *terms:* circumstances.

[144] *go back again:* revert to her former (sane) self.

[*Reads.*] "High and Mighty. You shall know I am set
naked[145] on your kingdom. To-morrow shall I beg
leave to see your kingly eyes; when I shall, first
asking your pardon thereunto, recount the
occasion of my sudden and more strange return.
Hamlet."

What should this mean? Are all the rest come back?   48
Or is it some abuse,[146] and no such thing?

Laertes. Know you the hand?[147]   50

King. 'Tis Hamlet's character.[148] "Naked"!
And in a postscript here, he says "alone".
Can you devise[149] me?

Laertes. I am lost in it, my lord. But let him come;
It warms the very sickness in my heart   55
That I shall live and tell him to his teeth
"Thus didest thou".

King.   If it be so, Laertes—
As how should it be so, how otherwise?—
Will you be rul'd by me?

Laertes.   Ay, my lord;
So you will not o'errule me to a peace.   60

King. To thine own peace. If he be now return'd,
As checking at[150] his voyage, and that he means
No more to undertake it, I will work him
To an exploit now ripe in my device,
Under the which he shall not choose but fall;   65

---

[145] *naked*: destitute.
[146] *abuse*: deception.
[147] *hand*: handwriting.
[148] *character*: handwriting.
[149] *devise*: explain to, advise.
[150] *checking at*: shying, turning away from (falconry term).

And for his death, no wind of blame shall breathe;
But even his mother shall uncharge the practice[151]
And call it accident.

Laertes.   My lord, I will be rul'd
The rather, if you could devise it so
That I might be the organ.[152]

King.   It falls right.   70
You have been talk'd of since your travel much,
And that in Hamlet's hearing, for a quality
Wherein they say you shine. Your sum of parts
Did not together pluck such envy from him
As did that one; and that, in my regard,   75
Of the unworthiest siege.[153]

Laertes.   What part is that, my lord?

King. A very riband[154] in the cap of youth,
Yet needful too; for youth no less becomes
The light and careless livery[155] that it wears
Than settled age his sables and his weeds,[156]   80
Importing health and graveness. Two months since
Here was a gentleman of Normandy—
I have seen myself, and serv'd against, the French,
And they can well[157] on horseback; but this gallant
Had witchcraft in't; he grew unto his seat,   85
And to such wondrous doing brought his horse,
As had he been incorps'd[158] and demi-natur'd[159]
With the brave beast. So far he topp'd[160] my thought,

---

[151] *uncharge the practice*: acquit the device of treachery.
[152] *organ*: instrument.
[153] *siege*: rank, status.
[154] *riband*: ribbon, decoration.
[155] *livery*: distinctive clothes.
[156] *sables and his weeds*: sober clothing (furs and garments).
[157] *well*: perform well.
[158] *incorps'd*: made one body.
[159] *demi-natur'd*: made sharer in two natures (half and half).
[160] *topp'd*: exceeded.

That I, in forgery[161] of shapes and tricks,
Come short of what he did.

Laertes.   A Norman was't?   90

King. A Norman.

Laertes. Upon my life, Lamord.[162]

King.   The very same.

Laertes. I know him well. He is the brooch[163] indeed
And gem of all the nation.

King. He made confession[164] of you;   95
And gave you such a masterly report
For art and exercise in your defence,
And for your rapier most especial,
That he cried out 'twould be a sight indeed
If one could match you. The scrimers[165] of their
    nation   100
He swore had neither motion, guard, nor eye,
If you oppos'd them. Sir, this report of his
Did Hamlet so envenom with his envy
That he could nothing do but wish and beg
Your sudden coming o'er, to play with you.   105
Now, out of this—

Laertes.   What out of this, my lord?

King. Laertes, was your father dear to you?
Or are you like the painting of a sorrow,
A face without a heart?

Laertes.   Why ask you this?

---

[161] *forgery*: invention.
[162] *Lamord*: taken from the French (*la mort*), meaning "the death".
[163] *brooch*: jewel, ornament.
[164] *confession*: testament, report.
[165] *scrimers*: fencers.

King. Not that I think you did not love your father;   *110*
    But that I know love is begun by time,
    And that I see, in passages of proof,[166]
    Time qualifies[167] the spark and fire of it.
    There lives within the very flame of love
    A kind of wick or snuff[168] that will abate it;   *115*
    And nothing is at a like goodness still;[169]
    For goodness, growing to a pleurisy,[170]
    Dies in his own too much. That we would do,
    We should do when we would; for this "would"
        changes,
    And hath abatements and delays as many   *120*
    As there are tongues, are hands, are accidents;
    And then this "should" is like a spend-thrift's sigh
    That hurts[171] by easing. But to the quick[172] of th'
        ulcer:
    Hamlet comes back; what would you undertake
    To show yourself in deed your father's son   *125*
    More than in words?

Laertes.   To cut his throat i' th' church.

King. No place, indeed, should murder sanctuarize;[173]
    Revenge should have no bounds. But, good Laertes,
    Will you do this? Keep close within your chamber.
    Hamlet return'd shall know you are come home.   *130*
    We'll put on those[174] shall praise your excellence,
    And set a double varnish on the fame

---

[166] *passages of proof*: experience, proved cases.

[167] *qualifies*: weakens, diminishes.

[168] *snuff*: residue of burned wick.

[169] *still*: always.

[170] *pleurisy*: excess.

[171] *hurts*: It was believed that sighs drew blood from the heart, thereby shortening life.

[172] *quick*: sensitive flesh.

[173] *sanctuarize*: protect from punishment.

[174] *put on those*: instigate persons who.

The Frenchman gave you; bring you, in fine,[175]
   together,
And wager on your heads. He, being remiss,[176]
Most generous, and free from all contriving,   135
Will not peruse[177] the foils; so that with ease
Or with a little shuffling, you may choose
A sword unbated,[178] and, in a pass of practice,[179]
Requite him for your father.

Laertes.   I will do't;   140
And for that purpose I'll anoint my sword.
I bought an unction[180] of a mountebank,[181]
So mortal that but dip a knife in it,
Where it draws blood no cataplasm[182] so rare,
Collected from all simples[183] that have virtue
Under the moon, can save the thing from death   145
That is but scratch'd withal. I'll touch my point
With this contagion, that, if I gall[184] him slightly,
It may be death.

King.   Let's further think of this;
Weigh what convenience both of time and means
May fit us to our shape.[185] If this should fail,   150
And that our drift[186] look[187] through our bad
   performance,
'Twere better not assay'd, therefore this project

---

[175] *in fine:* finally.
[176] *remiss:* negligent.
[177] *peruse:* examine.
[178] *unbated:* unblunted.
[179] *pass of practice:* thrust made good by treachery.
[180] *unction:* ointment.
[181] *mountebank:* oily salesman, quack.
[182] *cataplasm:* poultice.
[183] *simples:* also given as "simplex"; medicinal herbs.
[184] *gall:* scratch.
[185] *shape:* role, plan.
[186] *drift:* purpose, scheme.
[187] *look:* be seen.

Should have a back or second, that might hold
If this did blast in proof.[188] Soft! let me see.
We'll make a solemn wager on your cunnings[189]—   155
I ha't.
When in your motion you are hot and dry—
As make your bouts more violent to that end—
And that he calls for drink, I'll have preferr'd him
A chalice for the nonce;[190] whereon but sipping,   160
If he by chance escape your venom'd stuck,[191]
Our purpose may hold there. But stay; what noise?

Enter Queen.

Queen. One woe doth tread upon another's heel,
So fast they follow. Your sister's drown'd, Laertes.   165

Laertes. Drown'd! O, where?

Queen. There is a willow grows aslant[192] the brook
That shows his hoar[193] leaves in the glassy stream;
Therewith fantastic garlands did she make
Of crowflowers, nettles, daisies, and long purples   170
That liberal[194] shepherds give a grosser name,
But our cold maids do dead men's fingers call them.
There, on the pendent boughs her coronet[195] weeds
Clamb'ring to hang, an envious sliver broke;
When down her weedy trophies and herself   176
Fell in the weeping brook. Her clothes spread wide
And, mermaid-like, awhile they bore her up;
Which time she chanted snatches of old lauds,[196]

---

[188] *blast in proof*: blow up in performance.
[189] *cunnings*: skills.
[190] *nonce*: occasion.
[191] *stuck*: thrust.
[192] *aslant*: also given as "askant"; alongside.
[193] *hoar*: silver-gray.
[194] *liberal*: free-spoken, licentious.
[195] *coronet*: also given as "crownet"; a small crown.
[196] *lauds*: hymns.

As one incapable[197] of her own distress,
Or like a creature native and indued[198]   180
Unto that element; but long it could not be
Till that her garments, heavy with their drink,
Pull'd the poor wretch from her melodious lay
To muddy death.

Laertes.   Alas, then she is drown'd!

Queen. Drown'd, drown'd.   185

Laertes. Too much of water hast thou, poor Ophelia,
And therefore I forbid my tears; but yet
It is our trick;[199] nature her custom holds,
Let shame say what it will. When these are gone,
The woman[200] will be out. Adieu, my lord.   190
I have a speech o' fire that fain would blaze
But that this folly douts[201] it.   [*Exit.*]

King.   Let's follow, Gertrude.
How much I had to do to calm his rage!
Now fear I this will give it start again;
Therefore let's follow.   [*Exeunt.*] 194

---

[197] *incapable:* unconscious, unaware.
[198] *indued:* suited, endowed.
[199] *trick:* trait or the way of men.
[200] *woman:* womanly part (i.e., the sensitivity shown by tears).
[201] *douts:* also given as "drowns".

ACT 5

Scene 1. *Elsinore. A churchyard.*

Enter two Clowns[1] *with spades and picks.*

1 Clown. Is she to be buried in Christian burial[2] when
she wilfully seeks her own salvation?

2 Clown. I tell thee she is; therefore make her grave
straight.[3] The crowner[4] hath sat on her, and finds
it Christian burial.   5

1 Clown. How can that be, unless she drown'd herself
in her own defence?

2 Clown. Why, 'tis found so.

1 Clown. It must be "se offendendo";[5] it cannot be
else. For here lies the point: if I drown myself
wittingly, it argues an act; and an act hath three
branches—it is to act, to do, to perform; argal,[6]
she drown'd herself wittingly.   13

2 Clown. Nay, but hear you, Goodman Delver.

1 Clown. Give me leave. Here lies the water; good.
Here stands the man; good. If the man go to this
water and drown himself, it is, will he, nill he,[7] he
goes—mark you that; but if the water come to
him and drown him, he drowns not himself.

---

[1] *Clowns:* rural folks.
[2] *Christian burial:* in consecrated ground with the rites prescribed by the Church
(denied to those who have committed suicide).
[3] *straight:* at once.
[4] *crowner:* coroner.
[5] *se offendendo:* mistaken rendering of *se defendendo,* a legal term meaning "in
self-defense".
[6] *argal:* mistaken rendering of *ergo,* "therefore".
[7] *will he, nill he:* willy-nilly, whether he will or will not.

Argal, he that is not guilty of his own death shortens not his own life.

2 *Clown.* But is this law?   21

1 *Clown.* Ay, marry, is't; crowner's quest[8] law.

2 *Clown.* Will you ha the truth an't? If this had not been a gentlewoman, she should have been buried out a Christian burial.   25

1 *Clown.* Why, there thou say'st;[9] and the more pity that great folk should have count'nance[10] in this world to drown or hang themselves more than their even Christen.[11] Come, my spade. There is no ancient gentlemen but gard'ners, ditchers, and grave-makers; they hold up Adam's profession.   31

2 *Clown.* Was he a gentleman?

1 *Clown.* 'A was the first that ever bore arms.[12]

2 *Clown.* Why, he had none.   34

1 *Clown.* What, art a heathen? How dost thou understand the Scripture? The Scripture says Adam digg'd. Could he dig without arms? I'll put another question to thee. If thou answerest me not to the purpose, confess thyself—

2 *Clown.* Go to.   40

1 *Clown.* What is he that builds stronger than either the mason, the shipwright, or the carpenter?

2 *Clown.* The gallows-maker; for that frame outlives a thousand tenants.   44

---

[8] *quest*: inquest.
[9] *thou say'st*: you are correct.
[10] *count'nance*: privilege.
[11] *even Christen*: fellow Christians.
[12] *bore arms*: had a coat of arms, the sign of a gentleman.

1 Clown. I like thy wit well; in good faith the gallows
    does well; but how does it well? It does well to
    those that do ill. Now thou dost ill to say the
    gallows is built stronger than the church; argal,
    the gallows may do well to thee. To 't again,
    come.   49

2 Clown. Who builds stronger than a mason, a
    shipwright, or a carpenter?

1 Clown. Ay, tell me that, and unyoke.[13]

2 Clown. Marry, now I can tell.

1 Clown. To 't.

2 Clown. Mass,[14] I cannot tell.   55

Enter Hamlet and Horatio, afar off.

1 Clown. Cudgel thy brains no more about it, for your
    dull ass will not mend his pace with beating; and
    when you are ask'd this question next, say "a
    grave-maker": the houses he makes lasts till
    doomsday. Go, get thee to Yaughan; fetch me a
    stoup[15] of liquor.   [*Exit Second Clown.*]   60

[*Digs and sings.*] In youth, when I did love, did love,
    Methought it was very sweet,
To contract-o-the time for-a my behove,[16]
O, methought there-a-was nothing-a meet.

Hamlet. Has this fellow no feeling of his business, that
    'a sings in grave-making?   66

---

[13] *unyoke:* stop work for the day, or unharness powers of thought after a long
day of work.
[14] *Mass:* by the Mass, a colloquial exclamation.
[15] *stoup:* tankard.
[16] *behove:* advantage.

Horatio. Custom hath made it in him a property of
  easiness.[17]

Hamlet. 'Tis e'en so; the hand of little employment
  hath the daintier sense.[18]   70

1 Clown. [*Sings.*] But age, with his stealing steps,
      Hath clawed me in his clutch,
  And hath shipped me intil the land,
      As if I had never been such.   74

                                    [*Throws up a skull.*]

Hamlet. That skull had a tongue in it, and could sing
  once. How the knave jowls[19] it to the ground, as
  if 'twere Cain's jawbone,[20] that did the first
  murder! This might be the pate of a politician,[21]
  which this ass now o'erreaches;[22] one that would
  circumvent God, might it not?   80

Horatio. It might, my lord.

Hamlet. Or of a courtier; which could say "Good
  morrow, sweet lord! How dost thou, sweet lord?"
  This might be my Lord Such-a-one, that praised
  my Lord Such-a-one's horse, when 'a meant to beg
  it—might it not?

Horatio. Ay, my lord.   85

Hamlet. Why, e'en so; and now my Lady Worm's,
  chapless,[23] and knock'd about the mazard[24] with a

---

  [17] *property of easiness:* matter of indifference.

  [18] *daintier sense:* more delicate, sensitive feeling (because the hand is not calloused).

  [19] *jowls:* hurls.

  [20] *Cain's jawbone:* cf. Genesis 4, the killing of Abel by his brother Cain (traditionally, not biblically, with the jawbone of an ass).

  [21] *politician:* considered crafty.

  [22] *o'erreaches:* gets the better of, reaches over.

  [23] *chapless:* also given as "chopless"; lacking the lower jaw.

  [24] *mazard:* head.

sexton's spade. Here's fine revolution, an we had
the trick to see't. Did these bones cost no more
the breeding but to play at loggats[25] with them?
Mine ache to think on't.   90

1 Clown. [*Sings.*] A pick-axe and a spade, a spade,
                For and a shrouding sheet:
            O, a pit of clay for to be made
                For such a guest is meet.

                            [*Throws up another skull.*]

Hamlet. There's another. Why may not that be the
skull of a lawyer? Where be his quiddities[26] now,
his quillets,[27] his cases, his tenures,[28] and his tricks?
Why does he suffer this rude knave now to knock
him about the sconce[29] with a dirty shovel, and
will not tell him of his action of battery? Hum! This
fellow might be in's time a great buyer of land, with
his statutes, his recognizances,[30] his fines, his
double vouchers, his recoveries. Is this the fine[31] of
his fines, and the recovery of his recoveries,[32] to
have his fine pate full of fine dirt? Will his vouchers
vouch him no more of his purchases, and double
ones too, than the length and breadth of a pair of
indentures?[33] The very conveyances[34] of his lands
will scarcely lie in this box; and must th' inheritor
himself have no more, ha?

[25] *loggats:* small pieces of wood thrown in a game.
[26] *quiddities:* subtleties (from the Latin *quidditas,* "whatness").
[27] *quillets:* nice distinctions (variant of *quidditas*).
[28] *tenures:* legal holdings of property.
[29] *sconce:* head.
[30] *statutes . . . recognizances:* forms of legal acknowledgments of debt.
[31] *fine:* end.
[32] *fines . . . recoveries:* forms of legal transformations from a limited to a more absolute property ownership.
[33] *pair of indentures:* agreements, contracts in duplicate.
[34] *conveyances:* deeds.

Horatio. Not a jot more, my lord.

Hamlet. Is not parchment made of sheep-skins?

Horatio. Ay, my lord, and of calves' skins too.   110

Hamlet. They are sheep and calves which seek out
     assurance in that. I will speak to this fellow.
     Whose grave's this, sirrah?

1 Clown. Mine, sir.   115

     [*Sings.*] O, a pit of clay for to be made
          For such a guest is meet.

Hamlet. I think it be thine indeed, for thou liest in't.

1 Clown. You lie out on't, sir, and therefore 'tis not
     yours. For my part, I do not lie in't, yet it is mine.   120

Hamlet. Thou dost lie in't, to be in't and say it is thine;
     'tis for the dead, not for the quick;[35] therefore
     thou liest.

1 Clown. 'Tis a quick lie, sir; 'twill away again from me
     to you.   125

Hamlet. What man dost thou dig it for?

1 Clown. For no man, sir.

Hamlet. What woman, then?

1 Clown. For none neither.

Hamlet. Who is to be buried in't?   130

1 Clown. One that was a woman, sir; but, rest her soul,
     she's dead.

----

[35] *quick*: living.

Hamlet. How absolute[36] the knave is! We must speak
 by the card,[37] or equivocation[38] will undo us. By
 the Lord, Horatio, this three years I have took
 note of it: the age is grown so picked[39] that the
 toe of the peasant comes so near the heel of the
 courtier, he galls[40] his kibe.[41] How long hast thou
 been a grave-maker?

1 Clown. Of all the days i' th' year, I came to't that day
 that our last King Hamlet overcame Fortinbras.   *140*

Hamlet. How long is that since?

1 Clown. Cannot you tell that? Every fool can tell that:
 it was that very day that young Hamlet was
 born—he that is mad, and sent into England.

Hamlet. Ay, marry, why was he sent into England?   *145*

1 Clown. Why, because 'a was mad: 'a shall recover his
 wits there; or, if 'a do not, 'tis no great matter
 there.

Hamlet. Why?

1 Clown. 'Twill not be seen in him there: there the
 men are as mad as he.   *150*

Hamlet. How came he mad?

1 Clown. Very strangely, they say.

Hamlet. How strangely?

1 Clown. Faith, e'en with losing his wits.

---

[36] *absolute*: positive, a stickler for accuracy.
[37] *by the card*: by the compass card, accurately.
[38] *equivocation*: ambiguity.
[39] *picked*: refined.
[40] *galls*: chafes, meaning that the association between the peasant and the
courtier demeans the status of the latter.
[41] *kibe*: chilblain, a sore on the back of the heel.

Hamlet. Upon what ground?[42]   155

1 Clown. Why, here in Denmark. I have been sexton
    here, man and boy, thirty years.

Hamlet. How long will a man lie i' th' earth ere he rot?

1 Clown. Faith, if 'a be not rotten before 'a die—as we
    have many pocky[43] corses now-a-days that will
    scarce hold the laying in—'a will last you some
    eight year or nine year. A tanner will last you
    nine year.   163

Hamlet. Why he more than another?

1 Clown. Why, sir, his hide is so tann'd with his trade
    that 'a will keep out water a great while; and your
    water is a sore decayer of your whoreson[44] dead
    body. Here's a skull now; this skull has lien you i'
    th' earth three and twenty years.

Hamlet. Whose was it?   170

1 Clown. A whoreson mad fellow's it was. Whose do
    you think it was?

Hamlet. Nay, I know not.

1 Clown. A pestilence on him for a mad rogue! 'A
    poured a flagon of Rhenish[45] on my head once.
    This same skull, sir, was, sir, Yorick's[46] skull, the
    King's jester.   176

Hamlet. This?

1 Clown. E'en that.

---

[42] *Upon what ground?* for what reason? (taken by the clown to mean: "Where?").
[43] *pocky*: decayed by the pox (syphilis).
[44] *whoreson*: despicable or coarse person.
[45] *Rhenish*: Rhine wine.
[46] *sir, Yorick's*: also rendered as "Sir Yorick's", taken as an ironic or affectionate title.

Hamlet. Let me see. [*Takes the skull.*] Alas, poor Yorick!
  I knew him, Horatio: a fellow of infinite jest, of
  most excellent fancy; he hath borne me on his
  back a thousand times. And now how abhorred in
  my imagination it is! My gorge[47] rises at it. Here
  hung those lips that I have kiss'd I know not how
  oft. Where be your gibes now, your gambols, your
  songs, your flashes of merriment that were wont to
  set the table on a roar? Not one now to mock
  your own grinning—quite chap-fall'n?[48] Now get
  you to my lady's chamber, and tell her, let her
  paint an inch thick, to this favour[49] she must
  come; make her laugh at that. Prithee, Horatio,
  tell me one thing.

Horatio. What's that, my lord?   191

Hamlet. Dost thou think Alexander[50] look'd a this
  fashion i' th' earth?

Horatio. E'en so.

Hamlet. And smelt so? Pah!   195

                                    [*Throws down the skull.*]

Horatio. E'en so, my lord.

Hamlet. To what base uses we may return, Horatio!
  Why may not imagination trace the noble dust of
  Alexander till 'a find it stopping a bung-hole?[51]   199

---

[47] *gorge:* contents of the stomach.
[48] *chap-fall'n:* lacking the lower chop, jawless; also dejected or down in the mouth.
[49] *favour:* countenance, appearance.
[50] *Alexander:* Alexander the Great (356–323 B.C.), undefeated commander, conqueror of the known world in his time.
[51] *bung-hole:* opening in a wine or beer barrel.

Horatio. 'Twere to consider too curiously[52] to consider
   so.

Hamlet. No, faith, not a jot; but to follow him thither
   with modesty enough,[53] and likelihood to lead it,
   as thus: Alexander died, Alexander was buried,
   Alexander returneth to dust; the dust is earth; of
   earth we make loam;[54] and why of that loam
   whereto he was converted might they not stop a
   beer-barrel?   206
   Imperious Caesar,[55] dead and turn'd to clay,
   Might stop a hole to keep the wind away.
   O, that that earth which kept the world in awe
   Should patch a wall t' expel the winter's flaw![56]   210
   But soft! but soft! awhile. Here comes the King.

*Enter the King, Queen, Laertes, in funeral procession after
   the coffin, with Priest and Lords attendant.*

   The Queen, the courtiers. Who is this they follow?
   And with such maimed rites? This doth betoken
   The corse they follow did with desperate hand
   Fordo[57] it own life. 'Twas of some estate.[58]   215
   Couch[59] we awhile and mark.

                       [*Retiring with Horatio.*]

Laertes. What ceremony else?

Hamlet. That is Laertes, a very noble youth. Mark.

Laertes. What ceremony else?

---

[52] *curiously*: minutely or ingeniously.
[53] *with modesty enough*: moderately, without exaggeration.
[54] *loam*: clay used to seal the opening in a barrel.
[55] *Caesar*: a title used by the Roman emperors after Julius Caesar.
[56] *flaw*: gust of wind.
[57] *Fordo*: destroy.
[58] *estate*: rank.
[59] *Couch*: hide.

Priest. Her obsequies[60] have been as far enlarg'd   *220*
    As we have warranties. Her death was doubtful;[61]
    And, but that great command o'ersways the order,
    She should in ground unsanctified have lodg'd
    Till the last trumpet; for charitable prayers,
    Shards,[62] flints, and pebbles, should be thrown on
        her;   *225*
    Yet here she is allow'd her virgin crants,[63]
    Her maiden strewments,[64] and the bringing home
    Of bell and burial.

Laertes. Must there no more be done?

Priest.   No more be done.

    We should profane the service of the dead   *230*
    To sing sage requiem and such rest to her
    As to peace-parted souls.

Laertes.   Lay her i' th' earth;
    And from her fair and unpolluted flesh
    May violets spring! I tell thee, churlish priest,
    A minist'ring angel shall my sister be   *235*
    When thou liest howling.[65]

Hamlet.   What, the fair Ophelia!

Queen. Sweets to the sweet; farewell!

                      [*Scattering flowers.*]

    I hop'd thou shouldst have been my Hamlet's wife;
    I thought thy bride-bed to have deck'd, sweet maid,
    And not have strew'd thy grave.

---

[60] *obsequies:* funeral rites.
[61] *doubtful:* suspicious.
[62] *Shards:* broken crockery.
[63] *crants:* garlands, chaplets.
[64] *strewments:* i.e., of the grave with flowers.
[65] *howling:* i.e., in Hell.

Laertes.   O, treble woe   240
    Fall ten times treble on that cursed head
    Whose wicked deed thy most ingenious sense[66]
    Depriv'd thee of! Hold off the earth awhile,
    Till I have caught her once more in mine arms.

                                 [*Leaps into the grave.*]

    Now pile your dust upon the quick and dead,   245
    Till of this flat a mountain you have made
    T' o'er-top old Pelion[67] or the skyish head
    Of blue Olympus.

Hamlet. [*Advancing*]   What is he whose grief
    Bears such an emphasis,[68] whose phrase of sorrow
    Conjures the wand'ring stars,[69] and makes them
        stand   250
    Like wonder-wounded hearers? This is I,
    Hamlet the Dane.   [*Leaps into the grave.*][70]

Laertes. The devil take thy soul!

                            [*Grappling with him.*]

Hamlet.   Thou pray'st not well.
    I prithee take thy fingers from my throat;
    For, though I am not splenitive[71] and rash,   255
    Yet have I in me something dangerous,
    Which let thy wiseness fear. Hold off thy hand.

King. Pluck them asunder.

---

[66] *most ingenious sense*: of quickest understanding, a finely endowed mind.

[67] *Pelion*: in classical mythology, a mountain in Thessaly that the Titans piled together with Mount Ossa and Mount Olympus in an effort to reach Heaven.

[68] *emphasis*: exaggerated speech.

[69] *wand'ring stars*: planets.

[70] There are differing accounts of the early staging of this scene (with Hamlet jumping into the grave or Laertes jumping out of the grave), making it questionable who is the aggressor.

[71] *splenitive*: hot-tempered (from the spleen).

Queen. Hamlet! Hamlet!

All. Gentlemen!

Horatio. Good my lord, be quiet.

[*The Attendants part them, and they come out of the grave.*]

Hamlet. Why, I will fight with him upon this theme   260
    Until my eyelids will no longer wag.

Queen. O my son, what theme?

Hamlet. I lov'd Ophelia: forty thousand brothers
    Could not, with all their quantity of love,
    Make up my sum. What wilt thou do for her?   265

King. O, he is mad, Laertes.

Queen. For love of God, forbear him.[72]

Hamlet. 'Swounds,[73] show me what th'owt do:
    Woo't[74] weep, woo't fight, woo't fast, woo't tear
      thyself,
    Woo't drink up easel,[75] eat a crocodile?   270
    I'll do't. Dost come here to whine?
    To outface me with leaping in her grave?
    Be buried quick with her, and so will I;
    And, if thou prate of mountains, let them throw
    Millions of acres on us, till our ground,   275
    Singeing his pate against the burning zone,[76]
    Make Ossa like a wart! Nay, an thou'lt mouth,
    I'll rant as well as thou.

Queen.   This is mere[77] madness;
    And thus awhile the fit will work on him;

---

[72] *forbear him*: leave him alone.
[73] *'Swounds*: by God's wounds, a colloquial exclamation.
[74] *Woo't*: wilt thou.
[75] *easel*: vinegar.
[76] *burning zone*: sun's orbit.
[77] *mere*: absolute.

Anon, as patient as the female dove   280
When that her golden couplets are disclos'd,[78]
His silence will sit drooping.

Hamlet.   Hear you, sir:
What is the reason that you use me thus?
I lov'd you ever. But it is no matter.
Let Hercules[79] himself do what he may,   285
The cat will mew, and dog will have his day.

                                        [Exit.]

King. I pray thee, good Horatio, wait upon him.

                                [Exit Horatio.]

[To Laertes] Strengthen your patience in our last
    night's speech;
We'll put the matter to the present push.[80]—
Good Gertrude, set some watch over your son.—   290
This grave shall have a living monument.
An hour of quiet shortly shall we see;
Till then in patience our proceeding be.

                                      [Exeunt.]

Scene 2. Elsinore. The Castle.

Enter Hamlet and Horatio.

Hamlet. So much for this, sir; now shall you see the
    other.
You do remember all the circumstance?

[78] her golden couplets are disclos'd: The dove lays two eggs, and the newly hatched
young are covered with golden down.
[79] Hercules: in classical mythology, a hero who performed many great deeds
and won immortality with the gods; also, denoting a ranting boaster.
[80] present push: immediate action.

Horatio. Remember it, my lord!

Hamlet. Sir, in my heart there was a kind of fighting
    That would not let me sleep. Methought I lay   5
    Worse than the mutines in the bilboes.[81] Rashly,
    And prais'd be rashness for it—let us know,
    Our indiscretion sometime serves us well,
    When our deep plots do pall;[82] and that should
        learn us
    There's a divinity that shapes our ends,   10
    Rough-hew[83] them how we will.

Horatio.   That is most certain.

Hamlet. Up from my cabin,
    My sea-gown scarf'd about me, in the dark
    Grop'd I to find out them; had my desire;
    Finger'd[84] their packet, and in fine[85] withdrew   15
    To mine own room again, making so bold,
    My fears forgetting manners, to unseal
    Their grand commission; where I found, Horatio,
    Ah, royal knavery! an exact command,
    Larded[86] with many several sorts of reasons,   20
    Importing Denmark's health and England's too,
    With, ho! such bugs and goblins[87] in my life—
    That, on the supervise,[88] no leisure bated,[89]
    No, not to stay the grinding of the axe,
    My head should be struck off.

Horatio.   Is't possible?   25

---

[81] *mutines in the bilboes*: mutineers in fetters.
[82] *pall*: fail.
[83] *Rough-hew*: shape roughly.
[84] *Finger'd*: filched, stole.
[85] *in fine*: finally.
[86] *Larded*: enriched, garnished.
[87] *bugs and goblins*: imagined terrors (bugbears).
[88] *supervise*: perusal.
[89] *leisure bated*: time allowed.

Hamlet. Here's the commission; read it at more leisure.
   But wilt thou hear now how I did proceed?

Horatio. I beseech you.

Hamlet. Being thus benetted round with villainies—
   Ere I could make a prologue to my brains,   30
   They had begun the play—I sat me down;
   Devis'd a new commission; wrote it fair.
   I once did hold it, as our statists[90] do,
   A baseness to write fair, and labour'd much
   How to forget that learning; but, sir, now   35
   It did me yeoman's[91] service. Wilt thou know
   Th' effect[92] of what I wrote?

Horatio.   Ay, good my lord.

Hamlet. An earnest conjuration from the King,
   As England was his faithful tributary,
   As love between them like the palm might
      flourish,[93]   40
   As peace should still her wheaten garland[94] wear
   And stand a comma[95] 'tween their amities,
   And many such like as-es of great charge,[96]
   That, on the view and knowing of these contents,
   Without debatement further more or less,   45
   He should those bearers put to sudden death,
   Not shriving-time[97] allow'd.

Horatio.   How was this seal'd?

---

[90] *statists:* statesmen.
[91] *yeoman's:* foot soldier's.
[92] *effect:* purport.
[93] *palm might flourish:* cf. Psalm 92:12: "The righteous flourish like the palm tree".
[94] *wheaten garland:* symbol of peace.
[95] *comma:* i.e., something small.
[96] *charge:* burden or serious exhortation.
[97] *shriving-time:* time for confession and absolution.

Hamlet. Why, even in that was heaven ordinant.[98]
    I had my father's signet[99] in my purse,
    Which was the model[100] of that Danish seal;   50
    Folded the writ up in the form of th' other;
    Subscrib'd it, gave't th' impression, plac'd it safely,
    The changeling never known. Now, the next day
    Was our sea-fight; and what to this was sequent[101]
    Thou knowest already.   55

Horatio. So Guildenstern and Rosencrantz go to't.

Hamlet. Why, man, they did make love to this
    employment;
    They are not near my conscience; their defeat
    Does by their own insinuation[102] grow:
    'Tis dangerous when the baser nature comes   60
    Between the pass[103] and fell[104] incensed points
    Of mighty opposites.

Horatio.   Why, what a king is this!

Hamlet. Does it not, think thee, stand me now
    upon[105]—
    He that hath kill'd my king and whor'd my mother;
    Popp'd in between th' election[106] and my hopes;   65
    Thrown out his angle[107] for my proper[108] life,
    And with such coz'nage[109]—is't not perfect
    conscience

[98] *ordinant:* ordaining, ruling.

[99] *signet:* signet ring.

[100] *model:* counterpart.

[101] *sequent:* subsequent.

[102] *insinuation:* slipping in, meddling.

[103] *pass:* sword thrust.

[104] *fell:* fierce, cruel.

[105] *Does it not . . . stand me now upon:* is it not an obligation incumbent upon me.

[106] *election:* i.e., to the throne (the Danish monarchy was decided by election).

[107] *angle:* fishing line and hook.

[108] *proper:* own.

[109] *coz'nage:* trickery.

To quit[110] him with this arm? And is't not to be
   damn'd
To let this canker of our nature come
In further evil? 70

Horatio. It must be shortly known to him from England
   What is the issue of the business there.

Hamlet. It will be short; the interim is mine,
   And a man's life's no more than to say "one".
   But I am very sorry, good Horatio, 75
   That to Laertes I forgot myself;
   For by the image of my cause I see
   The portraiture of his. I'll court his favours.
   But sure the bravery of his grief did put me
   Into a tow'ring passion.

Horatio. Peace; who comes here? 80

Enter young Osric.

Osric. Your lordship is right welcome back to Denmark.

Hamlet. I humbly thank you, sir. [Aside to Horatio] Dost
   know this water-fly?[111] 83

Horatio. [Aside to Hamlet] No, my good lord.

Hamlet. [Aside to Horatio] Thy state is the more
   gracious; for 'tis a vice to know him. He hath
   much land, and fertile. Let a beast be lord of
   beasts, and his crib shall stand at the king's
   mess.[112] 'Tis a chough;[113] but, as I say, spacious[114]
   in the possession of dirt.

---

[110] quit: pay back, acquit.
[111] water-fly: a gaudy insect.
[112] mess: table.
[113] chough: jackdaw, chatterer.
[114] spacious: well off.

Osric. Sweet lord, if your lordship were at leisure, I
should impart a thing to you from his Majesty.   *91*

Hamlet. I will receive it, sir, with all diligence of spirit.
Put your bonnet to his right use; 'tis for the head.

Osric. I thank your lordship; it is very hot.

Hamlet. No, believe me, 'tis very cold; the wind is
northerly.   *95*

Osric. It is indifferent cold, my lord, indeed.

Hamlet. But yet methinks it is very sultry and hot for
my complexion.[115]   *99*

Osric. Exceedingly, my lord; it is very sultry, as
'twere—I cannot tell how. But, my lord, his
Majesty bade me signify to you that 'a has laid
a great wager on your head. Sir, this is the
matter—

Hamlet. I beseech you, remember.   *104*

[*Hamlet moves him to put on his hat.*]

Osric. Nay, good my lord; for my ease, in good faith.
Sir, here is newly come to court Laertes; believe
me, an absolute gentleman, full of most excellent
differences,[116] of very soft society and great
showing. Indeed, to speak feelingly[117] of him, he
is the card[118] or calendar of gentry, for you shall
find in him the continent[119] of what part a
gentleman would see.   *111*

---

[115] *complexion*: temperament.
[116] *differences*: distinguishing qualities.
[117] *feelingly*: appropriately.
[118] *card*: chart, map.
[119] *continent*: summary, containment.

Hamlet. Sir, his definement[120] suffers no perdition[121]
in you; though, I know, to divide him
inventorially would dozy[122] th' arithmetic of
memory, and yet but yaw[123] neither in respect of
his quick sail. But, in the verity of extolment, I
take him to be a soul of great article,[124] and his
infusion[125] of such dearth and rareness as, to
make true diction of him, his semblable[126] is his
mirror, and who else would trace him, his
umbrage,[127] nothing more.

Osric. Your lordship speaks most infallibly of him.   *120*

Hamlet. The concernancy,[128] sir? Why do we wrap the
gentleman in our more rawer breath?

Osric. Sir?

Horatio. [*Aside to Hamlet*] Is't not possible to
understand in another tongue? You will to't,[129] sir,
really.   *125*

Hamlet. What imports the nomination[130] of this
gentleman?

Osric. Of Laertes?

Horatio. [*Aside*] His purse is empty already; all's golden
words are spent.   *130*

Hamlet. Of him, sir.

---

120 *definement*: description, definition.
121 *perdition*: loss.
122 *dozy*: dizzy.
123 *yaw*: stagger, veer like a ship steering wildly.
124 *article*: traits, scope.
125 *infusion*: essential quality.
126 *semblable*: likeness.
127 *umbrage*: shadow.
128 *concernancy*: meaning, relevance.
129 *to't*: i.e., reach an understanding.
130 *nomination*: naming.

Osric. I know you are not ignorant—

Hamlet. I would you did, sir; yet, in faith, if you did, it
would not much approve[131] me. Well, sir.

Osric. You are not ignorant of what excellence Laertes
is—   *136*

Hamlet. I dare not confess that, lest I should compare
with him in excellence; but to know a man well
were to know himself.   *139*

Osric. I mean, sir, for his weapon; but in the
imputation[132] laid on him by them, in his
meed[133] he's unfellowed.

Hamlet. What's his weapon?

Osric. Rapier and dagger.

Hamlet. That's two of his weapons—but well.   *144*

Osric. The King, sir, hath wager'd with him six Barbary
horses; against the which he has impon'd,[134] as I
take it, six French rapiers and poniards,[135] with
their assigns,[136] as girdle, hangers,[137] and
so—three of the carriages,[138] in faith, are very
dear to fancy,[139] very responsive[140] to the hilts,
most delicate carriages, and of very liberal
conceit.[141]   *150*

---

[131] *approve*: commend.
[132] *imputation*: reputation.
[133] *meed*: merit, reward.
[134] *impon'd*: wagered, staked.
[135] *poniards*: daggers.
[136] *assigns*: accompaniments, appurtenances.
[137] *hangers*: straps by which the sword hangs from the belt.
[138] *carriages*: affected term for hangers.
[139] *dear to fancy*: finely designed.
[140] *responsive*: corresponding.
[141] *liberal conceit*: tasteful design.

Hamlet. What call you the carriages?

Horatio. [*Aside to Hamlet*] I knew you must be edified
by the margent[142] ere you had done.

Osric. The carriages, sir, are the hangers.

Hamlet. The phrase would be more germane to the
matter if we could carry a cannon by our sides. I
would it might be hangers till then. But on: six
Barbary horses against six French swords, their
assigns, and three liberal conceited carriages; that's
the French bet against the Danish. Why is this all
impon'd,[143] as you call it?   160

Osric. The King, sir, hath laid, sir, that in a dozen
passes between yourself and him he shall not
exceed you three hits; he hath laid on twelve for
nine, and it would come to immediate trial if your
lordship would vouchsafe the answer.   165

Hamlet. How if I answer no?

Osric. I mean, my lord, the opposition of your person
in trial.

Hamlet. Sir, I will walk here in the hall. If it please his
Majesty, it is the breathing[144] time of day with
me; let the foils be brought, the gentleman
willing, and the King hold his purpose, I will win
for him an I can; if not, I will gain nothing but
my shame and the odd hits.

Osric. Shall I redeliver you e'en so?

Hamlet. To this effect, sir, after what flourish your
nature will.   176

---

[142] *margent*: margin, explanatory comment.
[143] *impon'd*: wagered, staked.
[144] *breathing*: exercise.

Osric. I commend my duty to your lordship.

Hamlet. Yours, yours. [*Exit Osric.*] He does well to
  commend it himself; there are no tongues else
  for's turn.

Horatio. This lapwing[145] runs away with the shell on
  his head.   181

Hamlet. 'A did comply, sir, with his dug[146] before 'a
  suck'd it. Thus has he, and many more of the
  same bevy, that I know the drossy[147] age dotes on,
  only got the tune of the time and outward habit
  of encounter[148]—a kind of yesty[149] collection,
  which carries them through and through the most
  fann'd and winnowed[150] opinions; and do but
  blow them to their trial, the bubbles are out.[151]   188

Enter a Lord.

Lord. My lord, his Majesty commended him to you by
  young Osric, who brings back to him that you
  attend him in the hall. He sends to know if your
  pleasure hold to play with Laertes, or that you will
  take longer time.

Hamlet. I am constant to my purposes; they follow the
  king's pleasure: if his fitness speaks, mine is ready
  now—or whensoever, provided I be so able as
  now.   195

Lord. The King and Queen and all are coming down.

---

[145] *lapwing*: precocious bird that was thought to run immediately upon being
hatched.
[146] *did comply . . . with his dug*: was ceremonially polite to his mother's breast.
[147] *drossy*: frivolous.
[148] *outward habit of encounter*: superficial manner of meeting and conversing.
[149] *yesty*: frothy.
[150] *fann'd and winnowed*: select and refined.
[151] *out*: blown away.

Hamlet. In happy time.[152]

Lord. The Queen desires you to use some gentle
entertainment[153] to Laertes before you fall to play.   *199*

Hamlet. She well instructs me.   [*Exit Lord.*]

Horatio. You will lose this wager, my lord.

Hamlet. I do not think so; since he went into France I
have been in continual practice. I shall win at the
odds. But thou wouldst not think how ill all's here
about my heart; but it is no matter.   *205*

Horatio. Nay, good my lord—

Hamlet. It is but foolery; but it is such a kind of
gain-giving[154] as would perhaps trouble a woman.

Horatio. If your mind dislike anything, obey it. I will
forestall their repair hither, and say you are not fit.   *210*

Hamlet. Not a whit, we defy augury: there is a special
providence in the fall of a sparrow.[155] If it be now,
'tis not to come; if it be not to come, it will be
now; if it be not now, yet it will come—the
readiness is all. Since no man owes of aught he
leaves, what is't to leave betimes?[156] Let be.

*A table prepared. Trumpets, Drums, and Officers with
cushions, foils and daggers. Enter King, Queen,
Laertes, and all the State.*

King. Come, Hamlet, come, and take this hand from
me.

---

[152] *In happy time*: a polite response.

[153] *entertainment*: courtesy.

[154] *gain-giving*: misgiving.

[155] *the fall of a sparrow*: cf. Matthew 10:29: "Are not two sparrows sold for a
penny? And not one of them will fall to the ground without your Father's will."

[156] *betimes*: early.

[*The King puts Laertes' hand into Hamlet's.*]

Hamlet. Give me your pardon, sir. I have done you
    wrong;
  But pardon't, as you are a gentleman.
  This presence[157] knows,   220
  And you must needs have heard how I am punish'd
  With a sore distraction. What I have done
  That might your nature, honour, and exception,[158]
  Roughly awake, I here proclaim was madness.
  Was't Hamlet wrong'd Laertes? Never Hamlet.   225
  If Hamlet from himself be ta'en away,
  And when he's not himself does wrong Laertes,
  Then Hamlet does it not, Hamlet denies it.
  Who does it, then? His madness. If 't be so,
  Hamlet is of the faction[159] that is wrong'd;   230
  His madness is poor Hamlet's enemy.
  Sir, in this audience,
  Let my disclaiming from a purpos'd evil
  Free me so far in your most generous thoughts
  That I have shot my arrow o'er the house   235
  And hurt my brother.

Laertes.   I am satisfied in nature,
  Whose motive in this case should stir me most
  To my revenge; but in my terms of honour
  I stand aloof, and will no reconcilement
  Till by some elder masters of known honour   240
  I have a voice[160] and precedent of peace
  To keep my name ungor'd[161]—but till that time
  I do receive your offer'd love like love,
  And will not wrong it.

---

[157] *presence:* i.e., the royal presence, assembly.
[158] *exception:* disapproval.
[159] *faction:* party or political group in opposition to another group.
[160] *voice:* authoritative opinion.
[161] *ungor'd:* uninjured.

Hamlet.   I embrace it freely;
  And will this brother's wager frankly play.   245
  Give us the foils. Come on.

Laertes.   Come, one for me.

Hamlet. I'll be your foil,[162] Laertes; in mine ignorance
  Your skill shall, like a star i' th' darkest night,
  Stick fiery off[163] indeed.

Laertes.   You mock me, sir.

Hamlet. No, by this hand.   250

King. Give them the foils, young Osric. Cousin
      Hamlet,
  You know the wager?

Hamlet.   Very well, my lord;
  Your Grace has laid the odds a' th' weaker side.

King. I do not fear it: I have seen you both;
  But since he's better'd,[164] we have therefore odds.   255

Laertes. This is too heavy; let me see another.

Hamlet. This likes me well. These foils have all a
      length?

                              [*They prepare to play.*]

Osric. Ay, my good lord.

King. Set me the stoups of wine upon that table.
  If Hamlet give the first or second hit,   260
  Or quit[165] in answer of the third exchange,
  Let all the battlements their ordnance fire;

---

[162] *foil:* background of metallic leaf (often for a jewel); here, punning on the swords used.
[163] *Stick fiery off:* stand out in brilliant relief.
[164] *better'd:* improved.
[165] *quit:* repay by striking back.

The King shall drink to Hamlet's better breath,
And in the cup an union[166] shall he throw,
Richer than that which four successive kings   *265*
In Denmark's crown have worn. Give me the cups;
And let the kettle[167] to the trumpet speak,
The trumpet to the cannoneer without,
The cannons to the heavens, the heaven to earth,
"Now the King drinks to Hamlet". Come, begin—   *270*
And you, the judges, bear a wary eye.

Hamlet. Come on, sir.

Laertes. Come, my lord.   [*They play.*]

Hamlet. One.

Laertes. No.

Hamlet. Judgment?

Osric. A hit, a very palpable hit.

Laertes. Well, again.

King. Stay, give me drink. Hamlet, this pearl is thine;
    Here's to thy health.

                    [*Drum, trumpets, and shot.*]

    Give him the cup.   *275*

Hamlet. I'll play this bout first; set it by awhile.
    Come.   [*They play.*]
    Another hit; what say you?

Laertes. A touch, a touch, I do confess't.

King. Our son shall win.

---

[166] *union:* pearl.
[167] *kettle:* kettledrum.

Queen. He's fat,[168] and scant of breath.
    Here, Hamlet, take my napkin,[169] rub thy brows.   280
    The Queen carouses[170] to thy fortune, Hamlet.

Hamlet. Good madam!

King. Gertrude, do not drink.

Queen. I will, my lord; I pray you pardon me.

King. [*Aside*] It is the poison'd cup; it is too late.

Hamlet. I dare not drink yet, madam; by and by.   285

Queen. Come, let me wipe thy face.

Laertes. My lord, I'll hit him now.

King.   I do not think't.

Laertes. [*Aside*] And yet it is almost against my
    conscience.

Hamlet. Come, for the third. Laertes, you do but dally;
    I pray you pass[171] with your best violence;   290
    I am afeard you make a wanton[172] of me.

Laertes. Say you so? Come on.   [*They play.*]

Osric. Nothing, neither way.

Laertes. Have at you now!

[*Laertes wounds Hamlet: then, in scuffling, they change
    rapiers, and Hamlet wounds Laertes.*]

King. Part them; they are incens'd.

Hamlet. Nay, come again.   [*The Queen falls.*]

---

[168] *fat:* sweaty or out of training.
[169] *napkin:* handkerchief.
[170] *carouses:* drinks a toast.
[171] *pass:* thrust, strike (with a sword).
[172] *wanton:* spoiled child.

Osric. Look to the Queen there, ho!   295

Horatio. They bleed on both sides. How is it, my lord?

Osric. How is't, Laertes?

Laertes. Why, as a woodcock,[173] to mine own
    springe,[174] Osric;
  I am justly kill'd with mine own treachery.

Hamlet. How does the Queen?

King. She swoons to see them bleed.   300

Queen. No, no, the drink, the drink! O my dear
    Hamlet!
  The drink, the drink! I am poison'd.   [*Dies.*]

Hamlet. O, villainy! Ho! let the door be lock'd.
  Treachery! seek it out.   [*Laertes falls.*]

Laertes. It is here, Hamlet. Hamlet, thou art slain;   305
  No med'cine in the world can do thee good;
  In thee there is not half an hour's life;
  The treacherous instrument is in thy hand,
  Unbated[175] and envenom'd. The foul practice[176]
  Hath turn'd itself on me; lo, here I lie,   310
  Never to rise again. Thy mother's poison'd.
  I can no more. The King, the King's to blame.

Hamlet. The point envenom'd too!
  Then, venom, to thy work.   [*Stabs the King.*]

All. Treason! treason!   315

King. O, yet defend me, friends; I am but hurt.

[173] *woodcock*: proverbially gullible bird.
[174] *springe*: snare, trap.
[175] *unbated*: unblunted.
[176] *practice*: deception, trick.

Hamlet. Here, thou incestuous, murd'rous, damned
    Dane,
  Drink off this potion. Is thy union[177] here?
  Follow my mother.   [*King dies.*]

Laertes.   He is justly serv'd:
  It is a poison temper'd[178] by himself.   320
  Exchange forgiveness with me, noble Hamlet.
  Mine and my father's death come not upon thee,
  Nor thine on me!   [*Dies.*]

Hamlet. Heaven make thee free of it! I follow thee.
  I am dead, Horatio. Wretched queen, adieu!   325
  You that look pale and tremble at this chance,
  That are but mutes[179] or audience to this act,
  Had I but time, as this fell sergeant[180] Death
  Is strict[181] in his arrest, O, I could tell you—
  But let it be. Horatio, I am dead: 330
  Thou livest; report me and my cause aright
  To the unsatisfied.[182]

Horatio.   Never believe it.
  I am more an antique Roman[183] than a Dane;
  Here's yet some liquor left.

Hamlet.   As th'art a man,
  Give me the cup. Let go. By heaven, I'll ha't.   335
  O God! Horatio, what a wounded name,
  Things standing thus unknown, shall live behind
    me!
  If thou didst ever hold me in thy heart,

---

[177] *union*: pearl, also the marriage with Gertrude.
[178] *temper'd*: treated or mixed.
[179] *mutes*: performers without speaking parts.
[180] *sergeant*: court officer with powers of arrest.
[181] *strict*: just or inescapable.
[182] *unsatisfied*: uninformed.
[183] *antique Roman*: reference to old Roman fashion of suicide.

Absent thee from felicity[184] awhile,
And in this harsh world draw thy breath in pain,   *340*
To tell my story.

                [*March afar off, and shot within.*]

What warlike noise is this?

Osric. Young Fortinbras, with conquest come from
     Poland,
To th' ambassadors of England gives
This warlike volley.

Hamlet.   O, I die, Horatio!
The potent poison quite o'er-crows[185] my spirit.   *345*
I cannot live to hear the news from England,
But I do prophesy th' election[186] lights
On Fortinbras; he has my dying voice.[187]
So tell him, with th' occurrents,[188] more and less,
Which have solicited[189]—the rest is silence.   *350*

                                   [*Dies.*]

Horatio. Now cracks a noble heart. Good night, sweet
     prince,
And flights of angels sing thee to thy rest!

                          [*March within.*]

Why does the drum come hither?

*Enter Fortinbras and English Ambassadors, with drum,
     colours, and Attendants.*

Fortinbras. Where is this sight?

---

[184] *felicity:* i.e., the felicity of death.
[185] *o'er-crows:* overpowers (as a triumphant cock crows over its weak opponent).
[186] *election:* i.e., to the throne.
[187] *voice:* vote.
[188] *occurrents:* occurrences.
[189] *solicited:* incited.

Horatio.   What is it you would see?
    If aught of woe or wonder, cease your search.   355

Fortinbras. This quarry[190] cries on havoc.[191] O proud
        death,
    What feast is toward[192] in thine eternal cell
    That thou so many princes at a shot
    So bloodily hast struck?

1 Ambassador.   The sight is dismal;
    And our affairs from England come too late: 360
    The ears are senseless that should give us hearing
    To tell him his[193] commandment is fulfill'd,
    That Rosencrantz and Guildenstern are dead.
    Where should we have our thanks?

Horatio.   Not from his mouth,
    Had it th' ability of life to thank you: 365
    He never gave commandment for their death.
    But since, so jump[194] upon this bloody question,
    You from the Polack wars, and you from England,
    Are here arrived, give order that these bodies
    High on a stage[195] be placed to the view;   370
    And let me speak to th' yet unknowing world
    How these things came about. So shall you hear
    Of carnal, bloody, and unnatural acts;
    Of accidental judgments, casual[196] slaughters;
    Of deaths put on by cunning and forc'd cause;   375
    And, in this upshot, purposes mistook
    Fall'n on th' inventors' heads—all this can I
    Truly deliver.

---

[190] *quarry*: pile of corpses.
[191] *cries on havoc*: proclaims indiscriminate killing.
[192] *toward*: forthcoming.
[193] *his*: i.e., Claudius'.
[194] *jump*: precisely.
[195] *stage*: platform.
[196] *casual*: not humanly planned, inscrutable to human eyes.

Fortinbras. Let us haste to hear it,
    And call the noblest to the audience.
    For me, with sorrow I embrace my fortune;   380
    I have some rights of memory[197] in this kingdom,
    Which now to claim my vantage doth invite me.

Horatio. Of that I shall have also cause to speak,
    And from his mouth whose voice will draw on[198]
      more.
    But let this same be presently perform'd,   385
    Even while men's minds are wild, lest more
      mischance
    On plots and errors happen.

Fortinbras.   Let four captains
    Bear Hamlet like a soldier to the stage;
    For he was likely, had he been put on,[199]
    To have prov'd most royal; and for his passage[200]   390
    The soldier's music and the rite of war
    Speak loudly for him.
    Take up the bodies. Such a sight as this
    Becomes the field,[201] but here shows much amiss.
    Go, bid the soldiers shoot.   395

        [*Exeunt marching. A peal of ordnance shot off.*]

---

[197] *rights of memory*: unforgotten, remembered claims.
[198] *draw on*: influence.
[199] *put on*: to the throne.
[200] *passage*: death.
[201] *field*: field of battle.

Contemporary Essays

Reading *Hamlet*

Crystal Downing
Messiah College

Laurence Olivier begins his 1948 film adaptation of *Hamlet* with a voice-over stating, "This is the tragedy of a man who could not make up his mind." Such a reading of the play, even when more elegantly articulated, has almost become a cliché. After all, Hamlet seems unable to take action, even when goaded to revenge by his murdered father's ghost. He hesitates to kill not only Claudius, his father's murderer, but also himself, as signaled by one of the most well-known lines in the history of English literature: "To be, or not to be—that is the question" (3.1.56). This line, however, is often misread, reflecting a misreading of the play itself. And perhaps that is appropriate, for *Hamlet*, I will argue, is a play about reading and misreading, about the difficulties of interpretation.

When people pronounce Hamlet's famous line, they usually emphasize the "that", as though Hamlet cannot "make up his mind" about killing himself: "To be, or not to be— *that* is the question." Though the soliloquy from Act 3, scene 1, does indeed proceed to discuss the consequences of suicide, there is something far more subtle going on than "shall I, or shan't I?" Significantly, Shakespeare's iambic pentameter line accents five words, but never "that": To BE, or NOT to BE—that IS the QUESTION. What we see here is an emphasis on the verb of being; even the word "not" serves to modify the "to be" verb. Hamlet's soliloquy, as written by Shakespeare in his preferred blank verse format, renders not merely a mental battle over suicide; it expresses a desire to interpret the meaning of existence itself, what it means "to be". A failure to discover that meaning, then, elicits Hamlet's thoughts about suicide.

Hamlet's quest for understanding seems to begin when his mother weds Claudius. Queen Gertrude has married her husband's brother so soon after the king's death that "[t]he funeral bak'd-meats/Did coldly furnish forth the marriage tables" (1.2.180–81).[1] With a pun on "coldly", Hamlet implies that only a *cold* person could marry with so much haste that the leftovers from the wake might serve as *cold* cuts for the wedding. More importantly, Hamlet seems to question what this haste indicates about the nature of love—that upon which human existence depends. What did his father's "being" mean to his mother if she could so swiftly strip off her mourning clothes to jump into bed with her brother-in-law? Doesn't her "o'erhasty marriage" (2.2.57) insult her first husband's very essence? Wouldn't such indulging of animal "appetite" (1.2.144) call into question "[h]ow noble in reason! how infinite in faculties" any human might be? (2.2.304). What does it mean "to be" human?

Significantly, the first time in the play that Hamlet speaks to another character, he uses the "to be" verb. When Claudius asks him, "How is it that the clouds still hang on you?" Hamlet replies, "Not so, my lord; *I am* too much in the sun" (emphasis added; 1.2.66–67). Hamlet's "to be" verb distinguishes who he "is" from the newly married Claudius and Gertrude. Here he plays with words, as he did with his verb-less first statement in the play two lines earlier—"A little more than kin, and less than kind" (1.2.65)—which is an "aside": an Elizabethan convention for mental rather than spoken thoughts. Just as the word "kin", made up of three letters, is "a little less than" the word "kind" with its extra letter *d*, so Claudius, who has just addressed Hamlet as "kin" by calling him "son", is "a little less than kind" for marrying his sister-in-law: not an action his "kind" of person should take. Therefore, when Hamlet speaks aloud two lines later, he puns on the word with which Claudius addresses him: "son". By saying he is "too much

---

[1] All quotations from *Hamlet* are from the edition published by Ignatius Press: *Hamlet, Prince of Denmark*, ed. Joseph Pearce (San Francisco: Ignatius, 2008).

in the sun", Hamlet implies he does not appreciate being identified as his uncle's "son".[2]

Hamlet's first two lines in the play, then, are about his identity, the authenticity of his "being", a point reiterated in the
primary verb of his next two statements. When his mother,
Gertrude, crassly tells him that "all that lives must die", Hamlet replies, "Ay, madam, it *is* common" (emphasis added). And
then when she replies with "If it *be*,/Why seems it so particular with thee?" he finally lashes out: "Seems, madam! Nay, *it
is*; I know not seems" (emphasis added; 1.2.72–75). Just as Hamlet struggles to interpret Gertrude's marriage, so she struggles
to interpret his continued mourning; and we struggle to interpret Hamlet's puns and repetitions. From Hamlet's very first
appearance on stage, he is embedded in an interpretive ambiguity that is related to the significance of being.

Shakespeare signals that his play is about interpretation from
the very start. *Hamlet* begins with two sentinels unable to interpret each other's identity. Bernardo, on duty guarding the Elsinore castle, opens the play pronouncing, "Who's there?"
Rather than answering, Francisco, approaching to take over
Bernardo's watch, throws the question back at him: "Nay,
answer me. Stand and unfold yourself" (1.1.1–2). These
lines anticipate Hamlet's dilemma at Elsinore. Not only is
the "to be" verb implied by the play's opening contraction
as Bernardo questions the identity of Francisco, but the latter's request to "unfold yourself" looks forward to Hamlet seeking to unfold the purposes of the Ghost—even as Claudius
seeks to unfold the purposes of Hamlet. Echoing Bernardo and
Francisco, the play repeatedly shows Hamlet trying to read others just as they try to read him.

Reading, in fact, becomes an explicit motif in the play. When
the Ghost tells Hamlet to "[r]evenge his foul and most unnatural

[2] Marjorie Garber notes that Shakespeare's seventeenth-century audiences
would have been as disturbed by the "incest" between Claudius and Gertrude as
twentieth-century audiences have been by the Freudian relationship between
Hamlet and his mother. See *Shakespeare After All* (New York: Pantheon, 2004),
p. 482.

murder" (1.5.25), the son proclaims that he will turn his brain into a text that will be his sole reading matter:

> I'll wipe away all trivial fond records,
> All saws of books, all forms, all pressures past,
> That youth and observation copied there,
> And thy commandment all alone shall live
> Within the book and volume of my brain.
>
> (1.5.99–103)

As with many books, however, the volume of Hamlet's brain must be interpreted; ay, there's the rub. For how does one reach certitude about one's reading? Though confident of his first reading of the Ghost's words, Hamlet later comes to wonder about the legitimacy of his interpretation:

> The spirit that I have seen
> May be a devil; and the devil hath power
> T' assume a pleasing shape; yea, and perhaps
> Out of my weakness and my melancholy,
> As he is very potent with such spirits,
> Abuses me to damn me.
>
> (2.2.594–99)

Interpretation, Hamlet implies, is problematic for two reasons: the reliability of the speaker/writer, and the reliability of the listener/reader. In Hamlet's case, the one authoring the book and volume of his brain may be a duplicitous devil in disguise, and he as reader may be biased due to weakness of understanding or to melancholy over his mother's marriage.

Hamlet is not the only perplexed reader in the play. Claudius, Gertrude, and their officious adviser, Polonius, are all trying to read *him*. For not only is Hamlet depressed and angry about his mother's marriage, but he has "put an antic disposition on" (1.5.172), presumably to disguise his knowledge of the murder. Significantly, Polonius' first attempt to interpret Hamlet's strange behavior occurs as the latter is reading. When Polonius asks, "What do you read, my lord?" Hamlet answers, "Words, words, words", as though in recognition that the meaning behind words is not always self-evident. This point is illustrated by Polonius' next question: "What is the matter, my lord?" Hamlet responds with one way to interpret Polonius' statement, saying, "Between who?" which causes Polonius to clarify his intended meaning: "I mean, the matter that you read, my lord" (2.2.191–95). The inherent ambiguity of the phrase "What is the matter?" reflects the ambivalence Hamlet feels about the Ghost's words, words, words.

Hamlet decides he needs another text to confirm the book and volume of his brain, and so he writes one himself: a script for traveling players visiting the castle at Elsinore. Because "guilty creatures, sitting at a play / Have by the very cunning of the scene / Been struck so to the soul that presently / They have proclaim'd their malefactions", he will devise a play that reprises the scenario reported by the Ghost (2.2.585–88). In other words, he will set up a scenario by which he can read Claudius.

Just as Hamlet devises a play by which he might interpret Claudius, Polonius develops a less formal play in order to interpret Hamlet. Like a stage director, the pompous adviser choreographs his daughter's movements, saying, "Ophelia, walk you here", and, significantly, "Read on this book" (3.1.43–44). As Hamlet enters the scene, Polonius watches with Claudius from the wings, where they witness strange acting. However, even though all three "readers" of Hamlet hear him speak the exact same lines, they interpret his words, words, words differently. While Polonius reads Hamlet as sick from "neglected love", Ophelia reads him as mentally unstable: "O, what a noble mind is here o'er-thrown!" Claudius, however, rejects both these interpretations: "Love! His affections do not that way tend, / Nor what he spake, though it lack'd form a little, / Was not like madness" (3.1.178, 150, 162–63). If people hearing the exact same words at the exact same time cannot agree on an interpretation, how can we expect Hamlet to be confident about words from a ghost? Indeed, while directing Ophelia to put on an act of reading, Polonius acknowledges how often "with devotion's visage / And pious action we do sugar o'er / The devil himself" (3.1.46–48). No wonder

Hamlet worries that the ghost may be a devil sugared over with his father's image!

Confirmation of the Ghost's words arrives with Claudius' distressed reaction to Hamlet's scripted play. When the new king jumps up and calls for "lights" after watching *The Murder of Gonzago*, Hamlet tells Horatio, "I'll take the ghost's word for a thousand pound" (3.2.280–81). His newfound interpretive confidence enables him, then, to take revenge soon after. When he believes he detects Claudius hiding behind an arras in his mother's chamber, Hamlet immediately stabs him. The victim, of course, turns out to be Polonius, to whom Hamlet admits his misinterpretation: "I took thee for thy better" (3.4.32). Ironically, immediately before he discovers his error, Hamlet confidently justifies the stabbing with information given him by the ghost: "A bloody deed!—almost as bad, good mother,/As kill a king and marry with his brother" (3.4.28–29). However, after he discovers his interpretive mishap, Hamlet does not mention the murder of his father for the rest of the two-hundred-line scene, only once calling Claudius "[a] murderer and a villain" (3.4.96). Instead, he embellishes for his mother views he already held before he met the ghost: about the superiority of his father to Claudius and his disgust with Gertrude's "incestuous" marriage. He even uses the same metaphor to describe his father that he employed in his first, pre-ghost, soliloquy: "Hyperion" (1.2.140; 3.4.56). As Hamlet now verbalizes to Gertrude his earlier thoughts, he asks her, "What devil was't/That thus hath cozen'd you at hoodman-blind?" (3.4.76–77). Hoodman-blind, known today as blindman's bluff, is an apt metaphor for the inability to see the substance underneath the words, words, words one hears—just as Hamlet was unable to see the substance of Polonius underneath the arras. Furthermore, by calling Claudius a "devil", Hamlet seems to signal his own ambivalence about the ghost, who might be a devil hiding under an arras of words in order to cozen him. Not coincidentally, the ghost appears seventy lines after the discovery of Polonius' corpse, apparently to draw Hamlet back to his interpretive confidence.

Ironically, the appearance of the Ghost in Gertrude's chamber generates another interpretive ambiguity—not only for
Hamlet and his mother but also for us. Because Gertrude does
not see the Ghost, even when Hamlet talks to it, we have to
wonder whether it is really there. After all, the first time Hamlet encounters the Ghost, his companions, Horatio and Marcellus, see it as well, as did Francisco and Bernardo before them.
So why cannot Gertrude see it? Does the Ghost have power
to reveal himself to whomever he wills? Does Gertrude's marriage blind her to her former husband's presence? Has Hamlet
become genuinely "mad", as she asserts? Or is Hamlet merely
projecting his own desire for direction, the ghost a "coinage of
[his] brain" that might spur him to action (3.4.105, 137)? Like
Gertrude reading Hamlet, readers of *Hamlet* do not know, which
elicits various interpretations. Some directors put a ghost on
stage; others do not. All we have are the play's words, words,
words.

It is as though Shakespeare wants his audience to experience the interpretive ambiguity that stultifies Hamlet. Of
course, unlike Hamlet, we hear Claudius confess his sin:
"O, my offense is rank, it smells to heaven;/It hath the primal eldest curse upon't—/A brother's murder" (3.3.36–38).
Our ambivalence must come from elsewhere. Thus, in addition to the Ghost's questionable appearance, Shakespeare makes
us question Gertrude's actions in her chamber. After Hamlet
abjures her to refrain from his "uncle's bed", he exhorts her
to trust him, explaining, "I essentially am not in madness,/
But mad in craft." She seems to believe him, stating, "Be
thou assur'd, if words be made of breath/And breath of
life, I have no life to breathe/What thou hast said to me"
(3.4.159, 187, 197–99). Words are indeed "made of breath",
but can we trust she who breathes them? This, of course, is
Hamlet's question about the words of his father, who, as a
ghost, literally has "no life to breathe". Furthermore, just as
Hamlet has reason to suspect the Ghost, we have reason to
suspect Gertrude. For, in the very next scene, we see Gertrude telling Claudius that her son is "[m]ad as the sea and

wind" (4.1.7). How do we interpret her duplicity? Is she putting on an act for Hamlet or for Claudius? Or is she merely saying what each wants to hear? Words, words, words can be unreliable.

Meanwhile, having been thrown back into interpretive ambiguity, Hamlet finally uses it to his benefit. Claudius puts Hamlet on a ship bound for England, along with Rosencrantz and Guildenstern, who bear an official letter calling for Hamlet's beheading. While the two fickle friends are sleeping, however, Hamlet exchanges their letter for one he has written and sealed with the stamp of Denmark, ordering *their* execution (5.2.29–56). Words, even when they bear signs of the king, can be easily manipulated to create new meanings. And manipulated words, as the death of Rosencrantz and Guildenstern illustrates, can have deadly consequences.

Words can manipulate even after death, as Shakespeare implies in the first scene of Act 5. Two gravediggers discuss Ophelia, who drowned not long after Hamlet killed her father. One of the diggers gives two readings of what happens when someone drowns: "If the man go to this water and drown himself, it is, will he, nill he, he goes—mark you that; but if the water come to him and drown him, he drowns not himself. Argal, he that is not guilty of his own death shortens not his own life." Hence, only if the water came to Ophelia, proving she was innocent of the unforgivable sin of suicide, would she be allowed a Christian burial. Nonetheless, the coroner holds to that far-fetched interpretation, for he "finds it Christian burial". The second digger suggests the probable motivation behind the coroner's interpretation: "If this had not been a gentlewoman, she should have been buried out[side] a Christian burial" (5.1.16–20, 5, 23–25). The rich, in other words, often have words, words, words bent to their own self-interest.

Hamlet makes his reappearance at Elsinore in this graveyard, where he adds another level to readings of death. The diggers have unearthed a skull, and the prince tries to read its origin: "This might be the pate of a politician, . . . [o]r of a courtier; . . . There's another. Why may not that be the skull of a lawyer?" He then elicits even more interpretive ambiguity when, upon asking, "Whose grave's this, sirrah?" the digger responds, "Mine, sir"—merely because he is digging it (5.1.78, 82, 93–94, 114–15). As they continue to banter back and forth, the digger gives answers to Hamlet that seem false on the surface but are true when given the right reading. Words, like skulls, must be fleshed out to have meaning.

So what is the point? Why does Shakespeare so insistently call attention to verbal manipulations and interpretive ambiguity? The most obvious answer is that Shakespeare presents the dilemma facing any highly reflective person: How can one kill another human, destroying that person's very existence, his right "to be", unless one has certitude about the truth of his guilt? Of course, selfish, unthinking people take lives all the time—like Claudius, for example. But Shakespeare's Hamlet is neither selfish nor unthinking—as his long soliloquies imply.

A clue to Hamlet's sensibilities—and perhaps to Shakespeare's—is the university Hamlet attends: Wittenberg. Shakespeare repeats the name Wittenberg four times during the scene in which he introduces Hamlet to us. Claudius tells Hamlet not to return to Wittenberg, and Gertrude makes the same request six lines later. After they leave the stage, allowing Hamlet his first soliloquy, Horatio enters, and Hamlet asks him twice within four lines why he has left Wittenberg (1.2.113, 119, 165, 168). This insistent repetition—four times in fifty-five lines—draws attention to the name, as though signaling its historical significance: Wittenberg, in Germany, is usually associated with the origins of the Protestant Reformation. In 1517, Martin Luther, who taught at Wittenberg University, nailed to the door of the castle church ninety-five theses protesting the abuse of indulgences: a practice by which people could abbreviate, either for themselves or relatives, the temporal punishments of Purgatory. Though Luther had no intention of separating from the Church of Rome, his protest, based on commitment to salvation by grace alone, guided by the Bible alone, instigated a controversial new movement in Church history.

England became Protestant through King Henry VIII. Although denouncing Luther in a treatise that earned him the title "Defender of the Faith" in 1521, by 1529 Henry had summoned a "Reformation Parliament". His motivation, however, was quite different from Luther's. While the latter desired to uphold Mother Church, Henry primarily desired to uphold his genetic line by making a mother out of a woman other than his spouse. Because Catherine of Aragon, his devout Spanish wife, did not produce a male heir, Henry planned to divorce her so that he could marry his young mistress, Anne Boleyn. Employing interpretations of Leviticus garnered from Hebrew scholars, Henry tried convincing Church authorities that, since Catherine had been married to his older brother, he had committed incest by marrying a brother's widow. (Sound familiar?)[3] Because the pope had granted a dispensation for Henry to marry Catherine in the first place, the Church wasn't about to renege on her decision. Henry therefore ordered the archbishop of Canterbury to sanction his divorce, marrying Anne in 1533 (after she was already pregnant) and the next year declaring himself Supreme Head of the Church of England.

Ironically, Anne gave birth to a daughter rather than a son. Nevertheless, that child became one of England's most effective monarchs: Queen Elizabeth ruled from 1558 to 1603—during most of Shakespeare's lifetime (1564–1616). Shakespeare, then, whose troupe was sponsored by Elizabeth's lord chamberlain, certainly realized that political upheaval before and during Elizabeth's reign often stemmed from antagonisms between Roman Catholics and Protestants. Furthermore, he would have seen how interpretive ambiguity inculcated tensions between Roman Catholic and Protestant Christianity. Similar to Hamlet struggling to interpret the authority of the ghost, Shakespeare's contemporaries struggled to interpret the authority of the Church. Did the Church's authority lie in the pope? In the monarch? Or, as Luther, Calvin, and English Puritans averred, in Holy Scripture?

[3] See Garber, *Shakespeare*, p. 481.

The Bible itself was a focus of great controversy during the sixteenth century. Not long before Henry broke with Rome, William Tyndale was persecuted for translating the New Testament from Latin into English. It was reasoned, with certain legitimacy, that if anyone could read the Bible in his own tongue, problematic misreadings—if not self-serving manipulations—could lead people astray. Without an educated Church hierarchy to guide and authorize biblical interpretations, words, words, words could easily be quoted out of context to reinforce individual readers' prejudices. An English-language Bible would inevitably lead to interpretive ambiguity.

To address this problem, the Geneva Bible, published by Protestants in 1560, included interpretive glosses set into the margins of the biblical text. Even though it was the most popular English translation during Elizabethan times, serving as the source of biblical quotations in Shakespeare's plays, the Church of England repudiated it *because* of the glosses. As Alister McGrath notes,

> [T]he Geneva Bible's annotations in effect offered an interpretation of certain biblical passages that contradicted those found in the *Books of Homilies*—in effect, a collection of "authorized sermons" . . . which were intended to be read aloud in churches.[4]

The Church of England questioned the Genevan interpretation of the Holy Ghost that inspired Scripture. There are different ways, in other words, to read the Ghost.

The same could be said of *Hamlet*'s ghosts: the texts that lived before Shakespeare's play. Hamlet is based upon a character from Norse legend—Amlothi—that became part of Danish history in 1200. In 1576, the Hamlet story appeared in a French collection of tragic histories, followed by an anonymous English play of around 1589. Scholars believe that Shakespeare rewrote this play, which they call the *Ur-Hamlet*, in 1600 or 1601.

---

[4] Alister E. McGrath, *In the Beginning: The Story of the King James Bible and How It Changed a Nation, a Language, and a Culture* (New York: Doubleday, 2001), p. 125.

Though he did not invent the Hamlet story, Shakespeare nevertheless made significant changes to it. In the earlier stories, not only is there no ghost—at least not until the *Ur-Hamlet*—but "it is generally known [among the people] that Claudius killed Hamlet's father"—thus eliminating any interpretive ambiguity for Hamlet.[5] And in the 1576 French version, Gertrude quite clearly takes Hamlet's side after he confronts her in her chamber—thus eliminating any interpretive ambiguity for us. Therefore, though it is common knowledge that Shakespeare invented Hamlet's delay, it is my suggestion that Hamlet's hesitation reflects Shakespeare's own: a hesitation about Protestant emphasis on *sola scriptura*. If the Bible is our final authority, whose interpretation of the Bible do we follow? Without a clear source of interpretive authority, how can we be sure of proper action?

As Stephen Greenblatt illustrates in his 2004 biography, Shakespeare may have been raised with Roman Catholic leanings.[6] This would certainly explain why, in the most explicitly Christian of all his plays, Shakespeare foregrounds the problem with interpretation. It also intensifies the profundity of the play's last act—pun fully intended. For in the last act of *Hamlet*, Hamlet makes his last act. The pun, of course, is my own, for Shakespeare did not divide his plays into acts, a demarcation added by later publishers. But he did divide his plays into separate scenes, and in the last scene of *Hamlet*, Shakespeare ties the resolution of Hamlet (and of *Hamlet*) to Christian faith—a faith that transcends interpretive ambiguity.

The closing scene begins with a conversation between Hamlet and Horatio. Getting ready to recount how he discovered a commission for his beheading among papers held by

[5] Frank Kermode, introduction to *Hamlet, Prince of Denmark*, in *The Riverside Shakespeare*, ed. G. Blakemore Evans, et al. (Boston: Houghton Mifflin, 1974), p. 1137. My summary of the Hamlet story history is based on Kermode's overview. See pp. 1136–37.

[6] Stephen Greenblatt, *Will in the World: How Shakespeare Became Shakespeare* (New York: Norton, 2004), pp. 89–117. See also Stephen Greenblatt, *Hamlet in Purgatory* (Princeton: Princeton University Press, 2001).

Rosencrantz and Guildenstern, Hamlet says, "Sir, in my heart there was a kind of fighting/That would not let me sleep" (5.2.4–5). Though he is describing his experience on board ship, the word "sleep" reminds us of his famous mental battle, another "kind of fighting", demonstrated in his "To be, or not to be" soliloquy:

> To die, to sleep—
> No more; and by a sleep to say we end
> The heart-ache and the thousand natural shocks
> That flesh is heir to. 'Tis a consummation
> Devoutly to be wish'd. To die, to sleep;
> To sleep, perchance to dream. Ay, there's the rub;
> For in that sleep of death what dreams may come,
> When we have shuffled off this mortal coil,
> Must give us pause.
>
> (3.1.60–68)

Due to these different interpretations of death's end, Hamlet "lose[s] the name of action" (line 88). However, by the last scene of the play, Hamlet can conclude his speech about troubled sleep with reference to One who transcends all interpretive ambiguity: "There's a divinity that shapes our ends,/ Rough-hew them how we will" (5.2.10–11). While earlier in the play, the "pause" is all, now a faith-filled "readiness" is all, as Hamlet explains to Horatio: "[T]here is special providence in the fall of a sparrow. If it be now, 'tis not to come; if it be not to come, it will be now; if it be not now, yet it will come— the readiness is all. Since no man owes of aught he leaves, what is't to leave betimes? Let be" (5.2.211–16). Notice the number of "to be" verbs in this speech: nine times in little more than four lines. Hamlet's experience has come full circle: a quest to understand what it means "to be" ends in confidence that significant "being" does not depend on complete understanding.

Hamlet, perhaps like Shakespeare, does not know whether he can trust what has come out of Wittenberg: after all, Horatio, from Wittenberg, is completely dependable, whereas other school fellows, Rosencrantz and Guildenstern, mislead him. By the end of the play, however, Hamlet trusts a providential divinity that transcends distinctions between Roman Catholic and Protestant interpretations of truth. Once he trusts this Being who transcends all "being", Hamlet attains certitude: during his duel with Laertes, it becomes quite clear—thanks to Laertes' confession—that Claudius, by attempting to poison his nephew, has caused the deaths of Gertrude and Laertes. Hamlet can therefore take immediate action to revenge, if not his father's murder, his mother's, Laertes', and his own—with a cloud of witnesses to legitimize his action.

Hamlet comes to recognize that, even though we make bad choices, rough-hewing our lives with problematic actions due to interpretive ambiguity, we can rest in the knowledge that God is in control. Hamlet's last words in the play imply as much: "[T]he rest is silence." His questing and questioning are over; he can *rest* in the ensuing silence. And even though death—the end of *the rest* of his life—causes his silence, Hamlet can rest in that rest. Horatio puts it best: "Good night, sweet prince,/And flights of angels sing thee to thy rest!" (5.2.351–53).

To Play or Not to Play:
How to Lie or Tell the Truth in Hamlet's Denmark

Anthony Esolen
Providence College

Claudius, that "king of shreds and patches" (3.4.103),[1] a clever rhetorician who understands that one who would be a king had better be adept at *playing* the king before the audience of his court and nation, has been eyeing his nephew and now stepson, Hamlet. He is suspicious of the young man's purported madness and has suborned the friends of Hamlet's youth to serve as spies, to discover what only he and perhaps his queen Gertrude must fear: that Hamlet knows of the murder of the old king his father. But at the same time, Hamlet himself has been eyeing the King, circling about him, and putting on an "antic disposition" (1.5.172) to mislead his pursuers.

Finally, Hamlet hits upon the trap he needs: he will discover the player king by means of a player king, and a player queen, and a play murder. He who lives by the stage will die by the stage, hoist with his own ropes. What interrogation and direct accusation could never have done, the indirection of art accomplishes in a moment. For at an apparently innocent entertainment staged to please the troubled Hamlet (a murder melodrama aptly called *The Mousetrap*), with all the court watching the prince, and with Hamlet and his friend Horatio watching the unwitting king, Claudius witnesses a reprise of his own crime. His conscience is seized. Before he can regain *his* stage presence, he interrupts the proceedings, calling for the last thing a murderer should desire: "Give me some light. Away!" (3.2.263).

The King's shock comes not simply from Hamlet's having found him out. He is shocked also to have found *himself* out;

[1] All quotations from *Hamlet* are from this edition published by Ignatius Press: *Hamlet, Prince of Denmark*, ed. Joseph Pearce (San Francisco: Ignatius, 2008).

for art enlists our sympathies before reason can sort through them or, more precisely, before the words we use to deceive ourselves can marshal their mendacious evidence. That appears by what the King does immediately after he bolts from the crowd. The man is no fool, nor is he plagued by indecision. He dispatches his spies, Rosencrantz and Guildenstern, to smuggle Hamlet off to England; then he consents that his foolish counselor Polonius should stow himself in the Queen's chambers to eavesdrop upon her conversation with Hamlet—the Queen intends it to be an angry rebuke, but that overmatched actress is in for an unpleasant surprise. Yet once his audience is away and he remains alone on stage, Claudius can no longer sustain the pretense. For a few brief moments, the play is suspended—I mean the play of corrupted Denmark, directed by the King. Suspended is the merciless need to keep up appearances, to praise the capable servant, to indulge the fool, to deceive the gullible, to weep the natural tears for a brother suddenly deceased, to win the acclaim of a restive people, to outface the young upstart Fortinbras of Norway, to carouse with no joy in the heart, even to pretend to a sister-wife that all has been done with due decorum and holiness yet suspecting that she too must know or guess the truth and that she too has a difficult role to play. All of this in the rotten state of Denmark is for a few moments banished to the wings as, unutterably alone, the King drops his mask and appears to us as a man, a wretched man attempting to pray:

> O, my offense is rank, it smells to heaven;
> It hath the primal eldest curse upon't—
> A brother's murder!
>
>   (3.3.36–38)

In this mazelike court, it is refreshing to hear a statement so direct. We have long suspected the King; but only briefly, by a near-confession of his guilt, has he engaged our sympathy. Polonius has devised a mousetrap to catch Hamlet, setting his daughter Ophelia in the prince's way to see if she can elicit some proof that his madness has sprung from disappointed love. Meanwhile, he and the king are to watch, unseen—an audience for one of the several plays within this play. As one last directorial touch, Polonius hands Ophelia a stage property. It is evidently a prayer book: the design is that Hamlet should happen upon her while she appears immersed in holy contemplation. Now, the old meddlesome Polonius is a poor director, a worse actor, and a rhetorical trader in platitudes as flat as the plains of Kansas, and Hamlet will, as I interpret the scene that follows, spy the spies and act advisedly. But before he sends Ophelia out on stage, Polonius comments shrewdly to the King upon the political or rhetorical use of prayer. He seems uneasy in his conscience, as it occurs to him that man will turn even devotion into a mask and make the Almighty his prop:

> We are oft to blame in this:
> 'Tis too much prov'd, that with devotion's visage
> And pious action we do sugar o'er
> The devil himself.
>
> (3.1.46–49)

It is an artless comment, a providential stroke ad libitum, not in the spies' script. And for that very reason, the King is struck to the quick. Says he, aside:

> O, 'tis too true!
> How smart a lash that speech doth give my conscience!
> The harlot's cheek, beautied with plast'ring art,
> Is not more ugly to the thing that helps it
> Than is my deed to my most painted word.
> O heavy burden!
>
> (3.1.49–54)

That is all we have heard from Claudius, but it is enough to show that he suffers the oppression of a dreadful sin, whose exact nature we learn only now, after *The Mousetrap*. Ophelia was only pretending to be alone, pretending to pray; but now the King, believing himself alone, actually does struggle to pray.

He wants desperately *not to be acting*; he knows he must not simply appear to be a man at prayer, as he will appear in a moment to Hamlet, who enters the stage unseen and who declines to slay the King while he is "in the purging of his soul" (3.3.85–86). But Hamlet has it wrong; there is no purging for Claudius. The King himself, with terrible clarity, admits as much:

> Pray can I not,
> Though inclination be as sharp as will.
> My stronger guilt defeats my strong intent,
> And, like a man to double business bound,
> I stand in pause where I shall first begin,
> And both neglect.
>
> (3.3.38–43)

Claudius here confronts an ineluctable reality. It is not show, or custom, or the "words, words, words" that the justly suspicious Hamlet pretends to read when accosted by Polonius (2.2.192). It is not the airy shapes conjured by man's vanity, or the "yesty [yeasty] collection" of fashionable phrases current at court for such waterflies as Osric (5.2.194). Those insubstantialities shift like the clouds. To trust them, or even to *play* at trusting them, is to enter a life of appearances rather than of simple honesty:

Hamlet. Do you see yonder cloud that's almost in shape of a camel?

Polonius. By th' mass, and 'tis like a camel indeed.

Hamlet. Methinks it is like a weasel.

Polonius. It is back'd like a weasel.

Hamlet. Or like a whale?

Polonius. Very like a whale.

> (3.2.366–72)

But that life produces half-men, men of show, who must assume a virtue though they have it not. Having attenuated their beings, caught in the habit of living by words alone, they cannot muster the courage for a genuine turn of the soul. This actor's disease afflicts everyone among the Danish aristocrats, though only Hamlet is consistently aware of it. We may say that in struggling to pray, the King struggles to shrug off the dead weight of self-deception. A false skin clings to his unhappy soul; if he is to repent, he must suffer his birth into a fully human life. Reason alone will not suffice, not even the reason of sound theology:

> What if this cursed hand
> Were thicker than itself with brother's blood,
> Is there not rain enough in the sweet heavens
> To wash it white as snow? Whereto serves mercy
> But to confront the visage of offence?
> And what's in prayer but this twofold force,
> To be forestalled ere we come to fall,
> Or pardon'd being down?
>
> (3.3.43–50)

That is because reality will not allow it. For the guilty man wants to play the innocent and retain the profit:

> My fault is past. But, O, what form of prayer
> Can serve my turn? "Forgive me my foul murder"!
> That cannot be; since I am still possess'd
> Of those effects for which I did the murder—
> My crown, mine own ambition, and my queen.
> May one be pardon'd and retain th' offence?
>
> (3.3.51–56)

Finding an Honest Man

It is a commonplace among postmodern critics that disjointed Denmark under Claudius defines the human condition. One need not be a murderer playing an honest man to be caught in the toils of words. For words, we are told, are necessarily slippery, as are perceptions: "[T]here is nothing either good or bad," says Hamlet when his friends Rosencrantz

and Guildenstern remark that Denmark seems a perfectly fine
place to live, "but thinking makes it so" (2.2.249). But Shakespeare is careful to set in place for us a Denmark as it once
was or might be, near the court but not within it
nor caught in its verbal trickery. In this world, men acknowledge their duties by deed and not simply by words. When
they do speak, they search for the truth in meditation and,
most strikingly, in probing conversation. I am speaking of the
world that frames the play: that of the soldiers.

These men have parts to play too and play them well, but
they are more than actors. Their language is manly and direct.
They express what they feel when it is fit to do so, yet they do
not entangle themselves in their rhetoric. Even their silences
speak:

> *Bernardo.* 'Tis now struck twelve; get thee to bed, Francisco.

> *Francisco.* For this relief much thanks. 'Tis bitter cold,
>   And I am sick at heart.

>   (1.1.7–9)

The Ghost has appeared to them twice already, but they check
their suppositions, calling upon Horatio to help them determine what to do. "Thou art a scholar; speak to it, Horatio",
says Marcellus in understandable trepidation, urging him to
speak to the Ghost when it appears again (1.1.42). Yet though
they are plain men, they are neither foolish nor tongue-tied.
They too ply the art of persuasion, and when they are moved,
they speak with a delicate feeling and an eloquence that should
shame everyone else in the play—even Hamlet, who, though
he utters lines of astonishing honesty and frank appraisal of
man's wretchedness, is not free of the verbal disease, cursing
himself for having to "unpack [his] heart with words" (2.2.581).
For example, when Bernardo begins to tell Horatio how and
when the ghost first appeared, his description of the heavens
is both carefully factual and elegant:

> *Bernardo.* Last night of all,
>   When yond same star that's westward from the pole

Had made his course t' illume that part of heaven
Where now it burns, Marcellus and myself,
The bell then beating one—

   Enter Ghost.

          (1.1.37–39)

So too Horatio's address to the Ghost, whom with wise circumspection he calls a usurper of the night and of the "warlike form ... of buried Denmark" (1.1.48); so the men's
discussion of their heightened watch, an apparent preparation
for war that, as the amiable Marcellus puts it, "[d]oes not divide
the Sunday from the week" and "[d]oth make the night joint-
labourer with the day" (1.1.76, 78). But we hear their noblest
eloquence after the Ghost has appeared again, and again has
refused to speak to them. They draw their pikes to strike at it,
but it vanishes. Marcellus' comment is self-reflective and honest:

  We do it wrong, being so majestical,
  To offer it the show of violence,
  For it is as the air, invulnerable,
  And our vain blows malicious mockery.
       (1.1.143–46)

Whereupon Bernardo utters one laconic line of observation:

  It was about to speak when the cock crew.
       (1.1.147)

Horatio picks up the line and the hint:

  And then it started, like a guilty thing
  Upon a fearful summons.
       (1.1.148–49)

The lines unwittingly foreshadow the King's discomfiture at
The Mousetrap; but the crowing of the cock, in whom God
has planted foreknowledge, suggests also the trump of doom
on that last day when all souls shall hear and acknowledge
their true deeds. In the meantime, spirits flee at cockcrow,

people say, because they fear the light, "and of the truth herein",
Horatio muses, "[t]his present object made probation" (155–56).

In other words, Horatio and the soldiers try to "catch" the
ghost by observation and reason—not by that limited portion
of reason called deductive logic, and certainly not by ratio-
nalizing what they wish to believe. They test the apparition
against their pulses, keeping preconceptions at bay yet also using
whatever folk wisdom has to offer them. Humility and honesty open their hearts to a wider reality than the materialist
can know. Hamlet will say, after the Ghost has spoken to him,
"There are more things in heaven and earth, Horatio,/Than
are dreamt of in your philosophy" (1.5.166–67), but it must
be anybody's philosophy he means, yours or mine or that
fellow's in the schoolyard, because if Horatio has a philosophy, it clearly admits of divine order and the reasonableness
of wonders. For Marcellus notes, in words of quiet grace, that
there is one night too when people say ghosts will not walk
the earth:

> Some say that ever 'gainst that season comes
> Wherein our Saviour's birth is celebrated,
> This bird of dawning singeth all night long;
> And then, they say, no spirit dare stir abroad,
> The nights are wholesome, then no planets strike,
> No fairy takes, nor witch hath power to charm:
> So hallowed and so gracious is that time.
>   (1.1.158–64)

Then Horatio, no credulous spinner of folktales, nor what is
worse, a naïve rationalist, replies:

> So have I heard, and do in part believe it.
>   (165)

And when at last it is time to break the watch, these men,
clean of heart, agree among themselves to tell young Hamlet
what they have seen, "[a]s needful in our loves, fitting our duty"
(173).

This is exactly the honesty that Hamlet and the audience seek. It is more than social decorum. It is not the worldly-wise truth to oneself that Polonius recommends to Laertes as he travels to that nation of manners, France (cf. 1.3.59–80), wisdom that does not guard Laertes from overplaying his role as grieving brother (5.1.247–54) or from consenting to cowardly deception against Hamlet, playing at playing! This honesty is, rather, a deep integrity of being, made evident in the just and considered use of language.

Thus, the shift from the world of the soldiers to the world of the courtiers—from night into the murk of political daylight—should stun the audience, jarring the ear and heart. In his inaugural appearance before his assembled court, the King can hardly utter a line that does not clank like a tin coin. He knows he must pretend sorrow at his brother's death, yet, since he is no amateur, he knows also that it will sound suspicious if he protests too much. He cannot avoid mentioning the other object of his murderous desire, his hasty marriage with his brother's wife, yet he knows there is no way to speak decently about it. He has all the air of a man determined, as speedily as he can, to pass a few glittering words as gold and to move on to the business of ruling. The old Hamlet was our "dear brother" (1.2.1) whose memory is still "green" (2); we have borne "our hearts in grief" (3), with all the kingdom "contracted in one brow of woe" (4); and yet somehow we have managed "with wisest sorrow" (6), meaning with Polonian worldly wisdom, to remember ourselves. So keen has that memory of ourselves been that we have invited our sister, now our queen, to join us in ruling this warlike state, and in a kind of psycho-facial absurdity we have married

> with a defeated joy,
> With an auspicious and a dropping eye,
> With mirth in funeral, and with dirge in marriage,
> In equal scale weighing delight and dole.
>
> (10–14)

One eye raised and one eye drooping: as awkward as the king's self-justification and as unnatural as his deed.

We need look no further to find the source of Hamlet's profound disaffection, even before he learns of the murder. As the courtiers wink at a scandalous remarriage that they have apparently advised upon (1.2.14–16) and troop offstage to celebrate, why should he not groan?

> How weary, stale, flat, and unprofitable,
> Seem to me all the uses of this world!
>   (1.2.133–34)

Hamlet possesses that quick sense of beauty and tact whereof we have seen admirable flashes among the soldiers. Witness his description of the glory of the world and of man, and of their misery (2.2.305–16). By nature he does not enjoy gaudy display, as his endearingly lame poem to Ophelia shows and as he himself confesses (2.2.116–24); and he mocks the wearisome pomposity of Osric (5.2.114–22). But unlike the soldiers, who live as loyal men among loyal men, Hamlet must find his way in a world of actors trading in words. Nor is there anything so apt to destroy a man's faith in God and his world than is the sight of crime unpunished and wrapped in holy garb. When Hamlet remembers how his mother at her husband's funeral walked behind the coffin "[l]ike Niobe, all tears" (1.2.149) and then recalls how she feasted at the wedding soon after, well then, there need be no undue filial attachment to cause him to doubt that there is stability or substance or meaning in anything at all. Brooding and unsympathetic, Hamlet sometimes is vindictive, self-tormenting; he is possessed of a powerful but involuted intellect. Yet his world is Denmark, and we should not expect a clear complexion in one who must breathe the air of hypocrisy.

That explains Hamlet's ability to move from the world of the court to the lower but honest world of the soldiers and the gravediggers. He seeks a point of stability; he is looking for the friend whose fidelity will help him see again the beauty of a world that trumpery and jargon have debased. We see this longing as soon as he ends his first soliloquy, when Horatio and the soldiers enter to tell him about the Ghost. Hamlet has whispered to himself that he must be silent: "But break, my heart, for I must hold my tongue" (1.2.159), but that determination does not last long. He recognizes Horatio, a fellow student at Wittenberg whose integrity he admires. They are clearly not on the same social level, nor have they been intimates, but Hamlet's greeting is affable and generous, inviting Horatio to share the same ground with him:

Horatio. Hail to your lordship!

Hamlet.   I am glad to see you well.
   Horatio—or I do forget myself.

Horatio. The same, my lord, and your poor servant ever.

Hamlet. Sir, my good friend. I'll change that name with you.
                                   (160–63)

Then in the course of a natural conversation between two acquaintances meeting unexpectedly, Hamlet is surprisingly open, using wit both to reveal his own feelings and to search Horatio out. The humbler student is quick to apprehend:

Hamlet. But what is your affair in Elsinore?
   We'll teach you to drink deep ere you depart.

Horatio. My lord, I came to see your father's funeral.

Hamlet. I prithee do not mock me, fellow student:
   I think it was to see my mother's wedding.

Horatio. Indeed, my lord, it followed hard upon.

Hamlet. Thrift, thrift, Horatio! The funeral bak'd-meats
   Did coldly furnish forth the marriage tables.
   Would I had met my dearest foe in heaven
   Or ever I had seen that day, Horatio!
                                    (174–83)

As it turns out, Hamlet's trust in Horatio, and in the soldiers whose story he listens to most carefully and whom he

treats with easy respect, is well placed; unlike Claudius, who
cannot share the secrets of his heart with his own wife, much
less with his clumsy counselor Polonius, Hamlet will at times
turn to Horatio as to a rock of sanity, concealing nothing from
him. Note what happens after the Ghost reveals to Hamlet,
alone, that the old king was murdered by the new king. Instead
of ending the scene expeditiously with the disappearance of
the Ghost and a raving exit by Hamlet bent on revenge, Shakespeare presents us with a tableau of solemn oath-swearing, with
the Ghost making a dread auditory reappearance from the cel-
larage below. Hamlet commands the men on their personal
allegiance to him, "good friends,/As you are friends, scholars,
and soldiers" (1.5.140–41), to keep quiet about all they have
seen. Not only that, but Hamlet reveals to them—and takes a
tremendous risk in doing so—that he is going to embark upon
a period of *acting*. He warns them beforehand, lest they play
the part of men who pretend to keep a confidence while, by
offhand ambiguities, they reveal it (1.5.168–79). And by what
should they swear this most dread oath? By the same ultimate
reality that the king in his chamber will confront: "So grace
and mercy at your most need help you" (1.5.180). They do so
swear, whereupon Hamlet promises that he will not forget their
kindness. The watchword is loyalty:

> Rest, rest, perturbed spirit! So, gentlemen,
> With all my love I do commend me to you;
> And what so poor a man as Hamlet is
> May do t'express his love and friending to you,
> God willing, shall not lack. Let us go in together;
> And still your fingers on your lips, I pray.
>   (1.5.182–87)

This scene stands out all the more for being bracketed by scenes
of family life, Polonian-style, wherein no one really trusts anyone else and wherein vows are made to be broken. First we learn
of Hamlet's love for Ophelia, which her brother Laertes dis-
misses as empty and transitory and subject to being overridden
by political calculation, and which Polonius derides as a snare:

Ophelia. [He] hath given countenance to his speech, my lord,
    With almost all the holy vows of heaven.

Polonius. Ay, springes to catch woodcocks!

                                             (1.3.113–15)

Polonius warns Ophelia to be more careful of her maiden vulnerability and, in short, to play hard to get, setting her "entreatments at a higher rate/Than a command to parle" (1.3.122–23). Unexceptionable advice—except when one's lover is sick to death of the social masquerade. And Ophelia's yielding to the command of her father is one of those odd gears that set in motion the destruction of her family and of Hamlet's. For she can no longer respond with honest love when Hamlet approaches her again. The prince, says she, bursts into her room in what we would interpret as an extravagant theatrical display—his doublet unbraced, his stockings fouled, his knees knocking—did we not know that he has just been listening either to the spirit of his murdered father or to a demon magnificently skilled at playing that part. Then he takes Ophelia by the hand—and recall that she is the young daughter of his enemy's footstool and that in the intervening stage-time between her first appearance and this she has been holding aloof from him. Hamlet searches her countenance for truth, for fidelity, before he can take her into his confidence:

    Then goes he to the length of all his arm,
    And, with his other hand thus o'er his brow,
    He falls to such perusal of my face
    As 'a would draw it.

                                             (2.1.88–91)

But he does not find what he seeks. Henceforward, Ophelia will be a stranger to his thoughts.

Nor does he find truthfulness and fidelity in Rosencrantz and Guildenstern, with whom indeed he once was an intimate friend: "My lord, you once did love me", says Rosencrantz in a rare moment of honest regret (3.2.326). How unguarded is Hamlet's greeting when he first catches sight of these comrades of his youth! Their easy masculine banter suggests spirits who ought to understand one another at once:

> *Hamlet.* My excellent good friends! How dost thou, Guildenstern? Ah, Rosencrantz! Good lads, how do you both?
>
> *Rosencrantz.* As the indifferent children of the earth.
>
> *Guildenstern.* Happy in that we are not over-happy;
> On fortune's cap we are not the very button.
>
> *Hamlet.* Nor the soles of her shoe?
>
> *Rosencrantz.* Neither, my lord.
>
> *Hamlet.* Then you live about her waist, or in the middle of her favours?
>
> *Guildenstern.* Faith, her privates we.
>
> *Hamlet.* In the secret parts of Fortune? O, most true; she is a strumpet. What news?
>
> (2.2.223–35)

Hamlet then asks of them, several times over, the same question he asked Horatio: Why are you here? Only now the stakes are far higher. Yet such is Hamlet's friendship that he will allow them to shuffle and duck the question for a while and will even try to prod them into the truth: "I know the good King and Queen have sent for you" (2.2.280). When Rosencrantz continues to hesitate, Hamlet calls for a second oath-swearing, begging them with great earnestness to join him in a world that is not the Danish stage: "But let me conjure you by the rights of our fellowship, by the consonancy of our youth, by the obligation of our ever-preserved love, and by what more dear a better proposer can charge you withal, be even and direct with me, whether you were sent for or no?" (2.2.290–95). But they demur for a moment longer, and from then on Hamlet will trust them as he trusts "adders fang'd" (3.4.203) and will only play at being their friend, to suit his own purposes, as they are playing at being his friends, to suit the King's.

No Shuffling There

In such a world, art itself tends to lapse into rhetorical fads, a false manipulation of easy emotions. It is a grave mistake to suppose that Hamlet is a nervous aesthete. He loves the theater, we learn, not for show but for what art can do to compel us to behold the truth. Hence his dismay when he hears that the theater has been degraded by troops of boy actors (who were then all the rage in Shakespeare's England), who do not play Hercules but play at playing him, to the delight of an audience that likes its entertainment superficial. Hardly has Hamlet welcomed the players come to the castle to divert him—and he is cheerful, informal, personal, and deeply appreciative of their craft—when he requests a speech. His choice, a monologue describing the cruel death of Priam of Troy, is powerful for its relative restraint and artlessness. "I remember", he says of it, "one said there were no sallets in the lines to make the matter savoury, nor no matter in the phrase that might indict the author of affectation; but call'd it an honest method, as wholesome as sweet, and very much more handsome than fine" (2.2.435–40). And indeed, as Hamlet listens, he is caught unawares by its power. When Queen Hecuba finds her husband murdered, she, true woman, does what Queen Gertrude apparently only pretended to do, and Hamlet, abashed by the contrast, cannot hold his countenance:

> *Player.* But if the gods themselves did see her then,
>   When she saw Pyrrhus make malicious sport
>   In mincing with his sword her husband's limbs,
>   The instant burst of clamour that she made—
>   Unless things mortal move them not at all—
>   Would have made milch the burning eyes of heaven,
>   And passion in the gods.
>
> *Polonius.* Look whe'er he has not turn'd his color, and has
>   tears in 's eyes. Prithee no more.
>
> (2.2.506–14)

These manly tears Hamlet cannot hide must suggest his crucial plan: "The play's the thing/Wherein I'll catch the conscience of the King" (2.2.600–1). As he was moved, so may the king be moved. Thus he must remind the players, before the crucial performance of *The Mousetrap*, that the fiction of art is to be truer than fact. They must not allow rhetoric or spectacle or faddishness or self-display to impede the theater's purpose, "whose end, both at the first and now, was and is to hold, as 'twere, the mirror up to nature; to show virtue her own feature, scorn her own image, and the very age and body of the time his form and pressure" (3.2.21–25). Those that "o'er-step ... the modesty of nature" (19) may win applause but will fail to convict us of the truth. We will remain on our own stage; we will not open our eyes. Had the player overdone his description of the woe of Hecuba, Hamlet would not have wept; and if the players now merely play at playing, if they do not submit themselves to the aim of their art, then *The Mousetrap* will but alert the King to Hamlet's suspicions without surprising him into revelation. He must be struck to the heart.

Therefore, true art is unlike the spying of Polonius, who boasts that such wise men as he "[b]y indirections find directions out" (2.1.66). Indirect it may be, but we ourselves are not true and cannot be appealed to directly. Yet at its profoundest, it shows us not only what we are now but the parts we shall play on the great stage to come, where the thoughts of all hearts shall be revealed. Hamlet's own faith in that ultimate truth is fitful, though in the end he seems to accept, or resign himself to, a divine Director whose will cannot be gainsaid: "[T]here is a special providence in the fall of a sparrow" (5.2.211–12; cf. Mt 10:29). The King, Hamlet's "dearest foe", also teeters on the verge of despair, or of the even more terrible faith. Let us read the end of his soliloquy:

> May one be pardon'd and retain th' offence?
> In the corrupted currents of this world
> Offence's gilded hand may shove by justice;
> And oft 'tis seen the wicked prize itself

Buys out the law. But 'tis not so above—
There is no shuffling; there the action lies
In his true nature; and we ourselves compell'd,
Even to the teeth and forehead of our faults,
To give in evidence. What then? What rests?
Try what repentance can. What can it not?
Yet what can it when one can not repent?
O wretched state! O bosom black as death!
O limed soul, that, struggling to be free,
Art more engag'd! Help, angels. Make assay:
Bow, stubborn knees; and, heart, with strings of steel,
Be soft as sinews of the new-born babe.
All may be well.

(3.3.56–72)

Claudius is a miserable man, without a friend to confide in; his evil ensures that he can survive only in a world of lies. In that unreality the King can kneel, and fold his hands, and exclaim, and weep. But he can also see, in a flash of self-knowledge, the reality of his black bosom and the imperturbable light of God. Could he but fling himself upon that mercy more lovely than man's greatest beauty and more terrible than man's direst fear, he could yet be forgiven, and all might be well. But he does not. The temporary rewards of the play prove too strong. Words are all he mouths, and he is wise enough to know and to confess that God requires more. Thus he ends with the saddest words in the play: "My words fly up, my thoughts remain below./Words without thoughts never to heaven go" (97–98). Let all of us Danes heed the warning.

Psychology, Character, and Performance in *Hamlet*

Gene Fendt
University of Nebraska

Just as the family psychology of the court of Denmark has been a popular nexus for scholarship and directorial interpretation since Freud, the character of Hamlet's soul has been the playground of actors (and actresses), directors, and critics for centuries. In the latter half of the twentieth century, the psychosexual reduction was all too popular, but other errors about the human psyche and its relations have been played, and argued for by critics. It is, however, possible to lay out a *psyche*-ology that is less dogmatic than those available to modern and postmodern critics, a *psyche*-ology that, in laying out the permutations of human *psyche*, predicts as well the possibilities of other, more reductive, psychologies. Such a *psyche*-ology would allow insights not only into the characters and relations in *Hamlet* but also into the character of the variety of critics and directors, and their relation to *Hamlet*. It would, as well, open up some suggestions for performance.

The *psyche*-ology I speak of precedes the play; it can be found in Saint Thomas Aquinas, though much of what Aquinas' science lays out can be found in Saint Augustine (especially the latter books of *De Trinitate*) and Aristotle. In *Summa theologica* I–II, q. 28, Aquinas distinguishes the kinds of ecstasy. The question at issue there is whether ecstasy (which in the literal Greek means "to stand out away from", or "to stand outside of") is an effect of love, and the answer is "Yes—in as many ways as there are different kinds of love". So, in order to understand the kinds of ecstasy, we need to recall that love is something pertaining to appetite and so differs according to the difference of appetites. A bit earlier (q. 26), Saint Thomas had distinguished three types of appetite. The first is the natural appetite, "which arises from an apprehension existing not in

217

the subject of the appetite, but in some other" (I–II, q. 26, art. 1), such as the force that through the green fuse drives the flower. This vegetable love is not simply in the concupiscible power, for it is active in all things: even electrons in their shells (which, strictly speaking, have no such power) seek the state that is suitable for them, as that is known by the mind of God, and science. This is the physical analogy of ecstasy. Even atoms of nitrogen do not remain in a state of perfect immanence.[1] The thing, all unknowing, moves out of its present state toward another—*standing out* from what it is to what it is to be.

The second kind of appetite, and so (analogously) love, arises "from an apprehension in the subject of an appetite, but from necessity, not freedom" (I–II, q. 26, art. 1), such as that of a dog for a bone, or a baby for the breast. How clear these animal apprehensions are, and precisely what their status is, is a matter of unending debate, but the fact that there is some apprehension *in the subject*, which the flower and the lonely electron lack, is not much up for grabs with God, or science. This is the animal's analogical reduction of ecstasy (for the primary use of a word always refers to man). It is the nature of the animal that apprehension *necessitates*, and so, while the animal *moves knowingly* toward what it does not yet possess, it is not placed outside itself in such a way as to *know its principle of movement*. It eats, but does not choose. It moves toward what its appetite desires and does not have, but does not know itself as having appetite. "The animal is in the world like water in water."[2] On the other hand, *we* know what we are, and *why* we choose what we do.

---

[1] Contrast Georges Bataille, *Theory of Religion*, trans. Robert Hurley (New York: Zone Books, 1992), p. 19; Bataille uses the atom as the prime example of nonecstatic being.

[2] Ibid., p. 23. Bataille continues less poetically, and in agreement with Aquinas: "If need be, the animal can be regarded as a subject for which the rest of the world is an object, *but it is never given the possibility of regarding itself in this way*" (my italics). Religion, from Aquinas to Bataille, understands human life as essentially ecstatic; religions arise from this primary (f)act. Bataille's empiricism lies in his reduction of Aquinas' metaphysical understanding to an anthropological, perhaps psychological, fact. His use of Ockham's razor denies the possibility that there are more things in Heaven and earth than are dreamt of in empirical philosophy.

The third kind of appetite "follows freely from an apprehension in the subject of the appetite" (I–II, q. 26, art. 1).
This is will, or rational appetite. Here ecstasy is not used analogously, for the being of man, our natural state, is this ecstasy;
our (rational) appetite reaches out for what we do not now
possess or attempts to secure what we do not hold securely.
We move so knowing our principle of movement. We can move
ourselves in accord with appetites we share (in a way) with
animals; we can move ourselves in accord with appetites in
which animals do not share, such as a desire for justice. Laertes
describes the human situation perfectly when he says of his
sister's ecstasy:

> Nature is fine in love; and where 'tis fine
> It sends some precious instance of itself
> After the thing it loves.
>
> (4.5.158–60)[3]

It sends, in fact, itself after the thing it loves. But as rational appetite, our ecstasy has two variables within it. That
is, since human beings have both apprehension and appetite,
the placing outside oneself that is ecstasy "happens [both] as
to the apprehensive power and as to the appetitive power"
(I–II, q. 28, art. 3), and so there are four permutations of
ecstasy.

Consider, first, the ecstasy of the apprehensive power, "caused
by love dispositively" insofar as love, in dwelling intently on
one thing, draws the mind to it from other things; or, as Shylock says, "[A]ffection,/Master of passion, sways it to the
mood/Of what it likes".[4] Shylock and Laertes reflect the traditional teaching; Augustine, for example, says that "the force
of love is so great that the mind draws in with itself those
things upon which it has long reflected with love, and to which

---

[3] All quotations from *Hamlet* are from the Ignatius edition, edited by Joseph
Pearce (San Francisco: Ignatius Press, 2008).

[4] William Shakespeare, *Merchant of Venice*, in *The Complete Pelican Shakespeare*, eds. Brents Stirling and Alfred Harbarge (New York: Viking, 1969),
4.1.50–52.

it has become attached by its devoted care."[5] This ecstasy may take one of two directions, depending on what we turn our minds to. So, what we love may raise us to a higher knowledge than is proper to the composite being—for "the intellect has an operation in which the body does not share" (I, q. 84, art. 6)[6]—or debase us to a lower one: "Thus a man may be said to suffer ecstasy when he is overcome by violent passion or madness" (I–II, q. 28, art. 3).

In the world of the play, the Ghost provokes a decision about this matter. Hamlet, at first, calls the Ghost "King, father, royal Dane" (1.4.45), presuming that the vision he shares with Marcellus and Horatio is of the spirit of his father. As in life he saw and loved the spirit of the man through the body, his love now might be said to be seeing the body through the Ghost. Later he wonders whether some demon might be working through his own weakness and melancholy (2.2.595–600) to produce something pleasing out of his sadness and foul imaginings about his uncle (3.2.78–82). Hamlet knows that love can draw the mind either to higher or to lower things. He must test his apprehensions, and the play he designs does just that. Immediately after the play, at the last (dis)appearance of the Ghost, Gertrude raises the exactly pertinent question of ecstasy (3.4.137–40). Just as the play has proved his own apprehension of the Ghost to be honest rather than the creation of disappointed love, Hamlet's comparison of the portraits of the two brothers has made the case that Gertrude's desires have led her apprehension to consider lower matters so lovingly that she cannot smell, much less see, the most simple things of sense

---

[5] *De Trinitate* 10.7. See also *Confessions* 13.9.10: "My love is my weight, by it am I borne whithersoever I am borne." It is not a modern teaching that love "fixates" the soul upon its object; the modern merely limits the possible objects to the instinctual or empirical, and the manner of fixation to concupiscence.

[6] As Hamlet might say, perhaps less scholastically: "What a piece of work is a man! How noble in reason! how infinite in faculties! ... in action, how like an angel! in apprehension, how like a god!" (2.2.30–34). A. C. Bradley, in *Shakespearean Tragedy* (London: Macmillan, 1919), agrees; after quoting these lines, he says that "it is the language of a heart thrilled with wonder and swelling into ecstasy" (p. 111). Bradley speaks the literal truth, religiously understood.

correctly (3.4.70–82); seeing spirits—even believing in their existence—seems now beyond her apprehension.

Both of these apprehensive ecstasies are caused by love: because our apprehensions are linked to our appetitive powers, all apprehensions grow by what they feed upon, and so, in the case of Gertrude, her formerly free apprehension, while not growing to madness (as Othello's consideration of a handkerchief does to him), has carried her beneath the proper apprehensions of a human being, to sate itself on the garbage that is Claudius. Hamlet begins her cure by pointing out her error and suggests how she may yet achieve the ecstasy appropriate to human beings—that of seeing and enjoying spirits, not merely bodies:

> Mother, for love of grace,
> Lay not that flattering unction to your soul,
> That not your trespass but my madness speaks:
> . . . .
> Confess yourself to heaven;
> Repent what's past; avoid what is to come;
> And do not spread the compost on the weeds,
> To make them ranker. Forgive me this my virtue.
>   (3.4.144–46; 149–53)

It is because he is himself suffering the higher ecstasy (love for a just soul rather than for merely an attractive body) that he can judge and minister rightly to his mother's unseen infection. As we will see, one of the questions every performance of the play answers is whether this shriving works toward her salvation or not.

As the apprehensive aspect of our ecstasy has two possibilities, so too does the appetitive power; here there is the ecstasy that is a placing outside oneself *simply*, or unrestrictedly, which takes place by the love of friendship (*amor amicitiae*), and the placing outside oneself that, occurring by love of concupiscence (*amor concupiscentiae*), is *restricted* because it seeks the extrinsic good for itself and so recovers itself in satisfaction.[7] Friendship, on Aquinas' account, is an ecstasy without return; for in it our end is not our own good but the good of the beloved. This is the love that seeks not its own (1 Cor 13:5). Concupiscence goes out of itself but only to return with its object in satisfaction. When Hamlet doubts the Ghost is honest, he is clearly fearing that his own desires for satisfaction against his uncle are turning his apprehension of the Ghost. Gertrude has, no doubt, considerable experience of those lower restricted ecstasies that recover themselves in satisfaction. Claudius does as well, as he confesses (3.3.36–72, also 4.7.110–14). And since Gertrude's mind is turned that way by the disposition of her heart, she can understand her son's behavior only as an ecstasy of a similar order (that is, aimed at an empirical object, as hers is), though simple—an ecstasy without return (since he gets nothing out of it, his beloved being the dead father)—and so more frightening: she thinks he suffers the unrestricted ecstasy of madness. Shakespeare's audience would have known that the fact that she sees nothing when the loving Ghost appears is a sign that her apprehension of what love is present is restricted by her own loves, not that she is right about Hamlet or about love. Meanwhile, the Ghost, in his last appearance, seems most concerned with the "fighting soul" of his wife; this concern reminds us of Hamlet's earlier description of him as a man "so loving to my mother,/That he might not beteem the winds of heaven/Visit her face too roughly" (1.2.140–42). The Ghost (as the man) goes out of himself in a love of friendship for both the body and the soul of his wife, not for his own enjoyment but for her good: "Speak to her, Hamlet" (3.4.115).

---

[7] Aquinas' words for these ecstasies are *simpliciter* ("in amore amicitiae, affectus alicujus simpliciter exit extra se") and *secundum quid* ("quia ... talis affectio in fine intra ipsum concluditur") (*Summa theologica* I–II, q. 28, art. 3). The translation of ecstasy *secundum quid* as "restricted" is that of the good brothers, Fathers of the English Dominican Province (New York: Benziger Brothers, 1947). This whole story, by the way, answers to L. C. Knights' demand, in *An Approach to "Hamlet"* (London: Chatto and Windus, 1960), for "a closer examination of the intimate and complex relationship of thought and feeling" (p. 55). Actually, the answer preexists the demand.

We may diagram the whole account this way:

Ecstasy: Placing outside Oneself

power of apprehension:	drawn to lower things	drawn to higher things
power of appetite:		
drawn outside itself *simpliciter* (*amor amicitiae*)	madness/violent passion (Othello)	Hamlet seeing ghost in bedroom
	Gertrude's view of Hamlet	
	(B)	(A)
drawn outside itself *secundum quid*, or "restrictedly" (*amor concupiscentiae*)	Gertrude (for most of the play) Claudius (forever)	Laertes agreeing to Claudius' scheme? Kyd's best characters
	(C)	(D)

There would be, then, four versions of ecstasy (reading from Hamlet counterclockwise): the simple and higher (A), the simple and lower (B), the restricted and lower (C), and the restricted and higher (D). If there were no true religion—i.e., nothing beyond natural philosophy—the type of ecstasy that Hamlet represents would not be possible, nor would friendship be an ecstasy without return.[8] Friendship could, at best,

---

[8] Hamlet *is*, then, in a certain positivist understanding, "dominated by an emotion which is ... in *excess* of the facts as they appear", as T. S. Eliot says ("Hamlet", in *Selected Prose of T. S. Eliot*, ed. Frank Kermode [London: Faber and Faber, 1975], p. 48), but his emotion is *not*, for that matter, a fault; it is, in fact, the proper passion for a human being, one who *ought* to be dominated by a passion in excess of things as they appear. So far as he can, Bataille makes a similar point. He closes *Theory of Religion* "positing a religious attitude that would result from clear consciousness, and would exclude, if not the ecstatic form of religion, then at least its mystical form" (p. 109). This religious attitude, this clear consciousness (cf. Laertes' final state at 5.2.294), is Hamlet's. Its proper expression is wonder: the passion without an opposite. Banquo exhibits this higher kind of soul in *Macbeth*. See my "Banquo: A False *Faux Ami?*" *Notes and Queries* 250, no. 2 (June 2005): 204–6.

be an aid to civic virtue and find both its origin and its telos there.[9] While "achieving the end for a city is more divine", as Aristotle says (*Nicomachean Ethics* 1094b10), the individual still participates in the honor and achievement of that end, and his affections may well still be concupiscent. We may think Laertes is here when he agrees to the King's scheme for achieving "justice" without disturbing the Queen's affections (4.7.52–69), though perhaps he is drawn as much by his own sickness as a desire for justice for his family. In the end, he discovers that he is deceived about the higher good—justice—and repents his sickness for the sake of a justice that exhibits his own error and dishonor.

Many modern critics consider the restricted forms of ecstasy (C, D) to be the only sane cases; they train their apprehension through the empiricism of the body. Polonius seems to be just such a character in the play. He "knows" that Hamlet's affection and holy vows to Ophelia are "springes to catch woodcocks", extinct of both light and heat even in the promising (1.3.115–20). They are "implorators" not of a love of friendship but of a desire for satisfaction of the blood. They aim not at something holy but at "unholy suits". It seems he thinks that human nature can aim only at such concupiscent satisfactions, of which there are those that might provide honor, "true pay" (1.3.106), and good "investment" tender for the family (1.3.128), and those that aim at a more singular bodily satisfaction for the implorator: young men will do it if they come to it. The Polonial idea of a higher end is still one desired concupiscently. He considers that when Hamlet's concupiscent desires are entirely denied by Ophelia's obedient refusals, this lack of satisfaction drives Hamlet simply mad (2.2.91–151). An unsatisfied concupiscence is a desire that goes out of itself to no avail; madness results from the world's refusal of Id

---

[9] The idea that friendship can go beyond the *telos* of the worldly polis is precisely where Aquinas exceeds Aristotle, where religion exceeds natural philosophy, and where Hamlet exceeds Horatio—until the end.

demands.[10] This is the only form of ecstasy without return allowed in the modern dispensation. So it is that in an age that disbelieves even in the possibility of the supernatural, the higher simple ecstasy (A) must be considered a serious neurosis, and the higher restricted psychological type (D) a person whose superego function has been regularized in accord with social convention: familial honor, respect, the city's good. The same account is applicable to contemporary understandings of the Hamlet-Gertrude closet scene. If there is no "love of grace" that cannot be played out entirely through the body, then Hamlet is merely deceiving himself about his own empirical and concupiscent desires (of one sort or another, depending on the psychologist or director) in appealing to those putatively higher desires.

Shakespeare's contemporary, Thomas Kyd, wrote very popular tragedies using only the other three types of character. His best heroes are drawn to what are considered higher things—justice, for example—but they are drawn to them in a restricted way. They are satisfied *in nature* by the action of the play. Hamlet himself is tempted this way—to work in such a manner that justice accomplishes his sweet revenge. We should note here that it is not that groundlings seek only lower things; they don't: the groundlings loved Kyd's heroes crying for justice—a higher thing—as the mob loved Laertes rushing in upon the king in Act 4, scene 5, to threaten just such justice. In the play's Denmark, Laertes looks like and has the effect that Kyd's heroes have on an English audience. As the Danish dogs follow Laertes crying vengeance, so too the groundlings loved the way Kyd gave justice to his heroes: he gave it to them in a way that satisfied their appetite. And they bayed out their "Bravo!" As the mob is disappointed when Laertes leaves them outside the throne room, so too groundling critics are somewhat vexed at Hamlet, for he does not set about

---

[10] The Id is Freud's term for the most fundamental part or principle of the soul; its operation is directed by what he calls the pleasure principle. Every other operation of the soul is born from this.

to satisfy their appetite.[11] The real love of justice seeks not the justicer's own satisfaction.

Hamlet's pulse doth temperately keep time and makes as healthful music as his mother's. Yet he is ecstatic. He alone of all the characters in the play is placed outside the knowledge proper to a man in a higher way by the repeated visits of the Ghost; he dwells intently on the honest ghost's news and its value; his love for the bringer of that news is friendship simply, not concupiscent and restricted, as is his mother's: his is not a dull sublunary love whose soul is sense. In fact, Hamlet cannot even force himself to the mere bloody *satisfaction* that lesser dramatists (like Kyd) and lesser critics (legion) would foist upon him. He must have justice and have it justly served. He does not have justice serve *his* turn, as Laertes desires[12] and Kyd's heroes would; he will serve it. Precisely that difference between an unrestricted ecstasy and an ecstasy that seeks to recover itself in satisfaction is the difference between justice and revenge, between friendship's love (*amor amicitiae*) and the more erotic ecstasy that shares its name—love. Laertes, who has inherited his father's capacity to speak the words of practical wisdom, if not practice the wisdom he speaks, has

---

[11] As an example of such a groundling critic, consider G. Wilson Knight, who, in his essay on Hamlet in *The Wheel of Fire* (London: Metheun, 1945), says, "[I]f Hamlet had promptly avenged his father, taken the throne, forgotten his troubles, and resumed a healthy outlook on life, he would have all our acclamations. Laertes, entering in wrath at the death of his father, daring damnation and threatening Claudius, comes on us like a blast of fresh air after the stifling, poisonous atmosphere of Hamlet's mind" (p. 40). Hamlet should have "struck at once and restored perfect health to Denmark" (p. 45). Ernest Jones, in *Hamlet and Oedipus* (Garden City, N.J.: Doubleday-Anchor, 1955), agrees (p. 44). This proves that what is fresh air to a groundling may well smell of sulfur to the judicious; we should note how quickly that fresh French air turns to poison.

Shakespeare perhaps intends his play as physic for such morality, as Nigel Alexander says: "The realization that what they desire is a person like Laertes might cause the audience more reflection. The reaction of Laertes is a 'normal' and 'human' reaction. It leads to those normal and human activities of treachery and murder" (*Poison, Play and Duel: A Study in Hamlet* [London: Routledge and Kegan Paul, 1971], p. 11).

[12] "My lord, I will be rul'd;/ The rather, if you could devise it so/ That I might be the organ" (4.7.68–70).

recognized something of Hamlet's nature in this regard. He has the prince's greatness weighed and knows

> his will is not his own;
> For he himself is subject to his birth:
> He may not, as unvalued persons do,
> Carve for himself; for on his choice depends
> The sanity and health of this whole state;
> And therefore must his choice be circumscrib'd
> Unto the voice and yielding of that body
> Whereof he is the head.
>
> (1.3.17–24)

Here, Laertes recognizes that Hamlet is bound in love to something that exceeds Ophelia's person and his own. Like the good Greek whose name he bears, Laertes extends the operation of virtue and desire to the state and presumes this is true of Hamlet. Laertes presumes Hamlet is bound to a higher object but in a restricted way. But perhaps Hamlet's love is distinct in another way as well from what Laertes knows or from what Hamlet himself can say. In any case, it is not by a more extensive love of justice but only by a *simpler* love for justice—one that seeks not its own pleasure as part and sum of justice's accomplishment—that there *can* be a return to free and open polity in Denmark. The economy of justice is not self-subsistent in the state. No restricted higher ecstasy can explain itself, except reductively—that is, by reference to the lower objects of desire. So justice, for someone like Freud, is merely roughly equal distribution of Id repression;[13] it seems, in this case, merely self-contradictory madness to sacrifice oneself for it. We see that for Hamlet to accomplish justice will cost him all he would choose could he carve for himself according to concupiscence. Hamlet sees so too in the nunnery scene, where

---

[13] See, for example, *Civilization and Its Discontents*, ed. and trans. James Strachey (New York: W.W. Norton, 1961): "The final outcome [of the development of civilization] should be a rule of law to which all ... have contributed by a sacrifice of their instincts" (p. 49).

he returns twice—his desire to stay struggling against his knowledge that he must break with Ophelia.

That most of the characters in this play (or any other) never achieve the simple and higher kind of ecstasy, or do so only with great difficulty, is no claim against it. Neither do we in our lives. Aquinas is not the kind of philosopher who thinks that the truth about human nature is found by sociology. Indeed, if we delve one yard deeper, Aquinas' ideas explain the pattern of disease imagery in the play: the diseases are symptoms of improperly ordered souls. Like most of Shakespeare's characters, most of us are living versions of restricted ecstasy—and probably of restricted ecstasy aimed at lower objects, for how many of us love anything (or anyone) in the world for its own sake, "unmixed with baser matter" (1.5.104)? But in the last appearance of the Ghost—who has been in Purgatory all day for several months—his concern is with the *soul* of his spouse, and if earlier his love for her face was mixed with his own satisfaction, he is now beyond the possibility of that: his love for her has become *amor amicitiae*, for a higher good than the earthly being and happiness of his wife; his concern is for her "fighting soul", and for that he has come back from the very grave one final time.

Perhaps he even wins; his last visit pulls Hamlet from his anger at Gertrude, at which point Hamlet gives the calm and morally perfecting advice that was quoted above. She seems thereafter not to consider him mad, and she does not appear thereafter on the arm of the King. How to play her conclusion seems to me to be the test of the director's understanding of her character. If we think of all the things she has seen and undergone before the last act—Hamlet's play, the King's reaction, Hamlet's accusation and shriving in her closet, a letter from Hamlet's sailor friends (4.7.37) concerning his unexpected return from England (Hamlet himself having in his pocket the King's order for his death)—she has grounds to watch her new husband closely, and the preparation of a special drink for Hamlet should catch her eye. How then, does this last choice of hers play?

Queen. Here, Hamlet, take my napkin, rub thy brows.
     The Queen carouses to thy fortune, Hamlet.

Hamlet. Good madam!
King.   Gertrude, do not drink.
Queen. I will, my lord: I pray you pardon me.

                                        (5.2.280–83)

If her seeming early habit of concupiscent love for lower things (C) remains the state of her soul, perhaps she takes the cup of wine as she takes her other pleasures and considers the King's warning to be rather like her son's, a plea that she cease to be so thoroughly engaged to such concupiscence, or, we could say, cease to be so "alive to her desires". But she likes wine as she likes men; the satisfactions of such desires are the very stuff of life, and so she takes the drink because it pleases her, even though her husband is displeased. In this case her next line to Hamlet, "Come, let me wipe thy face", must be her indulgence of her own doting pleasure as mother; note that this would not be so much pleasure in her son as pleasure in her motherhood.

Perhaps she has attempted to break her concupiscent habits (B), fearing Hamlet may be right about her stewing in corruption, but she has failed, or reconsidered Claudius and still finds him a satisfying man. But having gone back to the "bloat King", here—at his warning phrase—she realizes that Hamlet was right about him all along and she now hates herself, despairs of any good in herself, and takes the drink full of disgust at herself and with him: "I will, my lord; I pray you pardon me" is muttered between the teeth, with acid and complete contempt for the desires she has sold herself to; disgusted with all such satisfactions, she suffers a madness in which she throws herself away, drinking poison to escape her self-disgust. She runs to nothingness.

There are two possibilities that she is meditating on higher things. Perhaps she has been considering Hamlet's accusation of treason against Claudius; she has, as queen, for decades taken as her concern the good of Denmark (D+A). There is evidence that this is so in her first lines to Hamlet: "[L]et thine eye look like a friend on Denmark" (1.2.69); perhaps part of her reason for marrying so hastily was misapprehension about the state. In this ecstasy, she has been considering that the good of the state requires a nontreasonous executive and her picking up of the drink is her test of Hamlet's testimony against Claudius. The King's warning is the confession of his guilt, and now she knows; she drinks for the good of Denmark and her son. It will reveal what Claudius is and so allow Denmark to be purged: a higher apprehension than the previous version, but one in which her own good as queen is involved. To wipe Hamlet's face then is symbolically to reveal the face of the true prince, begrimed through the work of the play and by her own earlier weakness.

Finally, it is possible that even her love for Claudius has converted from the restricted to the simpler kind (A): she knows, upon his warning, that he is a murderer; but rather than despise herself or him, she opens a way for him to free himself by confession and repentance of his sin, as Hamlet's shriving had, in her most need, graced her. She looks at him, knowing all his crimes, and offers him this chance to repent out of her now far simpler love: "I will, my lord; I pray you pardon me." She pauses, and in that pause Claudius makes the decision of eternity. Holding his eyes, she drinks it slowly. When she calls Hamlet to wipe his face, it is a final act of gratitude for his having done the same to her, in the spiritual sense, in the shriving scene. The Ghost had told Hamlet not to contrive against his mother but rather to "leave her to heaven" (1.5.86), trusting she had within her that kind of virtue and would be aided by that grace, which—in this performance of her ending—she does have. Only if Gertrude ends like this do we see that the Ghost's love for her apprehended her soul aright, that their marriage was not merely an arrangement for the limited ecstasies of embodied souls but was a sacrament taken up to encourage and practice the soul's simpler love for a being higher than either of them. That is the family psychology appropriate for royalty. It is a consummation devoutly to be wished.

The Nobility of Hamlet

Richard Harp
University of Nevada

It has become commonplace in the criticism of Shakespeare's play about Hamlet to so emphasize the Prince's melancholy and procrastination that it is difficult to see how he can be regarded as a hero at all. Nearly everyone, it seems, regards the name of "Hamlet" as synonymous with delay, indecisiveness, and the inability to act, so that the idea of nobility and heroism as being at the core of his character, and not confusion and overthinking, must seem very odd indeed. Hamlet is frequently appreciated as a modern character, even a modern hero (or antihero, as the case may be), but this is not so much because he is strong and vigorous but rather because he is said to worry every problem to death, in a way that it is presumed characteristic of modern sensitive and "artistic" temperaments. But I will argue that he is, in fact, heroic in an older and simpler way, which is of great interest to us not only for the intrinsic admirability of his actions and virtues but also because he must practice them in a world that has indeed become "modern" in a negative sense—that is, a world increasingly given over to deception, appearances, and broken trust and where the idea of loyalty has begun to look quaint.

To evaluate justly Hamlet's character, we must first appreciate the circumstances that enclose him. They are extreme. His father, whom he justly admires and whom he can still see in his "mind's eye", has recently died and been replaced on the throne of Denmark by Hamlet's uncle, Claudius, for whom Hamlet's "prophetic soul" has no regard; Hamlet compares his father to his successor as "Hyperion to a satyr" (1.2.140).[1] To compound

---

[1] All quotations from *Hamlet* are from the edition published by Ignatius Press: *Hamlet, Prince of Denmark*, ed. Joseph Pearce (San Francisco: Ignatius, 2008).

his isolation, he is distant from his mother because of her quick marriage to Claudius, noting wittily that the "funeral bak'd-meats/Did coldly furnish forth the marriage tables" (1.2.180–81). It is clear, too, that the hero does indeed have emotional attachments to his father and mother; he is no generic prince merely biding his time until he can rule or, worse, cold-bloodedly plotting for that day, as the biblical Absalom did over a period of years against his father, David. No, Hamlet loves his father—"'A was a man, take him for all in all,/I shall not look upon his like again" (1.2.187–88)—and feels deeply his mother's quick remarriage, as we see when he pleads with her in Act 3 to stay away from his stepfather's bed.

And this is just for starters. Before the first act is over, he will be told that his dead father has appeared to castle guards as a ghost, and his subsequent interview with that spirit compounds his problems immeasurably: the Ghost tells Hamlet that he was murdered by a man the Prince already detested and in circumstances that did not allow for the King to repent his sins. He then tells Hamlet to avenge this death and to tell no one of his charge. But this is still not enough: soon Hamlet will discover that his beloved Ophelia's loyalty to him may well be in question and that his old school chums Rosencrantz and Guildenstern, whose arrival at Elsinore has lightened his spirits, are in fact in the employ of his enemy Claudius. He has, that is to say, within the space of four calendar months, lost his father, his mother, his hopes of any immediate succession to the Danish throne, his beloved (to the machinations of her own father), and the affections of two former school friends. It is enough to make any man, and not just one who may be given to thinking too precisely upon events, think that in nature "things rank and gross ... [p]ossess it merely" (1.2.136–37). He can count only upon the friendship of another schoolmate, Horatio. He does not even have the common consolation of being able to pray for the repose of his father's spirit, for he knows that it is in fact not at rest, and its reappearances and disappearances have further upset the balance of Hamlet's own psyche—as whose would it not? Hamlet could surely say with more justice than King Lear, "I am more sinned against than sinning."

But he does not say this, nor does he unreasonably delay discharging the Ghost's commands. Hamlet has been taken to task for not acting immediately, but, of course, he does not know if the Ghost is of Purgatory or Hell. It would have been the height of presumptuousness for him to have enacted his revenge without allowing time for the human actors to confirm or disprove the Ghost's charges. For it is part of Hamlet's nobility that he seeks justice, not simply the blood revenge of Seneca's Roman tragedies, popularly revived upon the Elizabethan stage at the time Shakespeare was writing, or of the older versions of the Hamlet story, and had he immediately killed Claudius, what possible means would he have had to prove publicly the justice of his case? He could cite only the witness of a ghost. If, on the other hand, and as is sometimes suggested, he washes his hands of the whole matter, he leaves a possible crime, and one against his father and king, no less, unpunished and the kingdom open to the consequences of this inaction. It is true that two months do elapse between Acts 1 and 2, during which time Hamlet does nothing to prove or disprove the Ghost's charges, except to put on the "antic disposition" that allows him a modicum of camouflage until events begin to be sorted out. That his madness is assumed is clear, I think, from his comments to Horatio and to the other witnesses to the Ghost at the end of Act 1, where he tells them exactly what he is going to do, that is, assume the disguise of insanity (1.5.165–80). But it is hard to know what his critics would have him do in these two months. If the Ghost is diabolic, he is then luring Hamlet to his own destruction by an act of murder, and if he is telling the truth and some kind of retribution is called for, it must, again, be demonstrated plainly. Any action that he would take would have to be done in the hothouse atmosphere of a court where he has practically no allies or familial support and where there are rumors of foreign invasion. And Hamlet cannot call 911, because the telephone would be answered by Claudius.

But he is doing more, I would quickly add, than being cal-
culating and cunning in awaiting the proper time to act. He
does have these qualities—that is clear from the success with
which he contrives the play within a play, *The Mousetrap*, with
which he catches "the conscience of the King" (2.2.601)—
but no one could survive Elsinore or, we might conclude from
the evidence of Shakespeare's plays generally, survive the tran-
sition into the early modern world without them. Hamlet is
indeed forced to scheme and employ subterfuge, not on his
own initiative but in response to circumstances, but it is to a
noble end: to be neither a man of blood vengeance who was
naïvely credulous about the words of a ghost nor a man who
shirked his responsibilities to see justice done and the truth
known by the people of his state. This is surely at the very
heart of nobility: to seek the truth and to minister justice without using the basely corrupt weapons of those in power who
have no interest in either end.

Ophelia testifies to Hamlet's general character when she says,
during the throes of what she mistakes as his genuine madness, "O, what a noble mind is here o'er-thrown!" (3.1.150)
and goes on to testify to his past qualities as soldier, states-
man, and scholar. These have been in evidence from the play's
earliest scenes. The Ghost addresses him as a "noble youth"
(1.5.38), and after the Ghost disappears, Hamlet shows an easy
familiarity with his comrades Horatio and Marcellus when he
addresses them as "good friends" and requests that as they are
"friends, scholars, and soldiers,/Give me one poor request",
which is to "[n]ever make known what you have seen to-night"
(1.5.140–43). The typical Renaissance definition of good friendship is for friends to treat each other as a "second self", a classical version of loving one's neighbor as oneself, and Hamlet
is here asking his friends to observe the same silence about
what they have seen as he will himself. This same ease and
familiarity of Hamlet with friends is seen again when Rosencrantz and Guildenstern arrive at Elsinore: he calls them
his "excellent good friends" (2.2.223) and asks them "in the
beaten way of friendship, what make you at Elsinore?" (2.2.269).

This is indeed the key question, for in the subsequent dialogue it is apparent that they do not reciprocate the open honesty with which Hamlet has greeted them: they lie to him about why they were sent—"To visit you, my lord; no other occasion" (2.2.270)—and Hamlet's reply to them embodies both the old world of friendship and nobility while at the same time (the kind of juxtaposition Shakespeare does superbly) gives a glimpse of the new world of hidden motives and suspicions with which this nobility will have to contend. "Beggar that I am," he begins,

> I am even poor in thanks; but I thank you; and sure, dear friends, my thanks are too dear a half-penny. Were you not sent for? Is it your own inclining? Is it a free visitation? Come, come, deal justly with me. Come, come; nay, speak.
>
> (2.2.271–75)

In order to get a straight answer from his "friends", Hamlet must plead with them to speak the truth, and in so doing he makes clear that the old way of easy friendship has indeed been so beaten down that it is nearly effaced: "But let me conjure you, by the rights of our fellowship, by the consonancy of our youth, by the obligation of our ever-preserved love, and by what more dear a better proposer can charge you withal, be even and direct with me, whether you were sent for, or no?" (2.2.282–87). To even this appeal, capable of a very simple yes or no response, Rosencrantz is not prepared to answer ingenuously, asking in an aside to Guildenstern, "What say you?" (2.2.288), that is, "What do you think we should say?" and in observing this, Hamlet also observes right before his eyes the sea change that has taken place in friendship, saying in his own aside, "Nay, then, I have an eye of you" (2.2.289), as he will soon also see before his eyes the withering of his love for Ophelia in her being used as a pawn by the spying eyes of her father and Claudius.

This is not necessarily to say that Rosencrantz and Guildenstern, and certainly not Ophelia, have inherently bad characters. It is Shakespeare's gift—although at times in writing the tragedies, he must have felt it a curse—to show us an older world of nobility and courtesy, a world seen not merely through the lenses of nostalgia or romantic haze but through a poetry that concretizes it and makes it live, subject to pressures of manipulation, cunning, and contrivance that threaten to distort it out of all recognition. These, of course, are not new vices suddenly appearing in the England of 1600. What does seem to have particularly struck Shakespeare is the capacity of these things to tear down an entire social order. In Greek tragedy, larger forces such as fate clearly and almost tangibly could be seen to bring about disaster—the very word means "from the stars"—but in *Hamlet*, while there is, of course, the supernatural agency of the Ghost that alerts strikingly the hero to the "something rotten" in Denmark, the decay of the Danish nobility is also the product of human motives and actions that often are tawdry, as in the spying and evasiveness employed by Claudius with Rosencrantz and Guildenstern, and at other times are poignant, such as in the conflict of loyalties between father and beloved that so tear at Ophelia. That tender natures such as Ophelia's—much less those weak natures such as Rosencrantz's and Guildenstern's, which are easily swayed to cooperate in Claudius' plottings—are destroyed is hardly surprising. What is surprising, astonishing in the older sense of "arousing wonder" or "hardly believable", is Hamlet's ability to preserve basically his own nobility in the midst of this combination of supernatural terror and human contrivance.

To the vexed question of whether or not Hamlet merely feigns madness or does become in fact unhinged, the text provides other clear-cut indications in addition to those I have noted. In Act 2 he feigns madness, showing signs of it only when he plays the part of a jilted lover, which naturally disturbs Ophelia, and when he speaks sarcastically to Polonius when the old man clumsily tries to prove his case that his daughter is the cause of Hamlet's madness. The role of distraught lover was subject to much parody on the Elizabethan stage—the servant Malvolio's dressing cross-gartered and in yellow stockings to impress his socially superior mistress Olivia in *Twelfth Night* is but one of

Shakespeare's own examples—and it is one that Hamlet might be expected to infuse with his own keen satiric spirit. That Ophelia takes it seriously is not surprising, given her undoubted affection for Hamlet and the familial conflict that centers on her, her brother and her father both having told her to discourage the highborn Hamlet's attentions. But all of Hamlet's other interactions and speeches in Act 2 are rational and incisive and display his customary nobility and high-mindedness. We have looked at his conversation with Rosencrantz and Guildenstern above, and even after his suspicions of their mission have been aroused, he concludes his interview with them by grasping their hands and telling them, "Gentlemen, you are welcome to Elsinore" (2.2.366).

After that, he welcomes the acting troupe to Elsinore with this same characteristic generosity and hospitality. Their low social class notwithstanding, Hamlet tells Polonius to see to their needs; Polonius replies that he will "use them according to their desert" (2.2.521–22), to which the Prince makes one of his many famous retorts that Polonius should instead use them much better: "Use every man after his desert, and who shall scape whipping? Use them after your own honor and dignity: the less they deserve, the more merit is in your bounty" (2.2.523–27). These are neither the actions nor the words of a madman. And neither is the final famous soliloquy (beginning "O, what a rogue and peasant slave am I" [2.2.542]) of the noble Prince when he reflects upon the energy and passion he sees in the players' rehearsal of a scene from the *Aeneid* when the Greek warrior Pyrrhus kills the Trojan King Priam, to the accompaniment of the frenzied screams of Queen Hecuba. Hamlet castigates himself ("Why, what an ass am I"), it is true, for what he perceives as his shirking the call of justice against Claudius, but no sooner does he understand this than he exclaims, "About, my brains!" (2.2.584) and immediately thinks of the scheme of the *Mousetrap* play, where he can observe for himself Claudius' guilty or innocent reactions to the play's reenactment of the death of King Hamlet. He says that this is necessary since the ghost that visited him might

have been of infernal origin—"the devil hath power/T' assume
a pleasing shape" (2.2.595–96), a perfectly rational conclusion consistent with centuries of theological thinking. Hamlet's
soliloquies are intense, passionate, and at times tortured—
that is, they are consistent with the pressurized events that
are focused upon him—but they are not mad.

Another great speech in Act 2 is Hamlet's lament to Rosencrantz and Guildenstern that "I have ... lost all my mirth".
This is certainly an exaggeration—witness to the contrary, for
example, the many instances of wit that he displays throughout the play—but nonetheless it is his own acknowledgment
of his currently melancholy disposition, a contrast, as his remarks
make clear, to his former way of life. His famous description of
man in this speech, "How noble in reason! how infinite in faculties! in action, how like an angel! in apprehension, how like
a god!" (2.2.301–5), makes clear that the nobility of man is
still very much in his mind and imagination; there is no one
else in the play, or in just about any play, who can speak more
articulately on subjects like this. But the speech nonetheless
concludes, "And yet, to me, what is this quintessence of dust?
Man delights not me—no, nor woman neither" (2.2.306–8).

There are many other such speeches in contexts like this
that show Hamlet is a great but a tragic figure, that is, one
wounded but not destroyed by the circumstances that press
upon him. As befits one in the tradition of *homo ludens*, man
not as sapiential but rather as playful and festive, he rejoices
that the stage players have come to Elsinore to put on a performance and, again in famous lines, tells them how to speak
their lines, "trippingly on the tongue" (3.2.2); he defines the
"purpose of playing, whose end, both at the first and now, was
and is to hold, as 'twere, the mirror up to nature; to show virtue her own feature, scorn her own image, and the very age
and body of the time his form and pressure" (3.2.18–22). But
it is telling that one who so well understands the liberal ends
of the dramatic arts is at the same time moved to use them
for very practical and illiberal ends; in this instance, that is,
for Hamlet, "The play's the thing/Wherein I'll catch the

conscience of the King" (2.2.600–1). He will not be attending the players' performance of *The Murder of Gonzago* as one enjoying the play for its own sake or for its satiric revelation of society but rather for the very practical purpose of exposing the king, at least to his own satisfaction, as the murderer of his father.

Or to take another instance of something that is supposed to be for sport or enjoyment being used for some other end: Hamlet is fond of fencing and tells Horatio at the end of the play before his duel with Laertes that he has been practicing and will win the wager that the King makes on him, but the duel itself is not for sport or entertainment but is the result of a very devilish and contrived scheme to kill him; and the festive ritual of drinking sportive healths to the fellow revelers and guests, a hospitable custom much practiced by Claudius (too much so in Hamlet's estimation) is turned by the King into his backup plot of murder, a plot that of course misfires and results in Gertrude's death. And then there is Ophelia's fine lament to lost love when Hamlet tells her to go to a nunnery: "O, what a noble mind is here o'er-thrown! ... Th' expectancy and rose of the fair state,/The glass of fashion and the mould of form/Th' observ'd of all observers—quite, quite down!" (3.1.150–54). Here is a classic statement of what was perceived as Hamlet's nobility, but the last description, "Th' observ'd of all observers", is made ambiguous by the context: Ophelia undoubtedly means that Hamlet was an admirable model for emulation, but the audience, through dramatic irony, must also think of the spying being at that moment conducted upon him by Claudius and Polonius—and aided and abetted by Ophelia herself.

So the play in its action, its dramatic contexts, and its hero pits nobility and liberality against newfangled practices in statecraft, love, and friendship; as Hamlet says early on, "The time is out of joint. O cursed spite,/That ever I was born to set it right!" (1.5.189–90). But that is nonetheless what he tries to do. Tragic heroes are, of course, not perfect—this is what allows us to understand them: Hamlet is also frail and stained by the realpolitik that descends like a dark curtain over just about everybody in Denmark, and he remarks accurately that the country is like a prison (2.2.242). His overall ruling passions are melancholy and brooding and also the rashness and anger that lead him to thrust his sword, for example, into the arras in his mother's bedroom, killing Polonius, the one action for which Hamlet himself expresses remorse. His openness and spacious speech are indeed subdued when he is compelled by circumstances to put on his antic disposition or by his rash passion, which he calls a madness. As he acknowledges in a generous speech to Laertes before their duel in the play's final scene: "What I have done / That might your nature, honour, and exception, / Roughly awake, I here proclaim was madness" (5.2.222–24).

But willingness to acknowledge faults is itself a sign of nobility. Hamlet does not whine or cringe in the face of his difficulties, and this is one reason Laertes begins to repent of his own plotting with Claudius to kill Hamlet—after assuring the King that he will hit the Prince with his poisoned sword, he says in an aside, "And yet it is almost against my conscience" (5.2.288), which is a prelude to his full reformation of conscience when, after he is stabbed by the envenomed sword, he says, "The foul practice / Hath turn'd itself on me" (5.2.309–10). And then, as he dies, he implores the Prince, "Exchange forgiveness with me, noble Hamlet. / Mine and my father's death come not upon thee, / Nor thine on me!" (5.2.321–23), to which Hamlet replies, "Heaven make thee free of it!" (5.2.324). The nobility of Hamlet is testified to in many ways in these final scenes but not perhaps more movingly than in this exchange of forgiveness by two enemies. It is also notable that if, as is often said, only our most devoted enemies know us as well as do our best friends, both Laertes and Claudius (who has earlier called Hamlet "free from all contriving" [4.7.135]) are in agreement about Hamlet's generous nature.

For Heaven has indeed been "ordinant" (5.2.48) in many of Hamlet's actions. By not killing the King when he appeared to be praying, Hamlet was saved from an act of ignoble

homicide and was able to accomplish his ends of securing justice for his father's death and the deliverance of the state from
murderous usurpation without, ultimately, resorting to the
Machiavellian practices of his enemy. His deliverance from
the death sentence carried by Rosencrantz and Guildenstern
as they accompanied him to England comes by chance or, to
Hamlet's mind, by providence, for by a sudden inspiration he
is able to read Claudius' deadly message, and this gives to
him the sense of an active providential will at work in his
destiny. As he says to Horatio:

> [L]et us know,
> Our indiscretion sometime serves us well,
> When our deep plots do pall; and that should learn us
> There's a divinity that shapes our ends,
> Rough-hew them how we will.
>
> (5.2.7–11)

Hamlet knows that he is one "benetted round with villainies"
(5.2.29)—the problems he faced were too great for individual
solution—thus his so-called delay, which I am arguing is basically prudent and wise: he must find some way to validate the
ghost's charge, however much it was in accordance with the
premonitions of his heart, and at the same time he must not
give away his suspicions about the King, thus necessitating his
"antic disposition". The rashness in his behavior is a general
failing in Denmark; he remarks to Gertrude, for example,
concerning her sensual behavior with the King, that this is
"reason pander[ing] will" (3.4.87), and willfulness getting the
upper hand of reason is a constant phenomenon in the
play, as seen most egregiously in Claudius' murdering of his
brother from ambition and lust and his inability to repent
even when his reason gives him compelling reasons to do
so. But the reason that rashness for Hamlet is not deadly—
indeed, it is praised by him as an instrument of providence in
the crucial instance of his reading the King's murder warrant
for him—is precisely because of his being free from all contrivance: providence has room to operate within his character,

for he is, as he said of Horatio, "one who in suff'ring all that suffers nothing" (3.2.64); others do the plotting in Act 5 and they are, in another strong motif of the play, hoist with their own petard; or as Laertes says when he is dying by his own trickery, "The foul practice / Hath turn'd itself on me" (5.2.309–10).

So where does Hamlet rank in the pantheon of world literary heroes? Very high indeed. Of course, if he were simply the dithering, can't-make-up-my-mind-what-to-do figure of popular caricature, he would hardly merit a mention. The name of that type is Legion. But fortunately, that is not Shakespeare's creation. Like many towering tragic figures, such as Job or Oedipus, he is dealt a very bad hand. And also like Job, he complains about it—but in some of the world's greatest poetry. He is like these two great precursors, again, in that he ultimately chooses to suffer the slings and arrows of outrageous fortune rather than to take arms against them by ending his own life. Of Shakespeare's other greatest tragic heroes, Othello, Lear, Macbeth, and Anthony, Hamlet is the least responsible by his personal actions for the dilemma into which he is thrust. Here again he is similar to Job and Oedipus: it would almost seem that some outside agency has concocted this web of circumstance that so hems him in, as the wager between Satan and God was responsible for Job's time of trial and as the mysterious prophecy that Oedipus would kill his father and marry his mother seems to bring about the Greek's misery—the more the prophecy is seemingly evaded, the closer it is brought to realization. Among Shakespeare's heroes, Lear acts with vanity and choler in demanding that his daughters tell him how much they love him, Othello doubts the honor of the best woman in Venice for the flimsiest of reasons, Macbeth has a list of crimes a mile long, and Anthony gives up perhaps too easily any attempt to reconcile love and duty. I certainly do not mean to say that these figures do not themselves also win their way through to wisdom and noble stature, but their clear, sometimes criminal responsibility for their problems must figure in any judgments about them.

But Hamlet is faced with a horror not of his own making, and in some ways his situation is more difficult than even Job's or Oedipus'. Job must suffer the envy and ignorance of his three friends, who try to convict him of wrongdoing for which there is no basis at all, but he can at least vent his emotions and candor upon them in his memorable replies. And when God speaks to him out of the whirlwind, there is no question of who it is who is speaking: this, Job clearly understands, is no devil taking a pleasing shape but rather the God of Abraham, Isaac, and Jacob. Hamlet, on the other hand, cannot say what he thinks to those (except Horatio) who are closest to him but must speak his frustration only in soliloquies. And when the supernatural does speak to Hamlet, it is by means of a ghost of dubious origin. As for Oedipus, throughout most of *Oedipus Rex*, he thinks that he is the avenger of the curse of sterility brought upon his land of Thebes, as he is willing to pursue to the utmost the investigation to uncover the murder of the previous king, Laius. His recognition of his own involvement in the crime comes late. But Hamlet is introduced to the facts of his situation in the first act. Once Oedipus is aware of his guilt, he does not stop the truth from coming out, an act of heroism; Hamlet, though, is aware almost from the beginning of the need for actions that will put him in great danger and that, as he progressively sees, will take away from him nearly everything he holds dear. His delay is in order to assess the situation; his soliloquies are not to find a weak substitute for action but rather to explore articulately in the only way possible the complexities of his circumstances; and his resignation to providence in Act 5 is not a world-weariness but is a desire to bring matters to a head. As he says to Horatio, when his friend suggests he move slowly, if things are not resolved now, they will be soon: "[T]he readiness is all" (5.2.214–15).

For, ultimately, the greatness of Job, Oedipus, and Hamlet involves their touching a realm higher than the merely human; their suffering is of such a dimension and intensity, and their acceptance of it is sufficiently genuine, that they are given a glimpse of the transcendent. Yahweh speaks directly to Job at greater poetic length than he does to anyone else in the Old Testament and in a way that recalls the creation in Genesis; in the depths of his misery, Oedipus is called by his adversary Creon a "holy" thing; and Hamlet has at the end a decided sense of cooperating with a providential destiny. Only accepted suffering, tragedy seems to say, can bring about such transformations. Hamlet is admired by friends and enemies in the play, and at the very end tribute is given him also by a stranger, Fortinbras, who says he was apt to have "prov'd most royal" (5.2.389–90) had he lived. But the final words about Hamlet should always be those of Horatio: "Now cracks a noble heart. Good night, sweet prince, / And flights of angels sing thee to thy rest!" (5.2.351–52).

Hamlet's Envenomed Foil

Andrew Moran
University of Dallas

In his speech to the players before their performance of *The Mousetrap*, Hamlet insists that the clowns' improvisations should not distract from "some necessary question of the play" (3.2.41–42),[1] and in a play that, as Harry Levin observes, revolves around questions,[2] it is worth considering what may well be the "necessary question" of *Hamlet*: "Who's there?" (1.1.1). The play's first line, cried out in the cold and dark by the sentinel Bernardo, not only introduces the audience to an anxious Elsinore haunted by apparitions and frenetically preparing for war but also commences a series of questions about identity—what is the apparition? Is it a soul from Purgatory or a demon from Hell? Is Hamlet mad or mad only in craft?—that rarely receive satisfactory answers. Indeed, even Bernardo's apparently simple question does not receive a straightforward response from his fellow sentinel Francisco. So too does Francisco's similar question to Marcellus and Horatio, "Who is there?" (1.1.14), not draw from them their names. At the most, these characters identify themselves by political loyalty—"Long live the King", "[f]riends to this ground", "liegemen to the Dane" (1.1.14, 15)—a self-identification rendered dubious by the character and fate of Rosencrantz and Guildenstern, Claudius' "sponge[s]" (4.2.11–20). Likewise, Horatio's reply to Bernardo's

My thanks to Dr. Christopher Malloy of the University of Dallas and Dr. Joseph Stibora of the University of Dallas Rome Campus for directing me toward pertinent passages in the works of Martin Luther.

[1] All citations from *Hamlet* are from the edition published by Ignatius Press: *Hamlet, Prince of Denmark*, ed. Joseph Pearce (San Francisco: Ignatius, 2008). Citations from other plays are from *The Riverside Shakespeare*, 2nd ed., ed. G. Blakemore Evans (Boston: Houghton Mifflin, 1997).

[2] Harry Levin, *The Question of Hamlet* (New York: Oxford University Press, 1959), pp. 19–22.

question as to whether he is there—"A piece of him" (1.1.21)—
further contributes to the sense of confusion and insecurity. The
whole man is not there, and unambiguous answers about identity are not forthcoming. What next follows, Horatio's inquiry
of the ghost, "What art thou . . . ?" (1.1.46), meets with silence,
and the scholar and the sentries can only puzzle over how "like"
(1.1.41, 43, 58, 110) the apparition is to old King Hamlet but
not assert a definite identity. As Stephen Greenblatt explains,
Marcellus and Horatio's befuddlement—"Is it not like the King?" /
"As thou art to thyself" (1.1.58–59)—reflects back on themselves as it "raise[s] the possibility of a difference between oneself
and oneself."[3] Even before Hamlet is "not himself" (5.2.227),
even before he considers how man may be both "like an angel"
and "like a god" and yet the "quintessence of dust" (2.2.304–5,
307), even before he peers into the obscured identities of the
ghost, Claudius, Gertrude, Ophelia, and others, the play confronts us with its necessary question. "Who's there?" if not always
in so few words, is asked again and again and repeatedly left
unanswered—Hamlet is not the only one who cannot "[m]ake
you a wholesome answer" (3.2.313).

   Hamlet also receives an incomplete answer when he asks
what, other than a brief rejoinder to his mother, are his own
first questions: "And what make you from Wittenberg, Horatio? . . . But what, in faith, make you from Wittenberg?"
(1.2.164, 168). What one "in faith" makes from Wittenberg
are the teachings of Martin Luther. The prince is a student
at the Lutheran university, and his pronouncements frequently have a distinctively Lutheran resonance, and so a number of recent studies of *Hamlet* have examined the place of
Luther and Lutheranism.[4] Yet the inquiry into doctrinal and

---

[3] Stephen Greenblatt, *Hamlet in Purgatory* (Princeton: Princeton University Press, 2001), p. 211.

[4] For example, in "Certain Speculations on *Hamlet*, the Calendar, and Martin Luther", *Early Modern Literary Studies* 2, no. 1 (1996): 5.1–51, Steve Sohmer discerns a Lutheran parody of Catholic feast days and connections between the lives of Luther and Hamlet, with Horatio a type of Philipp Melanchthon, the logical defender of the Lutheran faith, as is present in his name: *ora* (pray) and

confessional influences may be deepened if one recognizes that, in a sense, Hamlet's questions and *Hamlet's* necessary question are one and the same. What one in faith makes from Wittenberg is not a reformed understanding of God but a reformed understanding of man. During the Reformation, Roman Catholics and almost all Protestants remained largely in agreement about the nature of God. The Trinity; the Incarnation; Christ's human and divine natures; his life on earth; his Passion, Resurrection, and Ascension—such doctrines, at the heart of the trinitarian and Christological controversies that split apart the early Church, were largely absent from the polemics of the sixteenth and seventeenth centuries. In the most literal sense, the Reformation was not a theological dispute; it was an anthropological one, an argument not about the nature of God but about the nature of man. Specifically, the Reformation began with an argument about the effects of sin on man and the manner in which sinful man can then be justified. The Catholic Church, as it would proclaim at Trent in the Decree on Original Sin (1546), understands that "the guilt of original sin is remitted by the grace of our Lord Jesus Christ conferred in baptism" and that the "inclination to sin" that remains after baptism is not sin itself.[5] Since true goodness and meritorious activity remain possible, the Decree on Justification (1547) asserts that those "cut off from God by sin may be disposed through his quickening and helping grace to convert themselves to their own justification by freely assenting to and cooperating with that grace."[6] In contrast, Luther taught that the concupiscence born from original sin is intrinsic to human nature and remains as sin after baptism. Hence, since man's inherent sinfulness makes him in no way able to cooperate in his own justification, for

---

ratio (reason) (see n. 21 below). It may be more germane that Melanchthon was a master of the *oratio*. Raymond Waddington, "Lutheran Hamlet", *English Language Notes* 27, no. 2 (1989): 27–39, also finds that Luther is a model for Hamlet.

[5] *The Teaching of the Catholic Church*, ed. Karl Rahner, S.J. (New York: Alba House), p. 139.

[6] Ibid., p. 386.

Luther justification consists of a gracious God's imputation of righteousness.

Thus, the necessary question of the Reformation was not "Who is God?" but "Who is man?"—"Who's there?" Bernardo is only repeating the question that had preoccupied Europe since the Reformation. Is man a fallen creature who, with the aid of God's grace, is still able to do some good and thus participate in his own salvation? Or is he "an evil tree and by nature a child of wrath and sin"?[7] This essay will seek to understand *Hamlet* and its treatment of human identity in the light of this Reformation controversy and will argue that the play—through Hamlet's concern with the "spots" of sin, his interest in drama and other representations, his death, and the contrast with his "foil" Ophelia—intimates a distinct understanding of Lutheran, or more generally Reformed anthropology. I do not, however, read Shakespeare as a propagandist any more than I read him as a proto-postmodernist exploiting the cultural energies of religious discourses. Shakespeare may very well be a much more subtle religious thinker than has been generally recognized, one not only conversant with the doctrinal controversies of his age but also thoughtful about their significance. Shakespeare, I presume, understands the implications of doctrine and is moralist enough to represent these implications.

Hamlet is famous for his indecisiveness and confusion, as one who works in the "interrrogatory" rather than the "exclamatory" mood,[8] and the whole play well represents the epistemological skepticism of the early modern period. *Hamlet*, writes Aaron Landau, "far from representing a systematic or even coherent line of thought, virtually subsumes the intellectual confusion of the age."[9] Yet Hamlet insists, and the play returns again and again, to his one surety: that man is not merely a

---

[7] Martin Luther, referencing Psalm 51:5, in *The Seven Penitential Psalms*, in *Luther's Works* (St. Louis: Concordia Publishing House, 1958), 14:169.

[8] Levin, *Question of Hamlet*, p. 31.

[9] Aaron Landau, "'Let Me Not Burst in Ignorance': Skepticism and Anxiety in *Hamlet*", *English Studies* 82, no. 3 (June 2001): 218–30.

sinner but one for whom sin is the defining element. Whether or not Martin Luther is a prototype, Hamlet, in his preoccupation with sin, shares Luther's anthropology.[10] Luther explains how his and all men's natures are defined by sin: "Behold, it is so true that before Thee I am a sinner that even my nature, my very beginning, my conception is sin, to say nothing of the words, works, thoughts, and life which follow. How could I be without sin if I was made in sin and sin is my nature and manner?"[11] Likewise, Hamlet tells Ophelia that to marry is to be "a breeder of sinners" such as himself:

> I am myself indifferent honest, but yet I could accuse me of such things that it were better my mother had not borne me: I am very proud, revengeful, ambitious; with more offences at my beck than I have thoughts to put them in, imagination to give them shape, or time to act them in. What should such fellows as I do crawling between earth and heaven? We are arrant knaves, all; believe none of us.
>
> (3.1.122–30)

As Harold Jenkins notes, Hamlet shifts from "I" to "we", an indication that he is thinking not of his own particular sins but those of mankind.[12] He can speak of mankind as thoroughly depraved because, he tells Ophelia, "virtue cannot so inoculate our old stock but we shall relish of it" (3.1.117–18). The taint of original sin, "our old stock", never vanishes, and that concupiscence, which for the Lutheran Hamlet is sin itself, obviates the virtue of any deed.[13] For "if it be considered as it

---

[10] Father Peter Milward recognizes this as well: "There is surely something Lutheran in [Hamlet's] brooding emphasis on the corruption of human nature." *Shakespeare's Religious Background* (Bloomington: Indiana University Press, 1973), p. 161. Roland Mushat Frye, *The Renaissance Hamlet: Issues and Responses in 1600* (Princeton: Princeton University Press, 1984), p. 177, finds Luther's "general understanding of human nature" present in Hamlet's speech to Ophelia in Act 3, scene 1, which he understands as evidence of laudable moral seriousness.

[11] Luther, *Penitential Psalms*, p. 169.

[12] The Arden Shakespeare, *Hamlet*, ed. Harold Jenkins, (London: Thomson Learning, 2003), p. 282.

[13] Hamlet had said essentially the same thing earlier to Horatio: "The dram of eale [evil]" blots out "all the noble substance" of a man (1.4.36–37).

really is in the judgment of God," according to Luther in his *Defense and Explanation of All the Articles*, "every work of the just is worthy of damnation and a mortal sin."[14] It follows that, since sin overwhelms everything, including what is seemingly good, Ophelia's beauty "will sooner transform honesty from what it is to a bawd than the force of honesty can translate beauty into his likeness" (3.1.113–14). Her beauty merely excites concupiscence. All human things begin and end in sin.

Hamlet's first soliloquy begins with a complaint about sinful human nature, "this too, too sullied[15] flesh" (1.2.129), a characterization of the flesh that decries both literal and spiritual carnality and that, R. Chris Hassel Jr. argues, brings "into the play's interpretive arena prominent aspects of Martin Luther's theology of justification by grace."[16] Here is the first of a number of references to things being "sullied" or spotted. In order that Reynaldo may learn of Laertes' activities in Paris, Polonius counsels him to defame his son before his acquaintances by fabricating flaws, such as fighting, drinking, and whoring, that seem to be "the taints of liberty", "slight sullies" on a young man who is "a little soil'd" (2.1.28–40). Hamlet is angry that the drunkenness of the Danish court "soil[s]" its reputation (1.4.20). Then again, that men are spotted, that there is "some vicious mole of nature in them", is inherent, something "in their birth, wherein they are not guilty,/ (Since nature cannot choose his origin)", but that still overcomes their "virtues", even in those "as pure as grace" (1.4.23–33). Again, there is the Lutheran notion of the ineradicability of original sin being the essential aspect of human nature, and indeed Lutheran teaching uses the metaphor of spots. *The Formula of Concord* (1580) rejects and condemns "the view

---

[14] Quoted in Johann Adam Möhler, *Symbolism*, trans. James Burton Robertson (New York: Crossroads, 1997), p. 22. Cf. Hamlet's remark to Polonius: "Use every man after his desert, and who shall scape whipping?" (2.2.524–25).

[15] I am using the rendering from the Second Quarto here, which reads "sallied" (that is, "sullied") rather than "solid".

[16] R. Chris Hassel Jr., "Hamlet's 'Too, Too Solid Flesh'", *Sixteenth Century Journal* 25 (1994): 609–22.

that this blemish [of original sin] may be removed as readily
as a spot can be washed from the face or color from the wall".
The *Formula* goes on to explain that this blemish "inheres in
the nature, substance and essence of man in such a way that
... man's nature is corrupted through original sin, innate in
us through our sinful seed and the source of all other, actual
sins".[17] Obviously, the metaphor of a spot standing for sin is
common enough and does not necessarily point to a Lutheran
subtext in *Hamlet*. But the fact that the spot overcomes all
human virtue is redolent of Lutheran teaching, as is the presence of that spot for men "in their birth" and as is, most especially, its permanence. Hamlet, attempting to teach his mother
how wickedly she has sinned by marrying her late husband's
brother, promises to "set ... up a glass/Where you may see
the inmost part of you" (3.4.19–20). After he compares her
second husband to her first and catalogs her sins, Gertrude is
convinced: "Thou turn'st my eyes into my very soul;/And
there I see such black and grained spots/As will not leave
their tinct" (89–91). The spots on her soul are irremovable.

The looking glass for his mother's soul is but one of Hamlet's
metaphorical mirrors, and his use of various media of representation may follow from and cohere with his religious beliefs.
Whether or not a Lutheran anthropology undergirds his mimetic
practice, it goes without saying that his favorite medium is theater. Rosencrantz finds in Hamlet "a kind of joy/To hear of"
the Players' arrival (3.1.18–19), and even from his first appearance, the Prince evinces a highly theatrical consciousness as
he tells his mother that his expressions of grief for his late father
"are the actions that a man might play" but nonetheless are
insufficient to denote his sorrow (1.2.76–86). As Michael
O'Connell notes, Hamlet will later continually call attention
to the theater so overtly—pointing to the ghost as being under
the stage (1.5.164), drawing Rosencrantz's and Guildenstern's
attention to the physical features of the Globe theater

---

[17] *The Book of Concord*, trans. Theodore G. Tappert (Philadelphia: Fortress
Press, 1959), art. 1, antitheses 5, 9, p. 468.

(2.2.299–301), and discussing with them London's theater wars (2.2.330–58)—that it seems that Shakespeare intends to distract his audience from his own play.[18] Hamlet himself, however, readily accepts such dramatic fictions, as in these he appears to find analogous truth and models by which to act. The Player's recitation of the death of Priam at the hands of Pyrrhus confirms Hamlet's desire for vengeance. Unclear as to whether the Ghost is his father or a demon that aims at his damnation, Hamlet resolves to stage a play, Claudius' reaction to which will confirm or deny guilt. Indeed, Hamlet lectures the Player that "the purpose of playing … is to hold, as 'twere, the mirror up to nature" (3.2.16–17); the play will so mirror the murder that Claudius watching it will exhibit his guilt.

Of course, neither the story of the fall of Troy nor *The Mousetrap* is perfectly analogous to Claudius' killing of his brother. Indeed, what should disquiet Hamlet is that the villain in the first is a black-clad son seeking revenge for his father, while in the second the villain is a nephew killing a king. Moreover, while Claudius is his brother's killer, the King's reaction to the play offers no sure proof of this, and the scene of a nephew committing regicide could to a neutral observer account for the King's displeasure. Every analogy limps, and Hamlet fails to recognize that these theatrical analogies correspond only so far. Despite his confidence that he has succeeded (3.2.260–88), it is questionable how well he has held the mirror up to nature. Likewise, the static images he displays may not so obviously prove his point. He believes that Gertrude, looking on the "counterfeit presentment" (3.4.54) of old Hamlet and Claudius, will recognize the nobility of the former and the baseness of the latter, and so the portraits will teach that her desire for her present husband betokens "black and grained spots" on her soul. Yet the compared portraits of Claudius and old Hamlet, even if the latter is hyperbolically likened to Hyperion, Jove, Mars, and Mercury (3.4.56–58), do not determine that Gertrude sins

---

[18] Michael O'Connell, *The Idolatrous Eye: Iconoclasm and Theater in Early-Modern England* (New York: Oxford University Press, 2000), p. 133.

in remarrying. When the Queen demands that Hamlet state her crime (3.4.39–40), Hamlet leaves unmentioned incest, her particular sin, while he evinces disgust that for his uncle, whose portrait he now puts to her face (3.4.53), she could feel desire. The image, he believes, should manifest that sin—and he does persuade her—but that same portrait, he had previously acknowledged, now commands up to one hundred ducats. The picture the Prince abhors the people adore. "Sblood, there is something in this more than natural, if philosophy could find it out" (2.2.363–64). What philosophy might find out is that these images and these performances, while not necessarily false, are not necessarily more true and authoritative than anything else. Hamlet is right to despise his uncle, the people wrong to honor him, but the contrast between his and their appreciation of the King's image, as well as the difference between his and popular theatrical tastes (2.2.428–35; 3.2.8–12; 3.2.22–43), ought to reveal to the Prince the ambiguity of these media. The whole of Claudius is not present in his portrait. As Magritte might write on it, "This is not the King." Indeed, Ophelia deprived of reason is only a "picture" (4.5.83) of herself; if Laertes does not truly mourn the death of his father, he is, says Claudius, only the "painting" of sorrow (4.7.108). This association of pictures with fragmented, misleading, or unstable identity all the more calls into question Hamlet's reliance upon images.

Shakespeare, of course, is a dramatist, a maker of images. And thus it is all the more ironic that his creation, who so trusts in representations, who as Scott Crider argues "does not acknowledge the limits of mimesis",[19] is yet unusually sensitive, famously so, to the disjunction between appearance and reality, the one whom we first see scorning hypocrisy and declaiming against "seems" (1.2.76). Indeed, his thinking moves beyond skepticism into nihilism.[20] His inveterate punning

[19] Scott Crider, "With What Persuasion: Shakespeare and the Ethics of Rhetoric" (unpublished manuscript), p. 4.

[20] "Shakespeare devotes much of the early and middle portions of the play to an anatomy of nihilism as it might be experienced in a soul formed by Christian belief yet untouched by Christian teachings upon hope" (John Alvis,

stems less from playfulness and more from a sense of the instability and ultimate meaninglessness of "words, words, words" (2.2.192). His apparent position, that the human perception and expression of a thing does not correspond to the thing itself, receives fuller formulation in his claim that "there is nothing either good or bad, but thinking makes it so" (2.2.248– 50). It is, of course, difficult to penetrate the levels of Hamlet's irony, especially considering his precarious position at Elsinore—in the above quotations, he is first mocking Polonius and then playing with Rosencrantz and Guildenstern, all the while shielding himself from their inquiries. But his subsequent assertion, that "by my fay [faith], I cannot reason" (2.2.264), whether he is being ironic after a game of logic chopping with his university friends or hinting at a Lutheran belief in the fallenness of human reason,[21] is all of a piece with his constant doubts about how one is to act and what one can actually know. Even conscience fails to provide direction; instead of regarding it as the faculty that distinguishes right from wrong, Hamlet redefines it as "dread", something that "does make cowards of us all" (3.1.78, 83).[22] And so Hamlet's confidence in reflections and representations is all

---

Shakespeare's Understanding of Honor [Durham, N.C.: Carolina Academic Press, 1990], p. 68). Alvis also notes that Hamlet "severely deprecat[es] human capacities for virtue" (p. 74).

[21] B. A. Gerrish, in *Grace and Reason: A Study in the Theology of Luther* (Oxford: Oxford University Press, 1962), notes that Luther in his last Wittenberg sermon called reason "the Devil's whore" and elsewhere "a beast", "the enemy of God", "a source of mischief", "carnal", and "stupid" (p. 1). Gerrish argues that in these instances Luther is criticizing reason that trespasses upon the domain of faith, that there is a proper sphere for natural reason in the consideration of purely temporal matters, and that there may even be a regenerate reason in service to faith. Nonetheless, as to moral issues, reason is only of formal value: it knows that there is a good that should be followed but does not know what it is. Hamlet will later speak of "godlike reason" (4.4.38) but in the context of reason serving ambition and revenge.

[22] In so redefining "conscience", Hamlet is not in very good company. Others who do so include Dionyza (*Pericles*, 4.1.4) and Richard III (*Richard III*, 5.3.179, 309, 311). Hamlet later will use "conscience" in the more typical sense but only to justify killing Rosencrantz and Guildenstern (5.2.58) and Claudius (5.2.67).

the more perplexing. Possibly the very absence of knowledge accessible through discursive reasoning and conscience accounts for this turn to mirrors, stories, and pictures.

Whatever the origins of his mimetic frenzy, in his employment of another medium, Hamlet moves from intellectual error to moral turpitude. Hamlet not only enjoys theater; he participates in it, staging scenes in which other people are the chosen medium. Hamlet calls his plan to have Rosencrantz and Guildenstern executed a "play" (5.2.31),[23] and Hamlet's treatment of Ophelia, which Samuel Johnson rightly describes as "useless and wanton cruelty",[24] is in part play-acting: while Hamlet may be sincere when he tells her to "get thee to a nunnery", his manic appearance in her closet (2.1.74–100) is a piece of stagecraft, as is his love letter (2.2.115–24). Laertes' sincere grief when she dies, Hamlet adapts as a prologue for his histrionic grief (5.1.263–65). The visiting players are not the only ones Hamlet uses to mirror nature.

What do they mirror? And what are the implications of regarding other people as mirrors? Critics have long noted that Laertes and Fortinbras are "foils" to Hamlet, that they reveal him by contrasting with him, as a thin metallic leaf contrasts with and so increases the brilliance of a jewel. When Hamlet and Laertes receive their foils before the fencing match, the former puns on this sense of the word: "I'll be your foil, Laertes; in mine ignorance/Your skill shall, like a star i' th' darkest night,/Stick fiery off indeed" (5.2.247–48). But a foil is as well the thin sheet of metal placed behind the glass of a mirror that produces a reflection. Like a metaphor, a foil, through the two meanings, is both unlike and like another thing. And so Laertes and Fortinbras are foils to Hamlet in that they mirror him, as all three are young men who seek to respond with violence to the killing of a father. Or, more often the case, he imitates them. Since Fortinbras, for honor's sake, is to fight a

[23] Crider, "With What Persuasion", 47.

[24] Samuel Johnson, *The Plays of William Shakespeare*, in *Samuel Johnson's Literary Criticism*, ed. R. D. Stock (Lincoln: University of Nebraska Press, 1974), p. 194.

bloody battle against Poland for a worthless piece of land, so too must Hamlet "find quarrel in a straw,/When honour's at the stake" (4.4.55–56). Since Laertes mourns at Ophelia's grave, so too must Hamlet,[25] and so too will he imitate any of Laertes' acts:

> 'Swounds, show me what th'owt do:
> Woo't weep, woo't fight, woo't fast, woo't tear thyself,
> Woo't drink up easel, eat a crocodile?
> I'll do't.
>
> (5.1.268–71)

Hamlet will later compliment Laertes as "a soul of great article" whose "semblable is his mirror" (5.2.116, 117–18), but he has already made himself that "semblable". His later pun is unnecessary: Hamlet already is Laertes' foil.

Hamlet does not, however, understand the implications of being another's foil. He continues his exaggerated compliment of Laertes by saying that anyone who would "trace him", as Hamlet has done, is "his umbrage", his shadow (119). The one's identity then becomes inseparable from the other's. The two not only mirror and spur to action, they also define and give being to each other. One's identity is dependent upon the other's, as is a shadow upon a substance. And if Hamlet has multiple foils—the two other young men most obviously, but also Horatio, Ophelia, Claudius, and even Pyrrhus and Lucianus—Hamlet can know "who's there" only by looking around a hall of mirrors. His self is fractured into a multitude of images. He is "distracted" (1.5.97, 3.1.5, 5.2.222), literally "drawn apart".[26]

To reduce others to mirrors not only fractures oneself, however. Hamlet, who is to remember his father, instead becomes

[25] René Girard also sees this: "The reflective mood of the conversation with Horatio gives way to a wild imitation of the rival's theatrical mourning" (*A Theater of Envy* [New York: Oxford University Press, 1991], p. 278).

[26] Because of mercury fumes, insanity was known in Venice to be an occupational hazard of mirror makers. See "The History of Mirrors", Vision2Form Design, http://vision2form.nl/mirror_history.html (accessed October 14, 2006).

a dismemberer, of himself and Elsinore. When Gertrude says her son has gone "[t]o draw apart the body he hath kill'd" (4.1.24), her words may signify not only Polonius' corpse but something more, a common body, for Hamlet's mirrors fracture human bonds. If one appraises oneself by another, the other becomes a threat; the other's success diminishes one if one is defined in opposition to the other. Hence, envy is the presiding sin of *Hamlet*. Old Fortinbras, for example, is spurred on to war by "a most emulate pride" (1.1.83), and Claudius presumably murders his brother out of envy for his crown and wife. Immediately after Hamlet envies Fortinbras for "find-[ing] quarrel in a straw", a gentleman says the mad Ophelia "[s]purns enviously at straws" (4.5.6). But it is Hamlet who is most beset with this sin, in particular with regard to his closest foil, Laertes. He resents that Laertes in his grief "outface[s] me" (5.1.272). Of Laertes' virtues that "pluck such envy from him", none "so envenom [Hamlet] with his envy" than his talent at fencing (4.7.74, 103). The King recognizes that Hamlet is so envious of Laertes that he can provoke him to a fencing match, at which Hamlet will be cut by an uncovered sword whose point is smeared with poison, by having Osric "praise [Laertes'] excellence,/And set a double varnish on [his] fame" (4.7.131–32). Hamlet, despite his and Horatio's misgivings, accepts the challenge: "[L]et the foils be brought"; "Give us the foils" (5.2.170, 246). Envy, occasioned by defining himself through the mirror of another, leads to his death: the foil is poisoned.

"The treacherous instrument is in thy hand", the dying Laertes informs Hamlet, its "point envenom'd" (5.2.308, 313). Previously, Hamlet had held another foil, to show Gertrude a point, or spot, which she then assumed was permanently ingrained on her soul. May it be that the spot, however, is on that mirror? He stigmatizes his mother, but the stigma—or "foil", yet another meaning of the word in Shakespeare's time[27]—may very well be on his looking

---

[27] *Oxford English Dictionary*, 2b. (Henceforth cited as *OED*.)

glass.[28] The black spot is projected by Hamlet, "the glass of fashion" (3.1.153): the troublesome mote is on his mind's eye. This is not to say that Hamlet initiates Denmark's corruption. Gertrude is guilty of incest and disloyalty, Claudius is a murderer, and Elsinore hosts a sinister cabal of spies and lackeys, and so one's initial sympathies go to the Prince. Yet Hamlet exacerbates the situation as his actions lead directly or indirectly to the deaths of Polonius, Ophelia, Rosencrantz, Guildenstern, the Queen, Laertes, the King, and finally himself. The student from Wittenberg's perception of and response to sin lead only to greater sin, and it may be that what Shakespeare represents as fatal and venomous is Lutheran teaching on the ineradicability of sin. The representation is, to be sure, hyperbolic but may be intimating that this doctrine has dangerous implications. As "disposition" is a term from rhetoric and logic for "[t]he due arrangement of the parts of an argument or discussion",[29] Horatio's answer as to what in faith he makes from Wittenberg—"a truant disposition" (1.2.169)—may have a meaning of which the scholar is unaware. If the spot of sin is ingrained, if that disfigurement is permanent and an essential, if not the essential, human characteristic, then the identity of human beings as creatures made in the image and likeness of God is obscured to the point of being forgotten or lost.[30] To the question "Who's there?" men now answer, "Arrant knaves, all." Such fellows should not be "crawling between earth and heaven" since the human likeness to heavenly things is tenuous at best. Since God is perfect, spotted human beings, the "quintessence of dust", can no longer be, like the eyes of Beatrice, mirrors that reflect back the divine image. Thus, there is a need for a new image of man to provide

[28] If the last drops of redundant mercury and tin did not drop off during production, a crystallization of the amalgam would be left on the lower part of the mirror ("The History of Mirrors").

[29] *OED*, 1c. The adjective "truant" then had the sense of "wandering, straying" (1).

[30] Alvis argues something similar: Hamlet denies "the capacity of limited creatures to show forth vestiges of their Creator's goodness" (p. 78).

self-knowledge. But having been dispossessed of a higher self-understanding, human beings can know their identity only through the mirror of other human beings, who for the Lutheran Hamlet are as besmirched as he is, sinners meriting contempt, rivals provoking envy.[31] The envenomed foil that kills Hamlet is the spot of sin that will not leave its tinct; the envenomed foil is the mirror that images men who share no resemblance to the divine image.

One last foil, now in the sense of a character who mirrors Hamlet, may indicate what is, for Shakespeare, the essential problem with Reformed anthropology. Ophelia, too, loses her mind after the murder of a father, and her death, seemingly unlike Hamlet's, has a symbolic resonance that links it with his. She dies when, while climbing a willow tree, an "envious sliver" (4.7.175) breaks from a branch, dropping her into the "glassy stream" (4.7.168), in which she drowns. But Ophelia is his foil, in the sense of a contrast, as well, both in her death and in her madness. She is not looking into the glassy stream but rather is climbing, ascending, to hang her "crownet weeds" (4.7.173), when the envious sliver sends her to her death. Some think her death a suicide, yet the "crowner" (5.1.4) judges her worthy of Christian burial. The alternative spellings of "coronet" and "coroner" may be significant: Has Ophelia merited an eternal crown, the crown with which she was seeking to ascend? Certainly her last thoughts are more pious than Hamlet's. His are not with his salvation nor with the welfare of anyone else but with his "wounded name" (5.2.336); that is, in his last three speeches, he speaks of his reputation, the "story" (5.2.341) that will be told about him, by which his identity will be mirrored to others and preserved after his death. She, in contrast, dies "chant[ing] snatches of old lauds" (4.7.179),

---

[31] A remarkable irony becomes apparent from this insight into Lutheran anthropology: the Reformed doctrine of inhering sin that can only be covered over by God, in some ways a reaction against the anthropocentrism of Italian Renaissance humanism and the Catholic belief in intercession, ultimately substitutes a more extreme anthropocentrism.

and the gravedigger complains that "she wilfully seeks her own salvation" (5.1.2). This subtle reference, to the Tridentine doctrine of human cooperation with grace in the justification and salvation of souls, is but one of Ophelia's Catholic associations. Her reading a book when Hamlet finds her is reminiscent of the Virgin in countless paintings of the Annunciation.[32] But more than her image, her actions are Catholic. While the visit to the cemetery provokes Hamlet to nausea and the thought of "[t]o what base uses we may return" (5.1.197), she thinks of the "true-love showers" (4.5.38) the dead are owed. Her final words are a song that ends with a prayer for the dead—"God-a-mercy on his soul"—followed by her own prayer: "And of all Christian souls, I pray God. God buy you" (4.5.196).[33] She prays for the salvation of souls; Hamlet wishes for or even actively seeks after their damnation (1.2.182, 3.3.73–96, 5.2.47).

Such malice is antithetical to love; Hamlet is loveless. "Love! His affections do not that way tend" (3.1.162), judges Claudius. For Hamlet, the suffering of others means little, and even his mother's death prompts nothing more than "Wretched Queen, adieu!" (5.2.325). Hamlet spurns Ophelia and even denigrates love itself.[34] He chooses to have staged *The Mousetrap*, in which the king argues that fortune is more powerful than love since the will is too weak to remain constant (3.2.195–208),[35] a claim then buttressed by its plot. Here

---

[32] Bridget Gellert Lyons, "The Iconography of Ophelia", *English Literary History* 44 (Spring 1977): 60–74.

[33] In what is otherwise an excellent argument, Anthony Low, in "*Hamlet* and the Ghost of Purgatory: Intimations of Killing the Father", *English Literary Renaissance* 29, no. 3 (Autumn 1999): 443–66, errs in stating that "[n]owhere in this play does anyone mention Purgatory or pray for the dead" (p. 459).

[34] Cf. Luther in his *Lectures on Galatians*: "A curse on a love that is observed at the expense of the doctrine of faith, to which everything must yield—love, an apostle, an angel from heaven, etc.!" *Luther's Works* 27:38. He as well asserts, "Let that expression 'faith formed' be damned!" (i.e., the Catholic doctrine of "faith formed by charity") (*Luther's Works* 26:273).

[35] Hamlet's foil Claudius also argues that love is transient because of the weakness of the will (4.7.110–26). The fatalism of these passages comports with Luther's belief, explained throughout *De servo arbitrio*, in the utter passivity of the will.

he again contrasts with Ophelia. After Hamlet accuses her of unchastity, she still prays for him and agonizes over his madness (3.1.134–61).[36] When she goes mad, her thoughts particularly turn to love. She sings of knowing one's "true love" (4.5.23), and in her song of a maid betrayed by a false lover, she swears "[b]y Gis [Jesus] and by Saint Charity" (4.5.56). Her meek response to her father's death—"I hope all will be well. We must be patient; but I cannot choose but weep to think they would lay him i' th' cold ground" (4.5.66–68)— contrasts to the violence of Hamlet and Laertes.

The mad Ophelia speaks obscurely, but there is a pattern in her words, an emphasis on love, including love for the dead, and that emphasis may relate to another of her seemingly random phrases: "Lord, we know what we are, but know not what we may be" (4.5.41–42). She alludes, in fact, to the First Letter of John: "Dearly beloved, nowe are we the sonnes of God, but yet it is not made manifest what we shall be: and we know that when he shalbe made manifest, we shalbe like him: for we shall see him as he is" (3:2).[37] Following John, "what we are", indicates Ophelia, are children of God. And while we "know not what we may be", John says we shall be like God. In Ophelia's mind, as opposed to Hamlet's, what is distinctive about human nature is the likeness to God, now as children, and ultimately as something even more. Further, "every man that hath this hope" of seeing God as he is and being like him, writes John, "purgeth himself, even as [God] is pure" (3:3). Those freed from sin then are ready for the message "heard from the beginning, we should love one another" (3:11). But if what is most essential to and omnipresent about man is sin, not just one's own but that of others, then it is hard to love

---

[36] It may be objected that she takes part in Polonius' and the King's spying on Hamlet. She does so, however, having been told that they intend to learn the source of his madness so that, Gertrude says, the Prince can be healed (3.1.28–42).

[37] *The Geneva Bible: A Facsimile of the 1560 Edition* (Madison: University of Wisconsin Press, 1969). Jenkins, *Hamlet*, p. 350, and Milward, *Biblical Influences in Shakespeare's Great Tragedies* (Bloomington: Indiana University Press, 1987), p. 43, also find that this passage alludes to John.

one another—and "he that loveth not his brother, abideth in death" (3:14). In *Hamlet* the Prince's Lutheran anthropology is presented as deadly because it impedes love. It is difficult to love the sinner and hate the sin if the sinner *is* sin, if "sin is [man's] nature, [his] very beginning, [his] conception ... [his] words, works, thoughts, and life".[38]

---

[38] Luther, *Penitential Psalms*, p. 169.

Who's in Charge?
Providence in *Hamlet*

Jim Scott Orrick
Boyce College

It seems that nearly everyone in *Hamlet* is attempting to manipulate persons and events to accomplish his own purposes. Perhaps the ghost is attempting to effect an unholy revenge when he prompts Hamlet to kill Claudius. Hamlet seems always in doubt as to whether or not it is an honest ghost (sent from Heaven as a prompter to the exercise of legal justice) even when he is convinced that the Ghost has told the truth concerning the death of King Hamlet. Claudius is unquestionably attempting to manipulate Hamlet through Rosencrantz and Guildenstern. Rosencrantz and Guildenstern are attempting to manipulate Hamlet and play him like a pipe (3.2.336–65).[1] Hamlet attempts to manipulate Ophelia through feigning madness. It is noteworthy that all these attempts at manipulation end disastrously.

A case might be made that the main purpose of the character Polonius is to function as the prototypical meddler. He attempts to manipulate Ophelia first in censoring her relationship with Hamlet and later in deliberately "[loosing his] daughter to him" (2.2.161) while Polonius and the King hide and listen to the encounter. Polonius attempts to manipulate Laertes while Laertes is in France. One wonders what the purpose of the entire interchange between Polonius and Reynaldo is if it is not to prove that Polonius is a meddlesome old fool trying to orchestrate the lives of his children to his own advantage. But his meddlesome nature leads to his untimely demise when Hamlet inadvertently stabs him while Polonius is eavesdropping on the interview between Hamlet and his mother in her

[1] All quotations from *Hamlet* are from the edition published by Ignatius Press: *Hamlet, Prince of Denmark*, ed. Joseph Pearce (San Francisco: Ignatius, 2008).

bedroom. Hamlet's comment is, "Thou wretched, rash, intruding fool, farewell! / I took thee for thy better. Take thy fortune; / Thou find'st to be too busy is some danger" (3.4.31–33). Hamlet later adds, "Heaven hath pleas'd it so". Though it was an accident, Hamlet asserts that God was governing the event to accomplish his own sovereign will, which, in this instance, Hamlet says is twofold: "To punish me with this, and this [Polonius] with me, / That I must be their scourge and minister" (3.4.174, 175). God, apparently, does not look kindly on manipulators.

In the beginning of *Paradise Lost*, John Milton invokes the aid of the Holy Spirit, asking, "That to the highth of this great Argument / I may assert Eternal Providence, / And justifie the wayes of God to men" (1.24–26). William Shakespeare might well have stated this to be his aim in writing *Hamlet*. Although various characters throughout the play attempt to control the destiny of others, it is ultimately divine providence that controls the persons and events. While God governs through providence, this does not preclude his using means, especially human reasoning, to accomplish his desired ends.

Providence

The word "providence" itself appears only twice in the entire play, but the concept is nearly ubiquitous. As for the actual appearances of the word, we have the following: first, when King Claudius learns that Polonius has been inadvertently slain by Hamlet, he says, "Alas, how shall this bloody deed be answer'd? / It will be laid to us, whose providence / Should have kept short, restrain'd, and out of haunt, / This mad young man" (4.1.16–19). In this first occurrence of the word, the King is simply saying, "I should have seen this coming and done something about it." Though Claudius is not referring to divine providence, his use of the word does give insight into what divine providence is: God's seeing the persons and events of the world and governing them according to his own will. The second occurrence of the word "providence" is in the conversation between Hamlet and Horatio just prior to the fatal contest with Laertes. After Hamlet expresses an indefinable uneasiness at the prospect of the contest, Horatio urges him, "If your mind dislike anything, obey it. I will forestall their repair hither, and say you are not fit." Hamlet answers, "Not a whit, we defy augury: there is a special providence in the fall of a sparrow. If it be now, 'tis not to come; if it be not to come, it will be now; if it be not now, yet it will come—the readiness is all" (5.2.211–15). Hamlet is making allusion to Jesus' words recorded in Matthew 10:29–31: "Are not two sparrows sold for a penny? And not one of them will fall to the ground without your Father's will. But even the hairs of your head are all numbered. Fear not, therefore; you are of more value than many sparrows." In other words, Hamlet is saying, "Horatio, there is someone governing even the smallest of things. I will die only when he has planned for me to die."

Both Catholics and Protestants are very close to one another in their understanding of providence. The *Catechism of the Catholic Church* contains the following articles:

> **321** Divine providence consists of the dispositions by which God guides all his creatures with wisdom and love to their ultimate end.

> **322** Christ invites us to filial trust in the providence of our heavenly Father (cf. Mt 6:26–34), and St. Peter the apostle repeats: "Cast all your anxieties on him, for he cares about you" (I Pt 5:7; cf. Ps 55:23).

> **323** Divine providence works also through the actions of creatures. To human beings God grants the ability to cooperate freely with his plans.

In a classic Protestant catechism, the Westminster Shorter Catechism, providence is similarly described as "God's most holy, wise, and powerful preserving and governing all his creatures and all their actions."

The Christian doctrine of providence asserts that God continues to be actively involved in the world he created. While God sometimes supernaturally intervenes in the created order and performs outright miracles, his usual modus operandi in providence is to superintend and work through natural events. In this belief, historic Christianity differs from Deism, which teaches that God created the world but that since its creating, God is no longer personally involved in governing it. Instead, according to Deism, when God created the world he set certain natural laws into motion, and he now allows those laws to govern the universe. The God of Deism is analogous to someone winding up a clock and then simply allowing the clock to run through its own mechanisms.

Note that, technically, providence is not equal to election and predestination. Election and predestination refer to God's plans and decrees, while providence refers to the execution of his plans and decrees. The Westminster Shorter Catechism states, "God executeth his decrees in the works of creation and providence."

Reason: The Vicegerent of Providence

Some persons object to the doctrine of God's absolute sovereignty, protesting that if God is absolutely sovereign, then the freedom of human agency is negated. Erasmus and Luther hacked this out admirably, but historic Christian confessions and catechisms, both Catholic and Protestant, agree in declaring that God utilizes means to effect his sovereign plan. God not only has foreordained the end; he has also foreordained the means for accomplishing that end. While God's decrees may remain hidden and inscrutable to human ken, he has revealed the rules of daily obedience. For humans to enjoy the benefit of being in harmony with God's secret will, they need to cooperate with the means God has ordained for the accomplishment of that secret will. In *Hamlet*, when it comes to ordering the lives of humans, the means God most often employs is the faculty of human reason in submission to God's revealed will.

This utilization of means is one of the factors that set the Christian doctrine of providence apart from mere fatalism or the rule of Fortune. In the rule of Fortune, events are determined and executed by mindless, unconcerned forces. *Hamlet* refers to Fortune as a "strumpet" (2.2.234), or whore. In a world dominated by Fortune, what good does it do to control passions and utilize reason? In contrast, the doctrine of divine providence teaches that although all the events of the created order are predetermined and inevitable, they have been planned by an all-knowing, all-wise, and benevolent God. In his inscrutable wisdom, God has mysteriously established a connection between reasonable behavior and what will inevitably happen. Consequently, providence encourages the utilization of reason, human effort is not denigrated to futility, and the freedom of human agency is affirmed.

It should not be surprising that reason is accorded such a crucial place in the unfolding of God's plans for humans. Many Christian theologians agree with John Calvin in his assessment that the *imago Dei* (image of God) in humans, while evident in the whole human constitution, is primarily expressed in the ordering of all human attributes according to and in submission to the faculty of reason or right understanding:

> I retain the principle ... that the likeness of God extends to the whole excellence by which man's nature towers over all the kinds of living creatures. Accordingly, the integrity with which Adam was endowed is expressed by this word, when he had full possession of right understanding, when he had his affections kept within the bounds of reason, all his senses tempered in right order, and he truly referred his excellence to exceptional gifts bestowed upon him by his Maker. And although the primary seat of the divine image was in the mind and heart, or in the soul and its powers, yet there was no part of man, not even the body itself, in which some sparks did not glow.[2]

Therefore, the use of human reason is a legitimate means of humbly submitting to God's providence. When Hamlet persists in grieving for his dead father, Claudius chides him, saying,

---

[2] John Calvin, *Institutes of the Christian Religion*, vol. 1, ed. John T. McNeill, trans. Ford Lewis Battles, The Library of Christian Classics, vol. 20 (Philadelphia: The Westminster Press, 1960), 1.15.3, p. 188.

> [T]o persever
> In obstinate condolement is a course
> Of impious stubbornness; 'tis unmanly grief;
> It shows a will most incorrect to heaven,
> A heart unfortified, a mind impatient,
> An understanding simple and unschool'd.
>
>   (1.2.92–97)

A person may not be able to immediately change his will or his affections, but, according to Claudius, he ought to be able to change his mind through sane reason and thereby mediately change his will and his affections.

Similarly, Hamlet rebukes his mother for apparently abandoning reason and allowing herself to be ruled by passion:

> Ha! Have you eyes?
> You cannot call it love; for at your age
> The heyday in the blood is tame, it's humble,
> And waits upon the judgment; and what judgment
> Would step from this to this? Sense, sure, you have,
> Else could you not have motion; but sure that sense
> Is apoplex'd; for madness would not err,
> Nor sense to ecstasy was ne'er so thrall'd
> But it reserv'd some quantity of choice
> To serve in such a difference. What devil was't
> That thus hath cozen'd you at hoodman-blind?
> Eyes without feeling, feeling without sight,
> Ears without hands or eyes, smelling sans all,
> Or but a sickly part of one true sense
> Could not so mope. O shame! where is thy blush?
> Rebellious hell,
> If thou canst mutine in a matron's bones,
> To flaming youth let virtue be as wax
> And melt in her own fire; proclaim no shame
> When the compulsive ardour gives the charge,
> Since frost itself as actively doth burn,
> And reason panders will.
>
>   (3.4.67–88)

The phrase "reason panders will" indicates that Gertrude is using her reason for the ignoble purpose of excusing her choice, and perhaps especially her choice to indulge in an intimate relationship that Hamlet thinks illicit.

Gertrude *ought* to be ruled by reason. Horatio, the only just man in the play, *is* ruled by reason. And it is this, Hamlet says, that makes him take Horatio into his heart of hearts:

> Since my dear soul was mistress of her choice
> And could of men distinguish her election,
> Sh'hath seal'd thee for herself; for thou hast been
> As one in suff'ring all, that suffers nothing;
> A man that Fortune's buffets and rewards
> Hast ta'en with equal thanks; and blest are those
> Whose blood and judgment are so well comeddled
> That they are not a pipe for Fortune's finger
> To sound what stop she please. Give me that man
> That is not passion's slave, and I will wear him
> In my heart's core, ay, in my heart of heart,
> As I do thee.
>
>   (3.2.62–72)

But it is not unaided human reason that allows persons to cooperate with God's providence. God has revealed his will in what Hamlet calls "his canon". As early as Act 1, scene 2, we learn that Hamlet is contemplating suicide. He is tired of living in this "weary, stale, flat, and unprofitable" world. He wants to die and be free from it. But he remembers ruefully that "the Everlasting [has] fix'd/His canon 'gainst self-slaughter" (1.2.131–32). He recoils from the thought of utilizing an illegitimate means to accomplish a desired end. It would be contrary to God's revealed will, his canon.

In the famous "To be, or not to be" soliloquy, Hamlet again expresses his desire for respite from the troubles of life. Suicide seems a quick and easy way of attaining that respite—but only as long as the uncomfortable events of this world are considered "the slings and arrows of outrageous fortune". Freedom from these vexations of fortune would be like sleeping. But

Hamlet's metaphor for death, namely "sleep", leads him to consider the possibility of dreaming—life after death. And in remembering the possibility of life after death, he ceases to think like a miserable pagan living in a world ruled by the strumpet Fortune, and he begins to think like a miserable Christian living in a universe governed by a God who has "fix'd / His canon 'gainst self-slaughter" (1.2.132). The bodkin remains in its sheath. Hamlet would rather face a sea of troubles in this life than face the "dread of something after death—/ The undiscover'd country, from whose bourn / No traveller returns" (3.1.78–80). He acknowledges that he cannot thwart God's providence through unlawful means.

While reason and obedience to God's canon are legitimate means of cooperating with God's providence, it is by no means certain that the purposes of even those persons with the noblest resolves will necessarily coincide with God's purposes. The player king observes, "Our wills and fates do so contrary run / That our devices still are overthrown; / Our thoughts are ours, their ends none of our own" (3.2.206–8). This is very similar to Proverbs 16:9: "A man's mind plans his way, but the LORD directs his steps." Hamlet concurs: "There's a divinity that shapes our ends, / Rough-hew them how we will." "That is most certain", agrees Horatio (5.2.10–12).

It should be noted that the "rough-hewing" that Hamlet mentions occurs when he obeyed not reason but rashness:

> Rashly,
> And prais'd be rashness for it—let us know,
> Our indiscretion sometime serves us well,
> When our deep plots do pall; and that should learn us
> There's a divinity that shapes our ends,
> Rough-hew them how we will.

$$(5.2.7–11)$$

Though Hamlet succumbed to rashness, God, in his providence, sovereignly overruled it to accomplish his purpose.

In the end, not just Polonius but also all the would-be manipulators die: Hamlet, King, Queen, Rosencrantz, and

Guildenstern. Hamlet acknowledges that the final scene of carnage may appear to be the result of chance.

> You that look pale and tremble at this chance,
> That are but mutes or audience to this act,
> Had I but time, as this fell sergeant Death
> Is strict in his arrest, O, I could tell you—
> But let it be. Horatio, I am dead:
> Thou livest; report me and my cause aright
> To the unsatisfied.
>
> (5.2.326–31)

It looks like the result of chance, but what would Hamlet's final words be had he but time? Would it be more of how divinity shapes our ends in spite of our rough-hewing? Only Horatio, the man of consummate reason, lives to tell the tale.

Residual Catholicism in *Hamlet*
Spiritual Freedom and Political Tyranny

R. V. Young
North Carolina State University

In his brief treatise on the writing of letters, Justus Lipsius maintains that not only the style but also the content of a letter, especially a letter to a friend, ought to radiate simplicity: "As for the thought, I take it that a kind of simplicity and forthrightness should shine throughout the composition and disclose the special candor of a free mind."[1] Such a personally revealing comment in the midst of a work ostensibly aimed at youthful students indicates how eloquence had become more personal. While it had always involved far more for Renaissance humanists than mere stylistic adornment, eloquence eventually began to constitute their sense of self and personal identity. As Lipsius adds, "For in nothing do the nature and individuality of anyone more clearly shine forth ... than in a letter."[2] The Flemish scholar thus furnishes an example of the increasing importance to many of the later humanists of private integrity as distinct from the political concerns and ambitions that were the preoccupation of the earlier generations of humanist scholars. By the end of the sixteenth century, disillusionment had arisen in the wake of the religious struggles of the Reformation:

---

[1] *Principles of Letter-Writing: A Bilingual Text of "Justi Lipsi Epistolica Institutio"* [1591], ed. and trans. R. V. Young and M. Thomas Hester (Carbondale and Edwardsville: Southern Illinois University Press, 1996), pp. 30–31: "At de Mente: ita intellego; ut simplex quiddam et ingenuum in tota scriptione eluceat, et aperiat candorem quemdam liberae mentis." While not claiming that Shakespeare was directly influenced by Lipsius, I do note that Ben Jonson, Shakespeare's sometime friend and colleague, translated parts of the *Epistolica* into his commonplace book, *Timber, or Discoveries*.

[2] Ibid.: "Nulla enim ex re magis natura cujusque et certa indoles elucet ... quam ex epistola."

the great expectations of earlier generations for peaceful, enlightened reform of social and religious institutions driven by humanist learning and education no longer seemed probable.[3] Indeed, public engagement—marked by peril, caution, and secrecy—seemed subject to inevitable moral compromise. Sincerity, the "special candor of a free mind", is made possible by that liberty and liberality of thought that attaches to the private individual and his relations with kindred spirits.

Among the specifically tragic developments of a number of Shakespeare's mature tragedies is the threat to this "special candor of a free mind". Even at its most overtly political, Shakespearean tragedy is concerned with the corruption of moral character, with the defilement of pure intentions, as much as with political institutions. What is ultimately *tragic* about tyranny is less the use of force to suppress public or political freedom than the spiritual deterioration, the diminished mental candor, which afflicts not only tyrants and their supporters but also those who resist them. The tragic hero of *Hamlet* is notoriously anxious over his own inner life—his sincerity and the firmness of his moral identity, or what Robert Ellrodt calls "self-consistency".[4] From its opening line, "Who's there?" till its final catastrophe, *Hamlet* broods upon the mystery of human identity, and its title character is in anguish over the candor and freedom of his mind, of his inner being. The action of the play arises out of the appearance of a ghost, whose nature, purpose, and provenance are of crucial concern to Hamlet:

[3] The classic work here is, of course, Hiram Haydn, *The Counter-Renaissance* (New York: Scribner's, 1950). On Lipsius' specific role, see R. V. Young, "Lipsius and Imitation as Educational Technique", in *Iustus Lipsius Europae Lumen et Columen: Proceedings of the International Colloquium, Leuven, 17–19 September 1997*, ed. G. Tournoy, J. de Landtsheer, and J. Papy, Supplementa Humanistica Lovaniensia 15 (Leuven University Press, 1999), pp. 268–80.

[4] Robert Ellrodt, "Self-Consistency in Montaigne and Shakespeare", in *Shakespeare and the Mediterranean: The Selected Proceedings of the International Shakespeare Association World Congress, Valencia 2001*, ed. Tom Clayton, Susan Brock, and Vicente Forés (Newark: University of Delaware Press, 2004), pp. 135–55.

Be thou a spirit of health or goblin damn'd,
Bring with thee airs from heaven or blasts from hell,
Be thy intents wicked or charitable,
Thou com'st in such a questionable shape
That I will speak to thee.

$$(1.4.40–44)$$

This apparition that appears to be the ghost of his dead father, claiming in all but use of the word to have returned from Purgatory and demanding that the young man prove his manhood by avenging his father's murder, brings Catholicism into the play in an equivocal fashion, which serves to dramatize the moral uncertainties generated by the religious oppression of the absolutist regimes emerging in the sixteenth and seventeenth centuries. Shakespeare thus calls upon what was, by 1600, the residual Catholicism of most of his audience to remind it of how the spiritual life of subjects was controlled by the government, thus intensifying their apprehension of his tragic hero's dilemma.

Among all Shakespeare's plays, *Hamlet* most explicitly addresses the reductive treatment of individual human identity that characterizes New Historicism. In the year 2000, John Lee observed, "*Hamlet* . . . plays the ghost in New Historicism's drama, but it is a ghost to which New Historicism has not spoken."[5] The following year, Stephen Greenblatt brought out *Hamlet in Purgatory* on the crest of a wave of recent conjecture regarding Shakespeare's Catholic boyhood and youth and its effects on his subsequent career.[6] A Catholic element

[5] John Lee, *Shakespeare's "Hamlet" and the Controversies of Self* (Oxford: Clarendon Press, 2000), p. 51.

[6] The seminal work remains John Henry de Groot, *The Shakespeares and "The Old Faith"* (1946; repr., Fraser, Mich.: Real-View-Books, 1994), which had largely been forgotten until republished with a postscript by Stanley L. Jaki. Recent interest is manifest in works such as E. A. J. Honigman, *Shakespeare: The "Lost Years"* (Totowa, N.J.: Barnes & Noble, 1985); Eric Sams, *The Real Shakespeare: Retrieving the Early Years, 1564–1594* (New Haven and London: Yale University Press, 1995), esp. pp. 11–16; Richard Wilson, "Shakespeare and the Jesuits: New Connections Supporting the Theory of the Lost Catholic Years in Lancashire", *Times Literary Supplement* (December 19, 1997): 11–13; and a special section, "Catholicism and English Renaissance Literature", of the *Ben Jonson Journal* 7 (2000).

in the play cannot be ignored, because there is no other explanation for the ghost of Hamlet's father except as a spirit come
back from Purgatory. Now, Greenblatt exerts himself mightily
to exhibit sympathy for the idea of Purgatory, or at least for
the benighted souls who have believed in it, but he musters
almost no understanding of the religious experience of the communion of saints. After more than 250 pages, the Protestant
view of Purgatory prevails, and Purgatory is reduced to a stage
play: "[A]s Gee [a Protestant polemicist] perceives, the space
of Purgatory becomes the stage where old Hamlet's Ghost is
doomed for a certain term to walk the night. That term has
now lasted some four hundred years, and it has brought with
it a cult of the dead that I and the readers of this book have
been serving."[7] In other words, Catholic beliefs and practices
make for wonderful theater—those Papists know how to put
on a good show!

Fortunately, Greenblatt does not exhaust the possibilities of
making sense of Hamlet's purgatorial ghost. Anthony Low shows
that Shakespeare makes a serious representation of Purgatory
and dramatizes it as an issue in Reformation England. He also
provides a portal into Prince Hamlet's soul and his anxiety about
sincerity and integrity—a condition that seems to arise at least
in part from the unsettled conditions of the fictional Danish
court, which seems as religiously ambiguous as the Tudor court
of Shakespeare's day. As Low points out, the ghost of old Hamlet demands revenge, but he also says, "Remember me" (1.5.91).
This injunction could be taken—and would have been taken
by Englishmen of an earlier generation—as a request for prayers,
but the Prince seems oblivious. Acknowledging the peril of arguing from absence about Shakespeare's motive, Low adds,

---

[7] Stephen Greenblatt, *Hamlet in Purgatory* (Princeton, N.J., and Oxford: Princeton University Press, 2001), p. 257. See the withering review of this book by
William Kerrigan, *Ben Jonson Journal* 8 (2001): 385–90, who points out that
"Greenblatt begins with the welcome admission that he has felt, and means to
explain in some measure, the literary power of *Hamlet*" (p. 385) but leaves us
with the observation that "[c]ultural poetics is here, as elsewhere, more cultural
than poetic" (p. 390).

What we can say with greater certainty is that even though
the Ghost plainly comes from Purgatory, and says so in terms
as explicit as may be, short of an open declaration, neither
Hamlet nor any of the younger Danes ever openly reveals that
he has heard of such a place as Purgatory. As was the case in
England, so in Hamlet's Denmark. Purgatory is not just abol-
ished but effectively forgotten, as if it never were.[8]

This great occlusion in Hamlet's consciousness, his inability
to come to terms with the situation of his father's soul, also
marks an emptiness in the young man's own soul. Hamlet is
ensnared by a situation in which he feels compelled to confront tyranny; his moral and spiritual integrity is imperiled by
his very efforts to deal with corruption: "The time is out of
joint. O cursed spite,/That ever I was born to set it right!"
(1.5.189–90).

When the Prince first appears in the second scene of Act 1,
he is visibly estranged from a court of which he does not
approve, although he does not as yet have evidence—or even
a suspicion—that his uncle is in fact a tyrant rather than merely
a scoundrel. It is immediately clear to the audience, however,
that Claudius is an accomplished politician, in both the Elizabethan and the contemporary sense of the term. A modern
officeholder could learn a good deal about how to conduct a
press conference from his rationalization of the blending of
"mirth in funeral" with "dirge in marriage" (1.2.12), which is
a masterly piece of evasive rhetoric. Claudius appears to han-
dle the crisis involving young Fortinbras with shrewd diplo-
macy and the petition of Laertes with aplomb. It is only the
young Hamlet with his "inky cloak", ostentatious sighs, and

---

[8] Anthony Low, "*Hamlet* and the Ghost of Purgatory: Intimations of Killing
the Father", in *Aspects of Subjectivity: Society and Individuality from the Middle
Ages to Shakespeare and Milton* (Pittsburgh: Duquesne University Press, 2003),
pp. 118–19. Jan H. Blits, *Deadly Thought: "Hamlet" and the Human Soul* (Lan-
ham, Md.: Lexington Books, 2001), p. 1, also sees the religious tension in the
play, but he assumes that it takes place "in the early sixteenth century", when
"Denmark is still a Catholic country." Much as I admire many elements in this
book, I am skeptical of Blits' attempt to align the fictional world of *Hamlet* with
specific historical realities.

grieving countenance who strikes a discordant note in the harmonious transfer of power from the deceased king to his brother. When both his mother and uncle accuse Hamlet of excessive mourning, his response is an assertion of sincerity and integrity that brings to mind the Lipsian ideal of the candor of a free mind: "I have that within which passes show" (1.2.85). Noble as these words sound, they settle nothing. Jan Blits notes that Hamlet severs the connection between "the internal and the external, the mind and actions, of a man. His identification of actions and playacting serves to deny the moral significance of actions as such."[9] Anthony Low provides an explanation: "When Hamlet's mother as well as his uncle accuses him of unusual excess in his grief, and therefore of dangerous impiety"—a viewpoint typical of Protestant sermons of the Tudor period—"he cannot grapple with the theological questions implied. Instead, he is driven inward, into the most famous of all early-modern gestures of radical individualist subjectivity."[10]

If we accept Low's thesis, that lying behind *Hamlet* is a cultural crisis of conscience occasioned by the Tudor abolition of Purgatory, then the anguished doubts and hesitations that beleaguer the Prince throughout much of the play show more consistency with his character and situation. Maynard Mack points out that from its opening scene, *Hamlet* "creates a world where uncertainties are of the essence", which stresses "the problematic nature of reality and the relation of reality to appearance."[11] Lying firmly at the base of this general haze of uncertainties, however, is the particular uncertainty of how to regard the dead. Elsinore implicitly seems to be a court that has moved from Catholicism to Protestantism between the death of old Hamlet and the accession of his brother. Discreetly declining to specify a clear analogue to the actual facts of history, Shakespeare succeeds in suggesting a situation that

[9] Blits, *Deadly Thought*, p. 55.

[10] Low, *"Hamlet and the Ghost of Purgatory"*, p. 124.

[11] Maynard Mack, *Everybody's Shakespeare: Reflections Chiefly on the Tragedies* (Lincoln and London: University of Nebraska Press, 1993), pp. 111–12.

would be uncomfortably familiar to an Elizabethan audience. The new king has hastily and incestuously married his brother's widow, presumably for reason of state. How could Shakespeare's audience *not* think of Henry VIII, the man who, in order to free himself from a marriage to his brother's widow, initiated the Reformation in England that outlawed prayers for the dead and confiscated the wealth of the institutions founded for the remembrance of departed souls? The resemblance is strengthened when this king promptly reproves his nephew and now stepson for dwelling impiously on his deceased father—an act of impiety only to someone who denies the existence of Purgatory and hence the efficacy of remembering the dead. And young Hamlet seems to be a part of this new, reformed world: surely it is no coincidence that he is a student at Wittenberg, Luther's university, and that he makes a punning reference to the Diet of Worms—"Your worm is your only emperor for diet" (3.4.22)—after killing Polonius.

But the death of his father and the debauchery of his mother change everything. Hamlet exhibits bravado in his scarcely veiled insults and defiance of Claudius and Gertrude, but his soliloquies reveal that what he has "within which passes show" are disillusion and despair:

> O, that this too too solid flesh would melt,
> Thaw, and resolve itself into a dew!
> Or that the Everlasting had not fix'd
> His canon 'gainst self-slaughter! O God! God!
> How weary, stale, flat, and unprofitable,
> Seem to me all the uses of this world!
> Fie on't! Ah, fie! 'tis an unweeded garden,
> That grows to seed; things rank and gross in nature
> Possess it merely.
>
> (1.2.129–37)

The famous "To be, or not to be" speech, which likewise broods upon suicide, discloses a similar disgust with life and fearful bewilderment in the face of death. Life is the realm of the "slings and arrows of outrageous fortune", of the "whips and scorns of time", and of a host of ills spelled out in morbid detail; but death is the realm of "dread", "[t]he undiscover'd country, from whose bourn/No traveller returns", which "puzzles the will,/And makes us rather bear those ills we have/Than fly to others that we know not of" (3.1.56–82). Beginning at least with Coleridge, critics have often wished to gloss over the inconsistency of this speech, which seems to deny the Prince's very recent encounter with the ghost of his dead father.[12] Inconsistency it surely is, but an inconsistency consistent with Hamlet's character and situation. The abolition of Purgatory has *made* death "an undiscover'd country" and explicitly denied the connection between the living and the dead that was so important in medieval Catholic piety. Hamlet has simply reverted to his usual mode of thinking, a mode of thinking encouraged by the Tudor authorities of Reformation England, a mode of thinking that has become typical of the modern, secular world, a mode of thinking that discourages reflection upon death, a topic that "puzzles the will". The invasion of this world by a spirit from that nonexistent place, that "undiscover'd country", who takes leave of his son with the injunction "Remember me", is understandably an occasion for confusion and emotional turbulence, for inconsistency.

Like the Brutus of Shakespeare's *Julius Caesar*, Hamlet longs for Stoic mastery of himself. Such is the burden of his praise of Horatio: "Give me that man/That is not passion's slave, and I will wear him/In my heart's core, ay, in my heart of heart,/As I do thee" (3.2.71–74). Hamlet is likewise a man who has been recognized for his virtues, both as exemplar and exponent of the humanist vision of excellence at its most optimistic. He expresses his disillusionment with this vision to Rosencrantz and Guildenstern: "What a piece of work is a man!

---

[12] *Coleridge's Writings on Shakespeare*, ed. Terence Hawkes, with an introduction by Alfred Harbage (New York: G. P. Putnam's Sons, 1959), p. 150. See also the note on the passage by G. R. Hibbard, ed., *Hamlet* (Oxford and New York: Oxford University Press, 1987), p. 241.

How noble in reason! how infinite in faculties! in form and moving, how express and admirable! in action, how like an angel! in apprehension, how like a god! the beauty of the world! the paragon of animals! And yet, to me, what is this quintessence of dust?" (2.2.303–8). His lapse from the exemplary status he once held is manifest in Ophelia's lament over his apparent madness:

> O, what a noble mind is here o'er-thrown!
> The courtier's, soldier's, scholar's, eye, tongue, sword;
> The expectation and rose of the fair state,
> The glass of fashion and the mould of form,
> Th' observ'd of all observers—quite, quite down!
>
> (3.1.150–54)

In the face of his father's death and his mother's degradation, the self-assurance of courtly humanism and of Stoic rational autonomy has crumbled. With the suppression of participation in the communion of saints made possible by the doctrine of Purgatory, there is nothing on which Hamlet may rely. Hence the Catholicism in the play is *residual* insofar as it marks an absence in the hero's world.

Cast adrift in "a sea of troubles", beset all around by a world of uncertainties, Hamlet enters into a deadly struggle of wits with Claudius; Hamlet attempts to defeat tyranny by its own means, by deviousness and deception, by staying one step ahead of a nimble adversary in a psychological guessing game. To his credit, Hamlet is not very adept at court intrigue; for that matter, he is not very adept at revenge. As Claudius recognizes and tells Laertes, as the two of them plot Hamlet's death in an ostensibly friendly fencing match, Hamlet, "being remiss", will not check the foils because he is "[m]ost generous, and free from all contriving" (4.7.134–35). Nevertheless, his innocence and honor are stained by the effort. In a remarkable sequence of events on the heels of his apparently successful *Mousetrap* play, Hamlet demonstrates a total inability as a schemer and avenger—had he been in Prince Hal's place, Hotspur would probably have become king of

England in Shakespeare's I *Henry IV*. Having been summoned by his mother, Hamlet comes upon Claudius at prayer
and refrains from killing him lest his soul be saved, so
Hamlet says, thus affording no true vengeance (3.3.73–96).
"This speech", writes Dr. Johnson, "in which Hamlet, represented as a virtuous character, is not content with taking
blood for blood, but contrives damnation for the man he would
punish, is too horrible to be read or to be uttered."[13] Now,
if we mistake Hamlet for Vindice of *The Revenger's
Tragedy*, with his elaborate scheme and poisoned skull, Dr.
Johnson has a point; but surely Coleridge is correct in
finding here "the marks of reluctance and procrastination"
rather than "impetuous, horror-striking fiendishness".[14] Hamlet is a "virtuous character" with a natural reluctance to stab
a defenseless man in the back, but having sworn vengeance,
he must devise for himself a satisfactory rationalization for
his hesitation.

Shakespeare's sly parody of the bloodcurdling features of the
typical revenge tragedy, including his own *Titus Andronicus*, is
in no way inconsistent with Hamlet's impulsive stabbing of
Polonius through the arras. Despite his own doubts about himself, Hamlet is quite courageous and capable of vigorous action
when threatened. Not only does he strike out at what he takes
to be Claudius behind the arras, but he also acts decisively in
dispatching Rosencrantz and Guildenstern and taking advantage of the opportunity afforded by the pirates. But the result
of his exertions is the pointless, unjust death of men who are,
at worst, merely meddlesome (we have no reason to believe
that any of them were in on the plot to kill the old king);
indirectly, the death of Ophelia; and eventually the death of
her brother Laertes and Gertrude, as well as his intended victim, Claudius. Although Hamlet is wittier than Claudius, he
has not outwitted him; the death of the fratricidal usurper is a

---

[13] *Samuel Johnson on Shakespeare*, ed. W. K. Wimsatt Jr. (New York: Hill and
Wang), p. 111.
[14] *Coleridge's Writings on Shakespeare*, p. 153.

result of the failure of his own machinations, not the success of Hamlet's.

Although Hamlet's "deep plots do pall", he still becomes the providential instrument of Claudius' punishment: "There's a divinity that shapes our ends, / Rough-hew them how we will" (5.2.10–11). What is more, Hamlet seems to grow in Christian self-awareness:

> There is a special providence in the fall of a sparrow. If it be now, 'tis not to come; if it be not to come, it will be now; if it be not now, yet it will come—the readiness is all.
>
> (5.2.211–14)

For this reason, interpretation of *Hamlet* is not enhanced by efforts to identify the apparition with theological specificity and to determine the Prince's eternal destiny. While critics like Roy Battenhouse and Eleanor Prosser are able to establish with what seems an airtight case that the ghost is a devil and Hamlet damned,[15] such confident doctrinal demonstrations seem irrelevant to the actual experience of this tragedy. The apparition, which looms so large in Act 1, returns only once and briefly in Act 3 and then is heard no more. Quite visible to Horatio and the soldiers in the first act, in the third act Gertrude can neither see nor hear her son's shadowy interlocutor. Hamlet faces the impossible political predicament of dealing with an apparently invincible tyranny, and the ghost (or devil?) warns his son, "Taint not thy mind" (1.5.85); but he offers little guidance, and the lost Catholic world of spiritual nobility and moral assurance that he represents vanishes with him. In his efforts to bring a murderer to heel, the young Hamlet becomes, ironically, an indiscriminate killer. Although his acknowledgment of providence may prepare him for a more

---

[15] Roy Battenhouse, *Shakespearean Tragedy* (Bloomington: Indiana University Press, 1969), pp. 244–65; Eleanor Prosser, *Hamlet and Revenge*, 2nd ed. (Stanford, Calif.: Stanford University Press, 1971), pp. 121–41. See Roy Battenhouse, ed., *Shakespeare's Christian Dimension: An Anthology of Commentary* (Bloomington and Indianapolis: Indiana University Press, 1994), pp. 382–414, for excerpts from these works and other essays.

hopeful death than the pagan Brutus or the despairing Othello suffers, Hamlet's mind is still "tainted".

Despite any gleams of affirmation, *Hamlet* remains tragic; its ambiguous ending is, indeed, an element of the tragedy. Hamlet's admonition applies to critics as well as to Guildenstern: "[Y]ou would pluck out the heart of my mystery" (3.2.356–57); and we must accede to the force of his final words: "[T]he rest is silence" (5.2.358). He dies with a great deal of bloodshed troubling his conscience—consider his extraordinary behavior at Ophelia's grave (5.1.217ff.) and his mention of his "conscience" twice within ten lines in the following scene. Although Hamlet claims that Rosencrantz and Guildenstern "are not near my conscience" (5.2.58), his mother's words about the player queen apply here as well: he "doth protest too much" (3.2.225). And Fortinbras, who has the Prince's "dying voice" (5.2.348), is, at best, an unknown quantity: How optimistic should we be about the fate of Denmark in the hands of "a delicate and tender prince" whose spirit is, nonetheless, "with divine ambition puff'd" (4.4.48–49)? At the end of the play, it still seems that "[s]omething is rotten in the state of Denmark" (1.4.90), and the Prince has never come to terms with the ghostly apparition of his father and the Catholic realm of the irreparably lost. He has learned only, perhaps too late, that the answer of a free mind to tyranny is not to imitate the violence and deceit of the tyrant, nor is it resignation. It is rather what he calls "readiness".

CONTRIBUTORS

Crystal Downing taught Shakespeare for several years at UCLA before taking a position at Messiah College in Pennsylvania, where she is professor of English and film studies. In addition to presentations at academic conferences, her work on Shakespeare has appeared in *College Literature* and *Literature/Film Quarterly*. Her two books explore the relationship between postmodernism and Christianity: *Writing Performances: The Stages of Dorothy L. Sayers* (Palgrave 2004) and *How Postmodernism Serves (My) Faith* (IVP Academic 2006).

Anthony Esolen is a professor of Renaissance English literature at Providence College in Rhode Island. Among his books are a three-volume translation of Dante's *Divine Comedy* (Random House), and *Ironies of Faith: The Deep Laughter at the Heart of Christian Literature* (ISI Press), and his recently released *Politically Incorrect Guide to Western Civilization* (Regnery). He is also a senior editor of *Touchstone* magazine.

Gene Fendt has been teaching philosophy at the University of Nebraska, Kearney, for over twenty years. His publications include *Is Hamlet a Christian Drama? An Essay on a Question in Kierkegaard* (Marquette University Press) and *Love Song for the Life of the Mind: An Essay on the Purpose of Comedy* (Catholic University of America Press).

Richard Harp is professor of English and director of graduate studies at the University of Nevada, Las Vegas. He is founding coeditor (with Stanley Stewart) of the *Ben Jonson Journal* (Edinburgh University Press), which publishes articles and reviews on all aspects of Renaissance literature.

Andrew Moran is an assistant professor of English at the University of Dallas. Previously he taught at UD's Rome Campus, Hillsdale College, and Ave Maria University. His dissertation is on *The Winter's Tale*, and his scholarship has focused on Shakespearean metadrama and representations of Reformation-era controversies.

Jim Scott Orrick received his Ph.D. from Ohio University and is professor of literature and culture at Boyce College in Louisville, Kentucky. He and his wife, Carol, have six daughters.

Joseph Pearce is associate professor of literature and writer in residence at Ave Maria University in Florida. He is author of *The Quest for Shakespeare* (Ignatius, 2008) and editor of the *Saint Austin Review* (www.staustinreview.com).

R. V. Young is professor of English at North Carolina State University. In addition to scholarly books and articles on literature, he has also published in journals such as *Touchstone*, *First Things*, *Crisis*, the *National Review*, and the *Saint Austin Review*.